Parenting…101
(Train up a Child)

DarNella K. Allen

PublishAmerica
Baltimore

First printing

ISBN: 1-4241-4731-X
PUBLISHED BY PUBLISHAMERICA, LLLP
www.publishamerica.com
Baltimore

Printed in the United States of America

I'd like to dedicate this book to my children: Toi, Jonathan, and Ethan, and to my grandchildren: Adam, Aron, and Chelsea.

With the constant reminder that insanity is truly inherited…we get it from our children, smile! And that no matter how complex life's issues, until you've been a parent or grandparent, nothing is more "The Real Deal" than standing face to face with someone who looks just like you, only…you don't know who they are!

And always, my dear husband John.

I love you guys!

Table of Contents

INTRODUCTION

Tucked safely away in the heart of every child are magnificent surprises, gifts, talents, and boundless potential that can only be seen with spiritual eyes and are contained within the hand of God.

The wonder of a child can only be expressed with one word…amazing! Imagine finding a treasure so precious and so priceless that no system of man can measure its value and its worth. That's a child!

See yourself sitting in this wonderful library with huge, comfortable, soft, fabric and leather chairs and ottomans, with thick, plush carpeting and huge bright windows that allow for absolutely perfect lighting. There are walls and walls of books that range in everything from A-Z…in size, subject expertise, even different in their covers, from bright, bright colors, elaborate artwork, landscapes, and the extremely imaginative "book jackets" used for other books, all so different…all so unique…all so special.

You're sitting and relaxing in this wonderful room, this splendid library, when suddenly one of the books is placed in your hands. Its cover is bright and cheerful brocade, with delicate gold-leaf pages, and feels very comfortable in your hands. You notice too, that the book has been dedicated to Mankind, the author is Jesus Christ, the inspiration is the Holy Spirit, and published by God, the Father, of Throne Room Publications.

After some years with your book, the author appears one day out of the blue, and asks to see your book. You're reluctant and even embarrassed because at first, you don't even know where you put it when last you were reading it, but eventually you find it and give it to the author. He asks, "Did you enjoy the book?" Your answer was sort of muffled, but He thought He heard you say, "It was fine, just fine." He looks at the book that He treasured so, and was so excited about lending you. He found that His once very beautiful book was torn, with the back binding completely destroyed, the pages stained and dog eared, and some valuable chapters were missing! The title of the book had been rubbed and rubbed so hard, that it was difficult for even the author to determine what it was titled.

You looked into His face, and were not only hurt, but shocked at what you saw. There was such a sadness and pain in His eyes, and immediately you repented of your sin, the neglect of this priceless book He loaned you. You asked if you could replace it in cost and value. His reply was simply, "How do you replace the sun, the moon, or the stars, my child?

Each child is loaned to us from God. And children, according to the Word of God in Psalm 127:3, "Lo, children are an heritage of the LORD: and the fruit of the womb is His reward." We have His charge to us in Proverbs 22:6, "Train up a child in the way he should go: and when he is old, he will not depart from it."

In the chapters to come we will trust the Holy Spirit to impart to us the true depth, weight and responsibility of this scripture to us as parents, to our children, to the body of Christ and for the Gospel's sake!

"Train Up A Child!"

Chapter I

You Can't Judge a BOOK...By Its Cover!

Let's get back to that library with just a few adjustments to the room. First of all, instead of a large comfortable leather or fabric chair you're sitting in, let's think of that chair as the arms of the LORD. Proverbs 16:20, "He that handleth a matter wisely shall find good: and whoso trusteth in the LORD, happy is he." The ottoman for your feet is the Rock of our salvation. The Gospel of Christ, Matthew 16:15-16, "He saith unto them, but whom say ye that I am? And Simon Peter answered and said, Thou art the Christ, the Son of the living God." Reading further down at verse 18, "And I say also unto thee, that thou art Peter and upon this Rock I will build my church; and the gates of hell shall not prevail against it."

Those huge windows that give this room such perfect lighting are the Word of God. Psalm 119: 105, "Thy Word is a lamp unto my feet and a light unto my path." Also in Psalm 143:8, "Cause me to hear thy loving kindness in the morning; for in thee do I trust: cause me to know the way wherein I should walk; for I lift up my soul unto thee." Now that you're resting in the arms of our LORD, your feet "propped" up on the Rock of our salvation, you'll need something cool and refreshing to drink...Try this, Isaiah 55:1, "Lo, everyone that thirsteth, come ye to the waters, and he that hath no money; come ye, buy and eat; yea, come buy wine and milk without money and without price."

Now for that book given to you by the author Jesus Christ, what type of book is it? Will the BOOK, unlike your other children, be difficult reading? Will this BOOK require other reference material, special outside help? Is this a thick BOOK that requires excessive reading to understand its content and worth totally? Is the BOOK filled with lots of colorful pictures, as in an active and creative imagination, extroverted and "non-stop" personality? Maybe by the time you reach out to read this BOOK, the pages are already worn, tattered and ripped, as with a foster or maybe adopted child. This kind of BOOK may also have marks of other abuse both emotional and spiritual, yet according to our author very much worth saving! Lastly, do you really want to read this BOOK, or has it been pushed on you or referred to you by others, as with an "unplanned" pregnancy? This can make a tremendous difference in your sincerely processing the data properly, and retaining and applying what you have read in the chapters of your BOOK, and what God has directed you to do, about this BOOK.

Above we have almost every example of "required reading" for parents. Each child that comes to us comes with different needs, and will place different demands upon you as the parent. But your only responsibility to the author is, to return the BOOK to the library…fit…for the Gospel!

The title of this chapter is: "You Can't Judge a BOOK…By Its Cover!" So many of us as parents refuse to read or study our children with the intent and purpose of "Train up a child in the way he should go: and when he is old, he will not depart from it," according to Proverbs 22:6.

What is our LORD telling us in this verse? As parents we are to train. And that word "train" means: "To make proficient with specialized instruction and practice!" Teach our children to honor authority, obey, and follow instruction. As their parents we are to discourage rebellion, stubbornness, and disobedience. These attributes cannot be discouraged or rendered ineffective without consistent discipline and corporal correction.

The biblical principals and wisdom used by Christian parents probably challenges our modern philosophies and practices of child rearing. According to the Word of God, we as saints are in warfare, spiritual warfare. 1 Corinthians 10:3-4, "For though we walk in the flesh, we do not war after the flesh: (4) For the weapons of our warfare are not carnal, but mighty through God to the pulling down of strong holds." A "stronghold" is an area dominated or occupied by a special group. We're also told in 2 Timothy 3:1-2, "This know also, that in the last days perilous times shall come. (2) For men shall be lovers of their own selves, covetous, boasters, proud, blasphemers, disobedient to parents, unthankful, unholy."

As parents we cannot rely on teachers, principals, their peers, neighbors, family, friends, psychologists, sociologists, etc., to do our reading for us. We must do our own reading. We must know our children from cover to cover, and the Word of God, likewise! This goes without saying. However, we need the help and input of others, especially those who have a devoted interest in children, and don't negate, or neglect the crucial spiritual aspects of their training.

You must know the author. If your background on the author is sketchy, or limited, and for some, non-existent, this is one author you cannot please or appreciate without understanding exactly "where He's coming from." It will most likely be a difficult read. In Hebrews 12:2, "Looking unto Jesus the author and Finisher of our faith; who for the joy that was set before Him endured the cross, despising the shame, and is set down at the right hand of the throne of God." Again, if you don't know this author if you don't have a relationship with Jesus Christ, you'll never understand the BOOK you're reading! Never!

Our children are bombarded daily with teachings, theories, and moral concepts that are absolutely contrary to the Word and Will of God for their lives. They are tested and tempted with everything from the way they dress, i.e., "who they're wearing," whether or not it is a designer label, to the ultimate fear of being found out that they're "still" virgins! They deal with smoking or non-smoking issues, to drink or not to drink…this is the question! Our children are pressured to accept "alternative" lifestyles as normal. In some schools a young lady would be given kudos to be pregnant with a certain boy's child! It's just too deep, and too crazy for us to be too lazy to read and study the BOOK that represents the child we are responsible for.

Don't forget, all children will resist being trained or raised. When you first became a child of God, didn't you resist, and aren't some of us still resisting God's instruction and purpose for our lives? Why? Because it's painful to be formed into anything other than the original and comfortable state.

Why do you think that God put Adam to sleep, when He decided to create Eve? It wasn't just to surprise him. Adam would not have been able to withstand such a painful invasion of his body. It would have destroyed him, and God never wants that! Neither should you! Never "throw the baby out with the bath water!" God only wants us to trust Him and seek Him in the shaping of the lives and ministries of our children.

Don't be angry when you are met with resistance. What you must determine to do is meet resistance with the proper resistance! The Word of God tells us in James 7:7, "Submit yourselves (as parents) therefore to God. Resist the devil (his attempt to undo the work of God in the life of your child!) and he will flee from you." Amen!

I know that I took a little liberty in that scripture to explain my point, but I feel it was proper, and after all…"All's fair in love and war!" And my friends, we are at war! When confronting your child or children with matters of discipline or concern, or both, ask them to go to their room while you get before God. It won't take long, but you must seek His Will concerning their discipline. He will establish excellent guidelines for each child He has blessed you with, only you must seek His counsel, especially until you're familiar with the BOOK you're reading. In Proverbs 3:6, "In all thy ways acknowledge Him, and He shall direct thy paths."

Never think that because your child is not a toddler that instruction and guidance are not still needed in their lives. You can't expect to know your child and their needs if the only thing you've devoted time to is the table of contents, in other words, the obvious traits and habits they possess. You must know and understand their needs, and not confuse them with your own. Your children will learn to respect you and your judgment not because they always understand it, but because God is on your side. Remember, you're His Child, and He will not leave or forsake you! In Luke 1:17, "And He shall go before him in the spirit and power of Elias, to turn the hearts of the fathers to the children, and the disobedient to the wisdom of the just; to make ready a people prepared for the LORD." See…He has your back! Trust Him!

Be encouraged by the Word of God in Phillippians 1:6, "Being confident of this very thing, that He which hath begun a good work in you will perform it until the day of Jesus Christ." In other words, God will perform the work that He has begun both in you and in your children! Praise God!

I can't imagine a more beautiful and scary feeling than the one we experience when we've given birth to this beautiful, precious, and vulnerable person. And then we're thrown out of the hospital, without warranties, guarantees or building instructions, not even the usual "some assembly required." Smile! No batteries, no charts, nothing. Nothing except this irreplaceable, precious responsibility! I know my husband and I always just looked at each other with this simple, stupid grin on our faces, not wanting to let anyone else know that we were scared to death of a little six-pound, eight-ounce package that didn't even have teeth! What a scary thought we must have been to our LORD; I'm certain He looked at the Father, more than once with, *Are we sure about them? after all, it is John and DarNella!* (Smile)

I'm serious. What happened between the periods of "BK" and "AK," that's Before Kids and After Kids? When we left the hospital with everything still smelling of baby powder, and we were so hopeful and full of possibilities. What happened to those young, eager, strong, beautiful, energetic, wide-eyed people? Children! That's what happened to them! Children! Oops…sorry, I got a little carried away, for a minute. Smile.

How do we or can we measure our success with our children when there in no parent report card? No real or tangible system of evaluation, or "checks and balances? The only real input we receive as parents is from our children, and they have been known to be somewhat biased, shall we say, in their reporting!

The Word of God tells us, "No Weapon Form Against Us"...oops...wrong scripture and application. How about the Word telling us to "Take the rod and beat that child before he or she stinks up the whole place?" Sorry, I'm paraphrasing.

Honestly, you are not alone! We've all hit that proverbial brick wall when it comes to understanding our child, but we can't allow our frustrations to distort the counsel God has given us. We must somehow get out of their faces and into their hearts! It's not a difficult task, but it will take sincere effort on your part as the parent.

Every child, like every book you read, is different. We are blessed in that the author of our BOOK is the same for each BOOK. Once you know and understand the author and the Inspiration (The Holy Spirit) behind the work, when you know without a doubt that according to Hebrews 13:8, "Jesus Christ [is] the same yesterday, and today, and forever," His work will not only be more appreciated by you, but bring joy to your life. You'll enjoy the BOOK so much you won't be able to put it down, so to speak. It will be a real page turner. Your children are more than worth any challenge they may present to you personally, and much too valuable to not devote any effort in their training. We're told in Hebrews 12:11, "Now no chastening for the present seemeth to be joyous, but grievous: nevertheless afterward it yieldeth the peaceable fruit of righteousness unto them which are exercised thereby."

It's a fact that there will be times when you'll feel as punished, as restricted and constrained as your child, and you are, you definitely are! When you became a parent, the stakes of the game of life doubled, for the body of Christ has changed. However, the magnificent possibilities you hold in your two hands cannot be measured or calculated by any man. Let's take a quick look at a beautiful example.

In the book of 1 Samuel, we have a wonderful story of hope, fulfillment and blessing, all through the birth of Samuel and the personal sacrifice of Hannah his mother. The story opens with Elkanah, Hannah's husband, and his second wife, Peninnah.

During one of Elkanah's times of yearly sacrifice in the tabernacle, his wife Hannah, who was childless, vows to dedicate her first child to the LORD if only God would bless her and open her womb. God answered her prayer, and Hannah was blessed with a son whom she named Samuel ("Heard by God"). When Samuel is weaned at the age of three, he is brought to Shiloh to serve with the resident high priest, Eli. There Samuel is loaned to the LORD according to the vow of Hannah. 1 Samuel 1:10-11, "And she was in bitterness of soul, and prayed unto the LORD, and wept sore. And she vowed a vow, and said, O LORD of hosts, if thou wilt indeed look on the affliction of thine handmaid, and remember me, and not forget thine handmaid, but wilt give unto thine handmaid a man child, then I will give him unto the LORD all the days of his life, and there shall no razor come upon his head."

Try to imagine the joy and happiness that Samuel brought Hannah, from the moment of his conception to his birth, and yes, even his being offered up to her LORD was a supreme sacrifice of joy. For Hannah did not just rejoice in the fact that God heard and answered her prayer, she rejoiced in the experience she'd longed for in his birth, nursing, and initial training. Three years was not a very long BOOK, but suffice to say, the BOOK was placed in the hands of God to complete and finish his training. Samuel was to serve the LORD at the tabernacle his entire life!

Hannah was blessed to read the introduction and dedication and acknowledgment pages, and because she was acquainted with the author her joy was fulfilled! In 1 Samuel 2:1-2, "And Hannah prayed, and said, my heart rejoiceth in the LORD, mine horn is exalted in the LORD; my mouth is enlarged over mine enemies; because I rejoice in thy salvation. There is none holy as the LORD; for there is none beside thee; neither is there any rock like our God." Again, I believe Hannah was familiar with the author and trusted His judgment and counsel in regards to her BOOK.

Does the whole thing really boil down to whether or not we love our LORD enough to trust Him with our child's destiny? Why do we hold so tightly that which does not belong to us? How can we possibly understand the innermost need and potential of our child, when all we have to go on is what we can see, feel, taste, smell, or touch? All things concerning our lives as Christians, all things are spiritual. We're either being blessed, directed, encouraged, up-lifted, edified, healed, delivered, prospered, etc., by the LORD, or being cursed, confused, discouraged, down trodden, debased, made sick, bound, destroyed, etc., by Satan! It's just that simple!

We cannot afford to view the raising and training of our children as anything less than a ministry, LOANED to us for the gospel's sake, just as it was with Samuel! Anything that you can see, taste, touch or smell, etc., you don't own, including your child, or the BOOK you are reading. It must be returned to the author with its value and worth potential increased.

We'll back track just a little bit by looking at the sons of Eli. Eli was given two BOOKS to read and train up, and he utterly blew it. You find their sin and immorality in 1 Samuel 2:12-17. "Now the sons of Eli were sons of Belial; they knew not the LORD." Stop. How you can be entrusted with two lives, as a high priest, and the Word of God refers to your children, your sons, as the "sons of Belial...Satan?" How is this possible? It's easy. Eli never sought the LORD for instructions and wisdom on how to train up his sons. Eli was obviously a lazy, self-centered, and self-indulgent priest.

Judgment was prophesied in 1 Samuel 2:27-29, "And there came a man of God unto Eli, and said unto him, thus saith the LORD, did I plainly appear unto the house of thy father, when they were in Egypt in Pharaoh's house? (28) And did I choose him out of all the tribes of Israel to be my priest, to offer upon mine altar, to burn incense, to wear an ephod before me? And did I give unto the house of thy father all the offerings made by fire of the children of Israel? (29) Wherefore kick ye at my sacrifice and at Mine offering, which I have commanded in my habitation: and honourest thy sons above me, to make yourselves fat with the chiefest of all the offerings of Israel my people?

The Word of God goes on through verse 36. Judgment was prophesied and a curse placed on Eli's line, but God declares He will raise up a man who will be faithful to all that is in God's heart and mind. See, that's' the key to raising our children...we must know the mind of God. And how can we know His thoughts, unless we do as He commands us in Proverbs 3:6, "In all thy ways acknowledge Him, and He shall direct thy paths." Again, in James 1:5, "If any of you lack wisdom, let him ask of God, that giveth to all men liberally, and upbraideth not; and it shall be given him." Lastly in Jeremiah 29:11, "For I know the thoughts that I think toward you, saith the LORD, thoughts of peace and not of evil, to give you an expected end."

The LORD has specific thoughts concerning our lives, and the lives of all His children, whether they are six hours old, or six hundred years old, He has a purpose and a plan for each of us, and for our children, we must find His purpose and His plan, then they will have good success. We don't want to leave Him with the"sons of Belial!

Samuel was a Nazarite (1 Samuel 2-11). A Nazarite vows abstinence from intoxicating drinks, self-denial, and separation from sensual indulgence, free growth of hair indicating the complete dedication of all the power of the head to God, and the avoidance of contact with a dead body as a token of absolute purity of life. All of this was the sign of a Nazarite, and man of God. But,

Samuel was also a priest and a prophet, an intercessor and a judge, a man, whose life was one of faith, honor and labor for the Will of God and…for the people of God!

What better gift could be given to our LORD after all He's paid for and accomplished through His own sacrifice for His children? What better gift than to give the body of Christ another Samuel, whose only desire was to serve and follow God, or another Hannah whose only desire was to fulfill her vow and purpose to the LORD.

The great difference between these two parents was that Hannah made her vow and commitment to the LORD before she even conceived! Samuel, whose name means "Asked of God" or "Offering of God," belonged to the LORD before he was even conceived. I can't say not thought of, for a child was forever in the heart and mind of Hannah, but definitely before he was conceived!

The call of God in Samuel's life came when he was weaned and dedicated by his mother. Samuel was approximately twelve years old when he received his first revelation from the LORD, which was a clear message of doom against Eli's guilty house.

We find in 1 Samuel 3:1, "And the child Samuel ministered unto the LORD before Eli. And the word of the LORD was precious in those days; there was no open vision." Reading down a little further we get to the heart of the matter in regards to Samuel's first experience with the voice of God. Continuing at the end of verse 3-8, "and Samuel was laid down to sleep; (4) That the LORD called Samuel: and he answered, Here am I. (5) And he ran unto Eli, and said, here am I; for thou calledst me. And he said, I called not; lie down again. And he went and lay down. (6) And the LORD called yet again, Samuel. And Samuel arose and went to Eli, and said, here am I, for thou didst call me. And he answered, I called not my son; lie down again. (7) Now Samuel did not yet know the LORD, neither was the Word of the LORD yet revealed unto him. (8) And the LORD called Samuel again, the third time. And he arose and went to Eli, and said, here am I, for thou didst call me. And Eli perceived that the LORD had called the child."

Now this is a crazy picture to me. Here you have the high priest who does not know the voice of God, until he speaks to this child three times! However, this is how non-existent the voice of the LORD was during this period. Remember what the Word of God tells us in verse 1 of this chapter, "and the Word of the LORD was precious in those days"? Our LORD didn't go through His high priest. He spoke to a child of twelve. How beautiful; don't forget Jesus Christ started His ministry in the temple at the age of twelve!

Getting back to this scripture at verse 9, "Therefore Eli said unto Samuel, go lie down; and it shall be, if He call thee, that thou shalt say, Speak LORD; for thy servant heareth. So Samuel went and lay down in his place. (10) And the LORD came, and stood, and called as at other times, Samuel, Samuel. Then Samuel answered, speak; for thy servant heareth."

Afterwards, Eli wants to know what the LORD said unto Samuel, and demands that he tell him all, and tells him to leave nothing out. Samuel tells Eli everything that the LORD told him, leaving nothing out, and at verse 19, "And Samuel grew, and the LORD was with him, and did let none of his words fall to the ground (20) And all Israel from Dan even to Beer-sheba knew that Samuel was established to be a prophet of the LORD."

This is a powerful story of love, sacrifice, devotion, honor and integrity, as far as Samuel is concerned. Looking at Eli and his sons, we have the exact contrast!

His sons were Hophni, whose name means "strong," and Phinehas, "face of trust" or "mouth of serpent." Both these young men had great potential when we look at their names, to be priests of strength, honor and trust, and yet, their father was indifferent. He failed to not only seek the LORD in regards to their training, but obviously forgot the Law of God himself, that was handed down from Moses. This indifference was a silent consent by Eli to "Do whatever you want, only, don't bother me," or maybe, "I'm just too tired to deal with the struggle of making you do what is right and honorable before God," or maybe, "I just love you too much; I can't bear to see you cry or be sad!"

This indifference on the part of Eli led his sons down a path of evil practices that brought a twice-pronounced curse upon their heads. Both were slain at the battle of Aphek, and this coupled with the loss of the Ark, caused the death of Eli. All these men were a total disgrace to their priestly office in more ways than one.

Eli never established the spiritual guardianship for his sons. We have two stark, very different examples of how to release your child into the hands of God and allow His divine wisdom to govern and direct their lives and training for ministry. My reason for saying ministry is because the great commission of our LORD, found in Matthew 28:19-20, "Go ye therefore, and teach all nations, baptizing them in the name of the Father, and of the Son, and of the Holy Ghost: (20) Teaching them to observe all things whatsoever I have commanded you: and lo, I am with you always, even unto the end of the world." Amen.

This vital call was given to the apostles, the disciples, the early church, passed down from our great grandparents, grandparents, on down, on down, to us, to our children, to their children, etc. At birth, we are called into the ministry, especially if we were born to Christian parents. There is no exception, only great responsibility. GO YE!

One other thing I'd like to point out about Samuel as a young man of twelve, remember when the LORD called him, and he thought it was Eli, this young man was in bed for the night, and yet at the voice of his spiritual father, the Bible tells, us at verse 5, "And he ran unto Eli, and said, here am I; for thou calledst me." Samuel responded immediately to what he thought was the voice of Eli. Teach your children to answer your call immediately, and to come quickly; if they're taught this from toddlers, when they are old, or older it will not depart from them; they will also be quick to hear and answer the call of God on their lives.

Our LORD has hidden within each of our children very special gifts and treasures, gifts that if properly nurtured will not only more than meet their need for material comfort, but will also provide for the body of Christ. Please don't allow your ambitions for your child or children to cloud the purpose God has for their lives; remember Samuel, the boy, the priest, the prophet, and the judge of Israel. There are no limits to what God wants to do and will do for our children, IF He is allowed the complete control or mastery over their lives. After all, how wonderful to think of your child as being the next Mother Theresa, or Billy Graham or John the Baptist, or Paul or Stephen or Esther or Deborah, and the possibilities go on and on!

To have a child who will stand in the gap for this generation and declare that God's Word never fails! To declare to a lost and dying world that the answer to all their heartache and pain, the answer to every perplexing question or thought, can be found in His Word. To have a son or daughter that will shout from the mountain tops, like in Isaiah 55:1, "Ho, everyone that thirsteth, come ye to the waters, and he that hath no money; come ye, buy, and eat; yea come, buy wine and milk without money and without price." Or that out of the depths of their soul they would cry out unto them from the Book of Revelation 7:16-17, "They shall hunger no more, neither thirst any more; neither shall the sun light on them, nor any heat. (17) For the Lamb which is in the midst of the throne shall feed them, and shall lead them unto living fountains of waters: and God shall wipe away all tears from their eyes."

How could any child of God not want this for their child of God? To tell the sick and dying that God will always heal if they would but dare to believe! That there is a Balm in Gilead. According to Jeremiah 8:22, "Is there no balm in Gilead; is there no physician there? Why then is not the health of the daughter of my people recovered?" This balm, the health and healing Jeremiah refers to is within easy reach, and available to all. "Whosoever will, let him come."

Remember we saw earlier in 1 Samuel 3:1, "And the child Samuel ministered unto the LORD before Eli. And the Word of the LORD was precious in those days; there was no open vision"

The Word of God tells us in Proverbs 29:18, "Where there is no vision, the people perish: but he that keepeth the law, happy is he." Also in Romans 10:13-14, "For whosoever shall call upon the name of the LORD shall be saved. (14) How then shall they call on Him in who they have not believed? And how shall they believe in Him whom they have not heard? And how shall they hear without a preacher!"

As parents we must determine within ourselves what part we will play in proclaiming the gospel to a dying world. First, if the people have no vision of what is to come, or what is to become of them without Christ, they will lose their eternal souls. Second, how can this word of salvation, deliverance, and of healing go forth without a preacher!

Again in Luke 10:1-2, "After these things the LORD appointed other seventy also, and sent them two and two before His face into every city and place, whither He Himself would come. (2) Therefore said He unto them, the harvest truly is great, but the laborers are few: pray ye therefore the LORD of the harvest, that He would send forth laborers into His harvest."

The gifts to the body of Christ are named and proclaimed in Ephesians 4:9-13, " (9) Now that He ascended, what it is but that He also descended first into the lower parts of the earth? (10) He that descended is the same also that ascended up far above all things. (11) And He gave some, apostles and some prophets; and some, evangelists, and some pastors and teachers, (12) for the perfecting of the saints, for the work of the ministry for the edifying of the body of Christ: (13) Till we all come in the unity of the faith, and of the knowledge of the Son of God, unto a perfect man unto the measure of the stature of the fullness of Christ."

How can these great tasks and assignments be completed without the hand of God on the lives of mankind, but, God cannot place into this earth the missionaries, preachers, teachers, apostles, evangelists, etc. without...you guessed it...our CHILDREN!

Notice the example that our LORD gives us in this scripture, that before ascending into heaven, He descended into the lower parts of the earth to fulfill His own commission found in 2 Peter 3:9, "The LORD is not slack concerning His promise, as some men count slackness; but is longsuffering to us-ward, not willing that any should perish, but that all should come to repentance."

How can they repent…without a preacher, how can they learn…without a teacher, how can they be healed…without faith, and how can faith come…without hearing?

Friends, there is no greater call on the life of each parent than to "Train up a child in the way he should go: and when he is old, he will not depart from it." (Proverbs 22:6). We're in a race, a race and a fight that is to the death, the death of the enemy and his plans or purpose for our lives, or the death of God's purpose and plans for our lives. According to Hebrews 12:1-2, "Wherefore seeing we also are compassed about with so great a cloud of witnesses, let us lay aside every weight, and the sin which doth so easily beset us, and let us run with patience the race that is set before us, (2) Looking unto Jesus the author and Finisher of our Faith; who for the joy that was set before Him endured the cross, despising the shame, and is set down at the right hand of the Throne of God."

Paul tells us in 2 Timothy 4:7, "I have fought a good fight, I have finished my course, I have kept the faith." If our children are to endure in this race, to finish their course set before them, you as their coach, their trainer, must be equipped with certain knowledge regarding their training and conditioning, which cannot be at all accomplished without your seeking God on their behalf with fasting, prayer, intercession, consecration, speaking the Word of God over them and to them, from the rising of the sun, until the going down of the same.

Only God can reveal to you the type of race or fight that is set before your child. After all, remember, He is the author and Finisher of our faith, He wrote the BOOK that you have in your hands, and only He knows what is needed for the good success of your child in this life, in the natural and spiritual sense.

Will you be like Hannah, who before conception dedicated the life of her child to the LORD, or like Eli, who had a form of Godliness, but denied the power thereof?

Chapter II

In This Way…You Shall Bless Your Children!

There is nothing more powerful, more necessary to our children than to have the approval and favor of their parent or parents. Even the youngest children have the look of contentment and peace that seems to cover their tiny faces when they know that they please you, or that they've done something that meets with your approval.

Remember your little ones, when they took that first shaky step towards you, when you held out your arms and called their name, bidding them to come? It was so exciting, and everyone, including any nearby neighbor had to hear the shrieks of sheer excitement at the joy of this very first step. Or when that first program or play at school came, and your child earned a special part, the entire family from great aunts and uncles, cousins, grandparents, etc. were all there, cameras clicking and flash bulbs flashing…All of this just because of the pride you felt at your child being chosen to perform something special. Perhaps the mere fact they were even participating, for with some little ones, to over come their fear and bashfulness is a tremendous feat in itself. But the happiness you felt, that unconditional love that surpasses even your ability to comprehend, cannot be expressed in simple words. Suffice it to say…they were the center of your life!

As they get older, and their grades, the choices they made with friends, social habits, colleges, careers, lifetime mates, all of these can cause pride and confidence in you for a job well done as their parent, especially if their choices meet with your approval.

The right choices our children make, the healthy attitude and self-esteem they possess help give them the inner strength and determination to fight and never give up, to remain determined, no matter how often or how severe the physical or emotional challenges that press against them, to face with steadfast boldness every hurdle life circumstances seem to bring into their lives, one right after the other. Failure to them, is not an option, but rather…a four letter word!

There are so many spiritual influences that mold and shape the lives of our children, seen and unseen factors that are worth more to them, and their good success, than we will ever know in this life. Only in eternity will we know the true weight and measure, the priceless value of our prayers and blessing that covered our children every day of their lives.

What every parent wants and needs for their children, the most invaluable gift you can place in their hands, is the Favor of God. We're told in 1 Corinthians 2: 9, "But as it is written, eye hath not seen, nor ear heard, neither have entered in the heart of man, the things which God hath prepared for them that love Him."

For them that love Him! Friends…that scripture is not for eternity only, but it applies for every day of their lives! When our children our taught to put Him first, to love their God with all their hearts, all their minds, all their souls and all their strength, "Eye hath not seen, nor ear heard, neither has it entered into the heart of man, the things which God hath prepared for them that love Him!"

The favor of the Father, our children will not know from the beginning what the favor and blessings of God will mean to their lives. You must teach them until they do fully understand. It's your blessing them according to the Word of God that will cause them to reap benefits beyond measure in their lives.

It's not your good wishes or your good intentions that will grant unto them divine intervention at a time when neither you nor your child will know it's needed. It's the favor of God that covers them because of the blessings you have proclaimed on their lives, and on their behalf from the very beginning…according to the Word of God!

Let's take a look at Isaiah 55:10-12. "For as the rain cometh down, and the snow from heaven, and returneth not thither, but watereth the earth, and maketh it bring forth and bud, that it may give seed to the sower, and bread to the eater: (11) So shall my Word be that goeth forth out of my mouth: it shall accomplish that which I please, and it shall prosper in the thing whereto I sent it. (12) For ye shall go out with joy, and be led forth with peace: the mountains and hills shall break forth before you into singing, and all the trees of the field shall clap their hands."

In these three verses of scripture alone, there is provision, food, water, joy, peace, victory over mountains, praises and adoration among the people.

Everything is here in these verses, including a covenant from our LORD, that when His Word is spoken, it will fulfill His own covenant towards us, towards our children, our homes, families, everything that involves us, so why would you use the empty shallow words of man, or your own intellect, hoping to fulfill what needs to be down for your child in areas of their lives you're not even aware of?

When you pray for your children, when you bless them, pray the Word of God! Pray the WORD! That is what will prosper them and make their path straight, and cause them to bring forth fruit for the gospel's sake.

As a parent there is nothing you would deny your child of this world's goods, or opportunities, certainly not the spiritual blessings and benefits you could bestow upon them. Every possible good thing you could think of, or that anyone else could think of, is how you would bless your children, if it were within your power to do so. Why not give that opportunity to their heavenly Father who can do…"Exceedingly abundantly above all we can ask or think…!" (Ephesians 3:20)

When you speak God's Word over your children, when you bless them by His Word, when you proclaim His Word concerning them, not your dreams, your hopes or ambitions, but what the LORD saith, according to His Word. It will do nothing but reap bountifully in their lives! He has declared it, and it's just so.

As with all spiritual matters there is a way to do everything. Remember when the disciples, after having watched Jesus when He prayed over everything imaginable from sickness, disease, demon possession, feeding the hungry, etc., saw that nothing was ever denied Him, they decided, hey, we need to know how to pray like Jesus prays. In Luke 11:1-4, "And it came to pass, that, as He was praying in a certain place, when he ceased, one of His disciples said unto Him, LORD, teach us to pray, as John also taught his disciples. (2) And He said unto them, when ye pray, say, Our Father which art in heaven, Hallowed be thy name. Thy kingdom come, thy will be done, as in heaven, so in earth. (3) Give us day by day our daily bread. And forgive us our sins; for we also forgive every one that is indebted to us. And lead us not into temptation; but deliver us from evil."

Incorporated in this prayer is: 1) The acknowledgment of who God is; 2) where He is and is Throne; 3) Giving reverence to His name; 4) Allowing for the power, presence and WILL of heaven to be accomplished in this earth, just as it is in heaven; 5) Asking for His provision for what we eat; 6) Asking for His forgiveness in our lives and in the lives of others, even those we are indebted to; 7) Order our steps according to His will and purpose and 8) Keep us out of mess…(Oops…sorry) keep us from evil. (Smile)

I don't understand why there's debate within the body of Christ as to whether or not this prayer was intended for us, or the disciples; what matters is that when we pray we should pray according to wisdom. What better wisdom is there than the wisdom of Christ? This prayer covers everything from A-Z! It doesn't matter if it's prayed word-for-word or not, what matters is that these components are at least included, Amen…Amen.

In Numbers 6:22-27, "And the LORD spake unto Moses, saying, (23) Speak unto Aaron and unto his sons saying, On this wise ye shall bless the children of Israel, saying unto them, (24) The LORD bless thee, and keep thee: (25) The LORD make His face shine upon thee, and be gracious unto thee: (26) The LORD lift up His countenance upon thee, and give thee peace. (27) And they shall put my name upon the children of Israel; and I will bless them."

The LORD was telling Moses to mark the children of Israel with this prayer, this blessing, that Aaron would use this blessing, this prayer as a spiritual branding iron, so to speak! That when He saw this prayer, this blessing upon them, because the prayers of the righteous have always accomplished much, He…God Himself, would move on their behalf in every facet of their lives!

We are encouraged to pray with understanding and wisdom, encouraged by our LORD to bless our children with our prayers. After all, isn't that what He told Aaron to do for the children of Israel? Wasn't He instructing him on how to pray for and bless Israel? We read in Matthew 7:7-11, "Ask, and it shall be given you, seek, and ye shall find; knock, and it shall be opened unto you: (8) For everyone that asketh receiveth; and he that seeketh findeth; and to him that knocketh it shall be opened. (9) Or what man is there of you, whom if his son ask bread, will he give him a stone? (10) Or if he ask a fish, will he give him a serpent? (11) If ye then, being evil, know how to give good gifts unto your children, how much more shall your Father which is in heaven give good things to them that ask Him?

The Aaronic Benediction captures the essential purpose of the priestly ministry that was to bless the people of God with God's presence in their lives and His provision on their behalf. It was to reflect God's goodness on their behalf. The same way God's presence was reflected on the countenance of Moses in Exodus 34:29, "And it came to pass, when Moses came down from Mount Sinai with the two tables of testimony in Moses' hand, when he came down from the mount, that Moses knew not that the skin of his face shone while he talked with him, (30) And when Aaron and all the children of Israel saw Moses, behold, the skin of his face shone; and they were afraid to come nigh him."

The New Testament establishes this as the Glory of God, which we behold with unveiled face as the Holy Spirit transforms us daily into His image, as seen in 2 Corinthians 3:18, "But we all, with open face beholding as in a glass the glory of our LORD, are changed into the same image from glory to glory, even as by the Spirit of the LORD!" Hallelujah! Give Him glory!"

Now back to the importance of blessing and anointing your children. Our desire for each of our children is that they grow as strong and fit spiritually, as they do physically. We desire for them this divine glory, the very visible presence of God on their lives. They must also grow in Him, grow beyond themselves and their limitations. They must be able to stand and face problems, conflicts, and make responsible choices. With the covering and protection of your prayers and blessings on them daily, from the womb and until forever, they will be able to do just that.

We cannot demand responsibility from our children if we have not given them the tools, both naturally and spiritually to make responsible choices and decisions. We look at Israel, and see them as children given a new lease on life, children that were enslaved, dependent, abused and even destroyed because of their ability to thrive even in the hostile environment in which they lived. As seen in Exodus 1:7, "And the children of Israel were fruitful, and increased abundantly, and multiplied, and waxed exceeding mighty; and the land was filled with them." At verse15-16 of Exodus 1: "And the king of Egypt spoke to the Hebrew midwives, of which the name of the one was Shiphral, and the name of the other Puah: (16) And he said, when ye do the office of a midwife to the Hebrew women, and see them upon the stools; if it be a son, then ye shall kill him: but if it be a daughter, then she shall live."

God's delivery of His people was essential, swift, sure, and without debate. Now that they had been redeemed from slavery, by God's great power, God knew His children needed guidance, boundaries, and help in shaping their bright new futures. He was there to provide all these things and more for them, because of His love for Israel. He did not abandon them after delivering them, nor did He expect from them what He had not provided. They had been taught God's will in the law that revealed much of His character. Provisions had been made to cleanse the Israelites from their sins that would inevitably come. The people had been instructed on how to live in fellowship with their God. They were provided with everything they needed to live a holy life, now they were responsible.

When we have provided our children with everything they need to grow, to flourish, and become productive and responsible adults, then they will be responsible for the choices they make, and the results of those choices. What you instill in them by the Word of God, your prayers and your blessings upon them will be a reflection of your obedience to God for their lives, and whether or not you "trained them up in the way they should go!" The rest of that verse reads, "and when he is old, he will not depart from it." It may take you child twenty-four years, or thirty years, or thirteen years to reach their potential in Christ. Your responsibility is to give them what they need to reach it. When they reach it, is up to them and their LORD. Rest, don't be too anxious. It's a very valuable BOOK. Please…handle it with care.

Now let's talk a little about your responsibility in praying for and blessing your child. Learning responsibility is difficult, difficult at any age, and even difficult for parents. Some of us learn responsibility only after great pain and heartache, and with some parents, it may be the only way they will learn. What we want to avoid is that late night telephone call, that crazy out-of-bounds relationship, or that battle with illicit drugs and alcohol. These and other issues may creep into our lives, but because of our prayers, our blessings, our speaking the Word of God into their lives, along with our training, the length of time and severity of these distractions will be greatly limited!

When I was told by my doctor that I was pregnant I began then, reading the Word of God aloud, not just for my benefit, also for my child's. I began speaking this prayer or what I consider a blessing over my children when they were in the womb. I received a new insight from a lady who came one Sunday to minister to the women of our church. I was a very young mother-to-be. The woman of God declared that what we speak over our children and what we speak into their lives would mold and shape their lives for the purpose and will of God. This concept changed and challenged my life in regards to what I thought needful and necessary to be a good mother, for my children to have God's best and His favor in their lives. It changed my life! Let's read this again, breaking it down according to what the Spirit of God gave me. What He gives you may be different, or your spirit may bear witness with mine in regards to this blessing of benediction. It's too deep and lengthy for me to tell you in complete detail, but it's my prayer that you will read for yourselves the scripture that the Spirit of God directed me to. Please read it and allow this

Word to become breath and life to you and your children! Let's read at Numbers 6:23-27: "Speak unto Aaron and unto his sons, saying, on this wise ye shall bless the children of Israel, saying unto them, (24) The LORD bless thee, and keep thee: (25) The LORD make his face shine upon thee, and be gracious unto thee: (26) The LORD lift up His countenance upon thee, and give thee peace. (27) And they shall put my name upon the children of Israel; and I will bless them."

Numbers 6, verse 24: "the LORD bless thee:" Deuteronomy 28:1-2, "And it shall come to pass, if thou shalt hearken diligently unto the voice of the LORD thy God, to observe and to do all His commandments which I command thee this day, that the LORD thy God will set thee on high above all the nations of the earth: (2) And all these blessings shall come on thee, and overtake thee, if thou shalt hearken unto the voice of the LORD thy God." Continuing with a brief statement of the verses:

Verse 4: Blessed shall be the fruit of their body—healthy children

Verse 5: Blessed shall be their basket and their store—no lack or hunger

Verse 6: Blessed when they come in or go out—safe traveling mercies

Verse 7: He shall defeat their enemies before your face

Verse 8: He'll not only bless their prosperity, He'll bless everything they touch!

Verse 9: If they keep His Word and commandments, He will firmly establish them in whatever they do

Verse 10: The entire world will know that God's hand is on their lives

Verse 11: Wealthy in this world's goods, in children and all their substance

Verse 12: He will open up the windows of heaven to rain on them, and bless them at work or play, and they shall not be in debt to any man!

Verse 13: They will take a back seat to no man if they will obey God!

Verse 14: They shall not detour from the establish path of His Word and His will for their lives!

The blessings that the LORD promised to bless the children of Israel with, they also belong to us. According to Hebrews 13:8, "Jesus Christ the same, yesterday and today and forever." In Malachi 3: 6, "For I am the LORD, I change not, therefore ye sons of Jacob are not consumed." The holiness of our God will not change. His desire for His people will not change. His willingness to bless us according to our obedience will not change!

When you pray the blessings of God on the lives of your children, you're proclaiming great wealth, health, prosperity, favor among men, favor in the work place, safety in all their traveling, with such abundance they will have more than enough; they will never be in debt! What else could you want for your children? Amen…Amen!

The wealth and prosperity of our LORD cannot be measured, or need it be measured, by the dollar sign only. Your children are wealthy when they can come and go, night or day, alone or in a crowd, never harmed or in danger of harm. They are wealthy when their bodies are strong and well, and respond to good food, exercise and rest, without the aid of medication. They are wealthy when they study and recall and can apply what they've studied with practical application. Wealth is the ability to have success in any environment.

You must remain faithful from the moment that new life begins within you. Speak the Word of God into the lives of your children. Anoint them with oil each day before they leave your home. I usually do this each morning before they even wake. When they're faced with challenges, and challenges will come, don't give them your philosophy; search the scripture for the answers God will give, and speak those answers into their lives concerning those challenges. This will accomplish two things: 1) You're teaching them where to go, and whom to look to for life's challenges, 2) You're also teaching them that the glory belongs to God for each victory! Amen!

The earlier your children realize not just the might and power of their God to deliver, not just the bounty of His provision, but His tender mercies, His love for His children, that He desires our fellowship our trust, adoration, and our love, the better for them.

They'll never know or understand what a blessing this knowledge is to them without their having seen it and experienced it through your life. We're told in Jeremiah 9:23-24, " Thus saith the LORD, Let not the wise man glory in his wisdom, neither let the mighty man glory in his might, let not the rich man glory in his riches: (24) But let him that glorieth glory in this: that he understandeth and knoweth me, that I am the LORD which exercise loving kindness, judgment, and righteousness, in the earth: for in these things I delight saith the LORD."

The LORD delights in that His child knows Who He is, and What He is, and that His every concern is only that we truly understand the above scripture.

When your feet touch the floor each morning, the praises of God, and the Word of God should be the first things out of your mouth! The fact that your hair is combed, or that you're dressed in a bright beautiful robe, that breakfast is not only prepared, but your table is also covered with this lovely table cloth and fresh flowers, with the ever-present, fresh-squeezed orange juice—these things are good, but have no eternal weight in glory! What matters is that your children hear your songs of praise and worship, that they are greeted with love and the blessings of the LORD, and as they leave the house, they feel anointed, prayed for and blessed! Your concern is not only that their homework is ready for the teacher, but that their lives would magnify and glorify the goodness of the LORD to those they will meet that day, and that they're not fearful of representing Christ!

That's what the LORD is talking about in the above scripture! Our lives and commitment as parents far surpass this world's concepts of good parents.

Remember in Job 1:8-10, "And the LORD said unto Satan, hast thou considered my servant Job, that there in none like him in the earth, a perfect and an upright man, one that feareth God, and escheweth evil? (9) Then Satan answered the LORD, and said, doth Job fear God for nought? (10) Hast not thou made an hedge about him, and about his house, and about all that he hath on every side? Thou hast blessed the work of his hands and his substance is increased in the land." Remember Deuteronomy 28:3-14? That's exactly what we have in place here, the total blessings of God...the hedge.

The dictionary gives this definition of *hedge*: To close in or bound, to hem in or hinder outside trespassing; to minimize and protect against loss; and a closely planted shrub or low growing trees forming a fence or boundary.

The hedge of God is the favor of God, provided for His children. When you bless your children and cover them with prayer, you're keeping the hedge of God's blessing about them. Even as adults, we must desire to be kept. Our gracious Father will never intrude upon our will, nor the will of our children. It is so crucial that every day we lay some new foundation within the lives of our children that cannot be uprooted! That the hedge the Holy Spirit has provided, is firmly rooted and grounded about them! For this to be accomplished, they must know who He is!

Remember in Matthew, the sixteenth chapter, when our LORD asked Peter, "Who do you say that I am?" (Matthew 16:15) Remember Peter's answer, Matthew 16:16, "And Simon Peter answered and said, Thou art the Christ the Son of the living God." Friends, do your children know and understand who Jesus is? If any man can call Jesus LORD, just as it was with Peter, it is by the Holy Spirit that this realization is made truth to them! This cannot just be your confession on behalf of your children; it must be the conviction of their own souls! When they are SAVED...and have really received and confessed the LORD as their Savior you will know and see that they are born, not of flesh and blood, but of the Spirit of the living God.

Maybe for some or for every one of your children, it may take months, or years before this heart-changing confessing truly becomes their own. That's why you must stand on the wall with a faithfulness and determination that will not waver. Our LORD has entrusted you with the life and training of His most valuable possession, your BOOK, an eternal soul. The reason and the only reason for the good success of any life is going back to Jeremiah (9:23-24), what He really delights in…is the personal confession of our hearts, that, "Thou art the Christ!" This knowledge is not just a hedge, but the very rock and foundation of our Faith, and the gates of hell shall not prevail against it! Hallelujah!

You also bless your children when you teach them the power of the name of Jesus! All things are possible to them through the name of Jesus! As it is written in Philippians 2: 9-11, "Wherefore God also hath highly exalted Him, and given Him a name which is above every name: (10) That at the name of Jesus every knee should bow, of things in heaven, and things in earth, and things under the earth; (11) And that every tongue confess that Jesus Christ is LORD, to the glory of God the Father." The awesome power of the Holy Spirit will help them to overcome everything that Satan may throw at them, through the name of Jesus. Bless them and teach them the power and authority His name. Instill within them the power, the virtue, and the glory of His name. Through His name they will have total access to our God.

The name of Jesus is the name they can utter even in a whisper, and demons will not only tremble, but must bow in their presence to the authority of His name. It is a blessed thing for your children to learn that God's Word never fails, even when parents do. That God will work mightily in their behalf, when they persist in believing Him despite the discouragements and disappointments they may face, knowing without a doubt that God is a reality, and that His Son Jesus Christ, and His name is the only authority they need in this earth to move mountains. This understanding and realization will be more valuable to them than silver or gold. Bless them with this knowledge on a daily basis. For God's will and purpose for their lives will never give way to human opinions, not even yours, if it's not His will for their lives. Whatever He has determined for them, what He has said regarding their lives, will come to pass in their lives, *if* you dare to teach them how to stand, and trust in His Plan, in His Purpose, and His Path for their lives.

This is the same authority Peter used when the lame man lay beside the temple gate called Beautiful, in Acts 3:6-7. " Then Peter said, Silver and gold have I none; but such as I have give I thee: In the name of Jesus Christ of Nazareth rise up and walk. (7) And he took him by the right hand, and lifted him up: and immediately his feet and ankle bones received strength."

When raising up little children, infants, toddlers, etc., all our efforts should not be spent by simply attending to their physical needs and discomforts. It's at this time in their lives that our prayers will water, prune back, and fertilize that spiritual hedge around them.

Here I want to try and convey the importance of your understanding of what you have in your hands. Whenever you look into the soft, warm eyes of your beautiful infant, or when you grasp the tiny chubby hands of your toddler, when you discipline your little son or daughter with a tear-stained face, that spirit man within them is ageless. Their spirit is as eternal and ageless as time itself! They need spiritual food for the developing of spiritual strength and maturity. As natural food affects the natural man, so spiritual food, the Word of God, affects the spiritual man! Our spirit man does not grow from eight days old to eighty years old! At the birth of your child, his spirit man, or his eternal soul, is as old as it will ever get, and rest assured, his spirit can handle anything you give it according to the Word of God! There is no such thing as baby spirit food! Feed that spirit the meat of the Word! Believe me, the Word you deposit within them will not return void.

We find that Jesus blessed the little children in Matthew 19:13-15. "Then were there brought unto Him little children that He should put His hands on them, and pray: and the disciples rebuked them. (14) But Jesus said, suffer little children, and forbid them not, to come unto me: for of such is the kingdom of heaven. (15) And He laid His hands on them, and departed thence."

Here in Matthew Jesus is teaching the crowds that followed close behind Him, listening, some very intently; others followed to ridicule and trap Him if at all possible. And there were those that followed out of their sincere need for a touch or miracle in their lives.

What we need to understand about the verse above are three statements made by our LORD, and an action Matthew noted for our information. 1) Allow the children to come; 2) Heaven is of such; and 3) He laid His hands on them.

A Jewish person becomes responsible for the Law of Moses, or responsible in relating to God through the Mosaic Law, at the age of twelve. These little children were too young to be under the Law, yet our LORD says let them come. His desire is always for an intimate personal relationship with His children, children of every age, and children that will respond willingly to His voice. What better age to start teaching them this, than as little children. He goes on to tell us that the fundamental essence of heaven is child-like eagerness, child-like willingness, and child-like faith. That's what heaven is all about.

The very emotional make up of a child is that of total trust. The only time your child may hesitate in doing anything you ask of them is if they've somehow experienced pain or some negative response due to some behavior of their own or someone else's. For example, if a child has never been bitten by a dog, he will run through a pack of dogs at your bidding! When she sees water, whether it be a small pool in the back yard, the family pool, or the ocean it's all the same to her…off she will run in with reckless abandonment, absolutely fearless!

Never fear to lay your hands upon your children and speak the blessing of God over them; Jesus did! He's always our most perfect and only true example. The earlier in their lives you begin this responsibility, this commitment, the sooner and the younger the age, you will see the magnificent fruit of your labor of love. For truly, that's exactly what it is…a labor of love. Isn't that what Jesus did for us on Calvary: a labor…of love?

It's the world's custom, at least professionally, to grab a child with talent, whether in sports, music, acting, golf, etc., at an early age. The younger they are, the better. Every athletic star or hero, every movie star, even those gifted with superior intellect, when it's discovered in them, they are immediately separated from the other children, and trained or developed from a very early age!

Parents are more interested in teaching their child to read at five months than to pray at five months. They would rather develop a particular skill in sports or something else, at two or three years of age, than to, at the same age, have her receive the LORD with clear understanding in her heart, as her LORD and Savior.

When you are blessed with a gifted child, give God the praise and the glory, for it is a blessed gift. However, please allow for the balance of their spiritual training to perfect all their gifts. What does it profit a man, or child to gain the world's acknowledgments and praise…and lose their souls? Allowing the balance the Holy Spirit will give you in training the whole child, is blessing them with God's favor!

The Word of God tells us in 1 John 2: 13-14, " I write unto you, father, because ye have known Him that is from the beginning. I write unto you, young men, because ye have overcome the wicked one. I write unto you, little children, because ye have known the Father. (14) I have written unto you fathers, because ye have know Him that is from the beginning. I have written unto you young men, because ye are strong, and the Word of God abideth in you, and ye have overcome the wicked one."

In the verses above we have a wonderful assurance in Christ, that even when we may not know or understand what we're doing, or why, God does, and God sees!

John seemed to have a beautiful confidence in the people he developed relationships with, often referring to the men, but don't forget what the Word of God that says in 2 Timothy 3:16-17, "All scripture is given by inspiration of God, and is profitable for doctrine, for reproof, for correction, for instruction in righteousness: (17) That the man [or woman, or child] of God may be perfect, thoroughly furnished unto all good works."

God's Word applies to all of us, man, woman or child. John was really trying to encourage the people of God that as little children they had made an initial commitment to Jesus, and their sins were totally forgiven! As fathers they had lived in relationship with God, a God who proved Himself again and again to them to be more than faithful! As young men, they were challenged in their faith by Satan, and because of God's strength and His Word in them, it enabled them to overcome!

Bless your children, by the Word of God, by the name of Jesus, by the Spirit of God, and of course...by the example of God! Amen, amen.

Chapter III

Calling Forth…the Calling

Within every child born, whether they are born to Christian parents, non-Christian, or to a single mother struggling for her own life's survival, whether they were abandoned at birth, or any other of one hundred and one possibilities that pertain to the birth of each child, they were born with not only a divine nature, having an eternal soul, but a divine purpose.

It is God's power through His Holy Spirit that has given us all things, and all things are directly related to knowing the LORD, becoming like Him, and growing in the character and virtue that represents His holiness.

The Christian life and walk cannot be accomplished in one day, one hour, and honestly, not even in one life time. It's a continuous effort of learning, re-learning, tearing down, building up, falling down, and getting up. All of this is a wonderful press towards the mark. Philippians 3: 14, "I press toward the mark for the prize of the high calling of God in Christ Jesus!"

In the Old Testament you'll find the word *elect* used to tell us that God has made a choice. God's choice was for His people Israel. Israel became God's people, not because they decided to belong to Him, but because He took the initiative and chose them. When looking at Israel, you don't see any particular outstanding virtue that they exemplified that would make them special. What you do see is God's faithfulness to their forefather Abraham and His covenant with him. Therefore, we understand that this word *elect* indicates God's prerogative in deciding what will happen, independent of human choice.

In the New Testament God's people are described as His elect or chosen ones, a term used by Jesus when speaking of the future time when the Son of Man will come and gather together God's people. As told to us in Mark 13:20, "And except that the LORD had shortened those days, no flesh should be saved: but for the elect's sake, whom He hath chosen, He hath shortened the days." We find in 1 Peter 2:9, "But ye are a chosen generation, a royal priesthood an holy nation, a peculiar people; that ye should shew forth the praises of Him who hath called you out of darkness into His marvelous light."

When Paul wrote Romans, he had not yet been to Rome, but was ministering powerfully and effectively throughout the Mediterranean world. Although Paul had never been to Rome, he had come to know many believers there, and was accustomed to introducing himself to others in this manner: Romans 1:1, "Paul a servant of Jesus Christ, called to be an apostle, separated unto the gospel of God." Paul was called and chosen by Jesus Christ on the way to Damascus.

How do you, as a parent, determine the call of God for your child? Is it something about them that will stand out powerfully and strong in their nature? Will you see it, or know it by the things they take pride and joy in doing? Or will they simply walk up to you one day and declare, "Mom, Dad, I want to be a preacher [or missionary, or evangelist]!" Well, they may do just that, especially if you've been praying, blessing them, and anointing them on a daily basis, and speaking God's Word into their lives. They may make it just that easy! (Smile)

Let's take a look at some of God's chosen people, those who were called. The first example is one who was called from the womb. In Luke 1: 15-17, "For he shall be great in the sight of the LORD, and shall drink neither wine nor strong drink; and he shall be filled with the Holy Spirit, even from the womb. (16) And many of the children of Israel shall he turn to the LORD their God. (17) And he shall go before Him in the spirit and power of Elias, to turn the hearts of the fathers to the children, and the disobedient to the wisdom of the just; to make ready a people prepared for the LORD." That's John the Baptist, the forerunner of our LORD and Savior, Jesus Christ!

John was a plain but powerful man, and a Nazarite. His parents were of priestly descent; his Mother, Elisabeth, a kinswoman of Mary, the Mother of our LORD, and his Father, Zacharias, was a priest in the Temple. As a Nazarite from birth, he developed self-reliance and spiritual strength as he communed with God in the desert solitude that he loved.

John the Baptist was not just separated by his customs and personal habits, nor because he was filled with the Holy Spirit from the womb. As a child, he came here differently and not just because we have a biblical record of his being filled with the Spirit from the womb. Everything about his birth and life sort of parallels with our LORD. The angel Gabriel appeared to his mother as he did the mother of our LORD. The birth of John the Baptist was a miracle because his mother, Elisabeth, was not only aged, she was also barren. The birth of our LORD was a miracle because His mother, Mary, had never known a man. Our LORD was given His name by His father, and the name of John was determined by his father. Our LORD, and John the Baptist started their work very young, died young, both had disciples, and they were also both sent from God. Everything about him was different, and compared to our LORD in so many ways. They were called.

Then there's Esther, who was chosen for "such a time as this." Esther was made queen to the king of Persia, Ahasuerus. She succeeded Queen Vashti, who would not obey the unjust command of her husband, to parade herself before his drunken and boisterous guests.

Esther was the ward of her cousin, Mordecai, a Benjamite official at the palace gate. We all know the story, but to shorten it, Esther and her people were placed in great danger by the jealousy and bitterness of one Haman, who sorely resented Mordecai because he did not give him the respect he thought he so richly deserved.

Haman plotted to destroy all the Jews, and Mordecai and Esther were naturally included in this plot. Mordecai told Esther that she would have to do something quickly; she must go before her king and petition for her people. At first Esther was fearful for her own life, but in Esther 4: 13-14, " Then Mordecai commanded to answer Esther, think not with thyself that thou shalt escape in the king's house, more than all the Jews. (14) For if thou altogether holdest thy peace at this time, then shall their enlargement and deliverance arise to Jews from another place; but thou and thy father's house shall be destroyed: and who knoweth whether thou art come to the kingdom for such a time as this?"

Esther fasted and prayed, and her people with her, and God delivered them, and Haman was hanged on the gallows he'd prepared for Mordecai.

Esther was called or chosen by God and separated from the masses by her grace and captivating beauty. She was an orphan who was loved, groomed, nurtured, and protected by her cousin, Mordecai. Her gift was her beauty, and the LORD used it to give His people a mighty deliverance from a silent enemy that sought to destroy them.

We have Timothy of Jewish and Greek ancestry, who was the spiritual son of the Apostle Paul. Timothy was a child of a Godly heritage, his mother, Eunice, was a devoted Christian Jewess, as was his grandmother, Lois.

As a child, he was a reader of the Scripture. In 2 Timothy 3:15, "And that from a child thou hast know the Holy Scriptures, which are able to make thee wise unto salvation through faith which is in Christ Jesus." There is a rich blessing when a child is cradled in the things of God!

Timothy, ordained by the presbytery, was nurtured and encouraged in his gifts by Paul, who was acutely aware of Timothy's unique gifts, especially that of evangelism (1 Timothy 4:14-16, "Neglect not the gift that is in thee, which was given thee by prophecy, with the laying on of hands of the presbytery. (15) mediate upon these things, give thyself wholly to them; that thy profiting may appear to all. (16) Take heed unto thyself, and unto the doctrine; continue in them: for in doing this thou shalt both save thyself, and them that hear thee."

Paul is giving complete instructions to his son by telling him: 1) Use your gift; 2) It's legitimate, coming from God; 3) Stay focused on what God has given you that others will be blessed; 4) Be careful of the truth, and stay within the truth; it will save you and others!

That's a perfect example of what we as parents are to do. When you determine the gifting within your child, you are to nurture it by the Word of God, and the confession of your mouth. We must also challenge our children to be responsible for what God has given them, especially if it's the word of the gospel.

We have many other wonderful people of God that were called, chosen or separated for His divine purpose for a season. There was Moses, Noah, David, Deborah, Ruth, Joseph, Abigail, Jael, and the list goes on, and on of God's sons and daughters that were used to protect, fight, deliver, provide and even kill for the gospel's sake, and the people of God.

When you look at your child, or spend time with them, what separates him from the norm, or is it the fact that he is so normal that catches your eye? Is he the type of child that does better by himself? Does he play, think, write, read or paint alone with pleasure and contentment? I'm not just saying that he doesn't interact; does he appear to be more productive working alone?

Is your daughter very easy to please, never needs or wants anything special in the way of how she chooses to dress, or wear her hair? Is she totally satisfied with whatever you do for her, with no argument? If so, have a golden statue of her likeness erected in the town's square, for she is a rare one indeed! (Smile)

Does your child give all his toys away no matter how hard you try to discourage him? Is she always willing to be last, and allow her friends to go before them, or take her turn? Is this the child you can always count on to pull flowers from someone else's yard (smile), and bring them to you? Or maybe you pick him up from school and he's starved, because he gave their lunch to someone else!

How about Little Mary who *always*…has the answer, even when she's not asked the question! She will insist on having the last word, and being the center of everyone else's conversation, and interests. How many times have you had to say, "Mary, give someone else a chance; it was your turn yesterday."

When you're out as a family, is it Mary who introduces everyone to everybody else? (Smile) Oh yes, one more thing. Is it Mary who knows everybody else's Easter Speech, or song, or just whatever? Leave it to Little Mary!

Do you have a child who seems to cry about everything, her pain, and the pain of others? Is she always protecting and taking care of someone…or something? When you're not feeling well, is this the child who will pray, or ask do you need anything? What about forever wanting to take your temperature whether you're sick or well!

Can you never put something down for more than one minute before Johnny will take it apart to fix it? Does Johnny fix everything in the house, beyond your ability to ever use it again? Has he fixed the alarm clock, your electric razor or maybe the doll of his little sister? How about his bike, that needed something…or…to be fixed. Smile!

I could go on and on with all these little telltale hints about our children: habits, talents, and sensitivities that our LORD has programmed in our children, like hidden treasure that we must not only find, but channel. Channel the gifts, or train these gifts in the way they should go.

Here's one more example. What about that child that always wants to sell something, whether it's lemonade or cookies, or maybe his very own toys? Does he use his own imagination to develop a product to sell his friends? Will he create an event for the neighborhood and charge an entry fee? Or like my younger son Ethan, who developed a comic strip series that he wrote, and had a friend of his do the art work because he "was better at drawing than me." My son, Ethan! Ethan sold a monthly copy of Cowboy Jeff to the kids at school for a monthly subscription fee of one dollar, or twenty-five cents a week, in the *fourth* grade! LORD! Please, please, help us! O-o-oh…when I found this out.…

Quickly, let's return to those things that are spiritual. Smile! Seriously, though, our LORD will never leave us in the dark about our children. Every day of their lives they're shouting out who they are, or what they want to be.

It's not difficult to see or to hear, but we must be willing to accept what we see or hear in them.

So many parents want to live their lives again, or reach for that second chance for their dream through their children. This is not only grossly unfair to them, it's also unfair to God, because what you're asking God to do is to accept a counterfeit of what was or could have been the real thing!

You may be a parent who has a child whose desire is to be just like Mommy or Daddy. She may want to be another doctor or lawyer, preacher, or teacher, etc. But your choice for them is not necessarily God's choice for them. For they will instinctively be drawn to whatever He's placed within them. Your desire can blur the lines of clear thinking. At times it may be difficult, but our command is to train up a child in the way he should go! Not in the way we wish or want, push or pull them to go!

We find that even within the body of Christ, our LORD has chosen to build His church around different gifts for different purposes. In Ephesians 4: 11, "And He gave some, apostles; and some, prophets; and some, evangelists; and some, pastors and teachers; (12) for the perfecting of the saints, for the work of the ministry, for the edifying of the body of Christ."

Not every child will belong behind the sacred pulpit, or on the hallowed grounds of the mission fields. Your child may not be called to evangelize the world in these last days. He may be chosen to bind up and heal physical bodies, or to teacher those that are young, bright, and hungry for knowledge. Others may stand on foreign battlefields or in our tortured streets where the young and old alike are crippled with drugs, alcohol, abuse, ignorance, and fear.

Maybe God has blessed you with the child that will write the most beautiful music to comfort and sooth the hearts of millions, or to paint His creation with the grace and beauty that only His Spirit could reveal to them. Maybe their words and humor will cause a saddened and hardened people to forget their pain and their sorrow. It's all good, and the Word tell us in James 1:17, "Every good gift and every perfect gift is from above, and cometh down from the Father of lights, with whom is no variableness, neither shadow of turning." Amen...Amen.

Earlier we talked about the little telltale hints and signs the LORD has programmed within our children, the hidden treasures of His kingdom, that we must not only find, but train, channel, nurture and cause to mature, into what He has called them to be.

A child who exhibits the courage to speak up for herself or others is a born leader. She can and should become anything that offers her the opportunity to lead or speak for those who can't speak for themselves. However, if this gift is not properly trained, this very same person could become a bully or dictator or one who manipulates others without mercy or conscience. A child that loves to fix or repair things, could be a mechanic, contractor or architect. But on the other hand, if these gifts are not properly trained, he might tear down instead of building up. The child that is neglected and is never given an opportunity to be heard or to grow, who must always fight for attention, might become one who abuses her body by using chemicals to poison her system, or causing harm to others by committing crimes on society to gain the attention she never received as a child.

What does your child need…what are they telling you every day of their lives? Have you ever listen to the Spirit of God, while reading your BOOK? Do you try to concentrate on your BOOK, in the midst of noise and other distractions, so that you have to read the same pages over and over again, before it sinks in?

Are you a parent who has left the majority of your reading assignment to someone else? Are you relying on their understanding of your BOOK to communicate to you the needs of your child? Many parents must work out of the home. With today's economy it can be difficult, but raising your children with your influence can still be accomplished if you're willing to spend quality time with them whenever possible. If when you're away from them your prayers continue, and you have left them in the care of the LORD, not a sitter. Working is not an excuse to neglect or transfer the responsibility of raising your child to another. Working out of the home creates a challenge and an essential partnership with the Holy Spirit. This is a must!

We're told in 1 Peter 5:7, "[Cast] all your care upon Him; for He careth for you." In other words, cast all the care of your child upon the LORD, because HE cares for your child! Surely if He knew the circumstances that would take you out of the home to provide or help provide for your family before you did, I'm certain that He's more than willing to stand in your place as a protector tutor guide, as their shield and covering. Don't forget the spiritual hedge the Word speaks about in Job; it's especially true for our children. You don't have to fear because you can't always be right there for them. Who's right there for them when you're sleeping? Right…our LORD! He is more than able and He will do "Exceeding abundantly above all, we can ask or think according to the power that worketh in you." (Ephesians 4:20)

Just as we have so many different types of BOOKS in libraries all over the world, everything from encyclopedias, journals, magazines, short stories, novels, children's books, fiction, non-fiction, mysteries, books on cooking, gardening, home repairs, etc., everything from A-Z, so it is with God's library, BOOKS of every size, shape, color potential, gifts, mysteries, talents, strength, and weaknesses, everything you can imagine, and some things you can't imagine. Add to this the different circumstances under which each parent was given her BOOK and the only common denominator in all our lives is Jesus Christ our LORD. It is upon Him that we must totally rely, even when the reading conditions and the lighting seem to be just perfect, any trust and reliance upon your own abilities should be quickly dismissed.

King Solomon was, and I guess still is, the hallmark of wisdom for all mankind. When it came time for him to reign over God's children, Israel, he knew that he was not equipped to do it alone. We find Solomon in 1 Kings 3:5-9. "In Gibeon the LORD appeared to Solomon in a dream by night: and God said, "Ask what I shall give thee. (6) And Solomon said, Thou hast shewed unto thy servant David my father great mercy, according as he walked before thee in truth, and in righteousness, and in uprightness of heart with thee; and thou hast kept for him this great kindness, that thou hast given him a son to sit on his throne, as it is this day. (7) And now, O LORD my God, thou hast made thy servant king instead of David my father: and I am but a little child: I know not how to go out or come in. (8) And thy servant is in the midst of thy people, which thou hast chosen a great people that cannot be numbered nor counted for multitude. (9) Give therefore thy servant an understanding heart to judge thy people. That I may discern between good and bad: for who is able to judge this thy so great a people?"

Solomon knew who he was, and he also knew who God is! He was chosen for this short season to reign over God's chosen people, and he was honest enough to know that the task was too great for him alone. When we can stand before God and say out of our hearts that we don't even have a clue and that without God's help and guidance the task will not only overwhelm us, but might possibly overtake us, we have already made great strides towards their good success.

Our children are to bring great joy into our lives, not tears of sorrow, frustration, and in some cases, even dread. Your child is exactly what you need to become more like Christ, and you are exactly what your child needs to become more like Christ. Keep your eyes on the author! If you can do this, believe me...your BOOK will be an easy read!

When you look at Solomon's life, how he started out with such promise, such hope, and yet he ended with the kind of hopelessness and despair that left him bitter, angry, and seemingly ungrateful. He had no regard for the things of God, nor did he for the Laws of God. His life was filled with worshiping the gods of his many foreign wives in their high places, material gains of every sort, the wealth of gold and silver, cattle, oxen, chariots, even people. People admired him, and were even in awe of his wisdom, and yet…this meant nothing. Why? Because even Solomon needed someone to keep him "pressing towards the mark." Solomon's search for meaning in life apart from God was foolishness, futile, and he was right, vanity! The very request he put before God became a stumbling block unto him, for he tended to trust in his own wisdom rather than in the guidelines given in God's Word.

Starting out right with your children doesn't mean that when they can make decisions for themselves they will always make the right ones, that their friends will always have their best interests at heart, or that at times they may test your very soul. What it does mean, however, is that your work as the parent is never done! We're to never give up! Never give up!

I thank God for the example of Jacob. Jacob is an outstanding illustration of the presence and conflict of the two natures within a believer. And his mother, Rebekah, a great example of "calling forth the calling!" In the *wrong* way!

Jacob was a victim of his mother's partiality. Rebekah loved Jacob. The birthright, which is the right or the privilege belonging to the firstborn son in a Hebrew family, belonged to the eldest son who ranked highest after the father, and he also had all responsibility of the father in his absence.

Jacob's name means, "he that supplanteth or followeth after." He was the second son of Isaac and Rebekah, and the twin brother of Esau. With the above custom in mind you can begin to see what Rebekah's plight was when it came to what she wanted for her second son, Jacob; she wanted the birthright or privilege of the family blessings placed up him.

Now don't get me wrong, it wasn't all Rebekah. I know she was the mother and held that place of authority in his life, but Jacob could not have been party to her plans if it had been against his nature. Jacob was selfish and a con man. When Esau came in from the fields, hungry, Jacob would not give him food without bargaining over it! How do you deprive your brother of something to eat when he's hungry, and then demand something as priceless as a birthright in exchange for a bowl of bean soup!

Genesis 25: 29-34 says, " And Jacob boiled pottage: and Esau came from the field, and he was faint: (30) And Esau said to Jacob, feed me, I pray thee, with that same red pottage; for I am faint: therefore was his name called Edom. (which means red) (31) And Jacob said, sell me this day thy birthright. (32) And Esau said, behold, I am at the point to die: and what profit shall this birthright do to me? (33) And Jacob said, swear to me this day; and he swore unto him: and he sold his birthright unto Jacob. (34) Then Jacob gave Esau bread and pottage of lentils; and he did eat and drink, and rose up, and went his way: thus Esau despised his birthright."

Now the plans of his mother. Genesis 27:8-13 says, "Now therefore, my son, obey my voice according to that which I command thee. (9) Go now to the flock, and fetch me from thence two good kids of the goats; and I will make them savory meat for thy father, such as he loveth: (10) And thou shalt bring it to thy father, that he may eat, and that he may bless thee before his death. (11) And Jacob said to Rebekah his mother, behold, Esau my brother is a hairy man, and I am a smooth man: (12) My father peradventure will feel me, and I shall seem to him as a deceiver: (seem to him as a deceiver…give me a break!) and I shall bring a curse upon me, and not a blessing. (13) And his mother said unto him, upon me be thy curse, my son: only obey my voice, and go fetch me them."

Jacob really started the ball in motion when he bargained with Esau for his birthright with a bowl of soup. If he weren't naturally crafty and deceitful, if it wasn't a part of his nature to con or trick people, this deed would have been almost impossible for him to carry out. Jacob had a voice, and could have refused to be used in such an ugly manner, and possibly holding on to some of his integrity and honor.

Jacob deceived his blind father with the covering of kid skins. He deliberately lied to obtain a spiritual blessing that was not his birthright, but a stolen right. He further sinned upon the most sacred ground, when he blasphemously used the name of the LORD to further their evil plans. (Genesis 27: 20, "And Isaac said unto his son, how is it that thou hast found it so quickly, my son? And he said, because the LORD thy God brought it to me.") That is just too deep! Jacob definitely needed some back-shed time! Amen…amen!

The only thing Jacob had to do was to not go through with the plans. He could have waited until Esau returned, or dropped the dish of food. But he was just too expert in what he did, and that's the ugly side of taking matters, God's matters, into your own hands.

We're told in Psalm 84:11, "For the LORD God is a sun and shield: the LORD will give grace and glory: no good thing will He withhold from them that walk uprightly." This scripture declares that God will not keep from His children anything that He has ordained for their lives. We're also told in Proverbs 18:16, "A man's gift maketh room for him, and bringeth him before great men."

We don't have to make room for our gift, or the gifts of our children; our LORD already has His perfect plans for their good success, and He will not be deterred. A wonderful scripture and comfort to the hearts of all God's children, or at least it should be, is found in Jeremiah 29:11, "For I know the thoughts that I think toward you, saith the LORD, thoughts of peace, and not of evil, to give you an expected end."

The LORD has magnificent plans for our children, plans that He expects to come to pass in their lives, plans that will bring them good success, plans that will make room for them, and bring them among people of renown."

Imagine…see yourself trying to get through a crowded room, to safety, or trying to get the attention of someone that everyone else in the room wants to see. You're pushing and being pushed, then suddenly, you hear the voice of the LORD saying, "Be still, and know that I am God: I will be exalted among the heathen, I will be exalted in the earth." (Psalm 46:10)

Nothing will prevent Him from doing what He has planned for our children. Our only effort is to be faithful until the end, and we will benefit from our labor as in Galatians 6:9, "Let us not be weary in well doing: for in due season we shall reap, if we faint not."

Just as you find joy in your children, there is great joy in being God's child. You're not alone in the training of your child, or in developing within them the character and nature of God, that His perfect will might be fulfilled in their lives. He has not asked of you, what He hasn't already completed. He has declared Himself to be mightier than every opposing power in this earth. There is not a problem or challenge that He is not more than able to help you through, or if necessary, deliver you from!

The same power that raised Christ from the dead also dwells in you! As God's children we are secure in His provisions for us. God has chosen to shape redeemed men in the likeness of His Son, Jesus Christ. It is our destiny to be like Jesus. Our LORD is committed to produce in all of us the love, all the joy, all the patience, all the long-suffering, all the goodness, and all the gentleness of Jesus Christ.

This divine commitment means that ultimately we win! If we can really grasp this confidence, and know that we are not alone, because we belong to Him, then why would we think God to be less than our heavenly Father, by not providing us with whatever we need to fulfill the commission He has entrusted to us? It makes no sense. The victory is ours, not just for our children, but victory in our lives as His children!

Our children shall become all that they can be in Christ, through Christ, and because of Christ!

We are not sufficient within ourselves to dare to think of anything as being from ourselves; our sufficiency is from God. Our Christian life and Christian faith is built upon our absolute faith in God's sufficiency in everything that pertains to our lives and the lives of our children and our families.

Parents, you must grow as close to our LORD and His Word as possible. His Word is His voice to us, and the nearer we are to Jesus, the more we'll understand the principles and purpose of His plans for our children and their lives. But you cannot possibly know the will of God concerning your children if you don't know His Word concerning your children. The BOOK you have in your hands, your child, must be supported by the Word of God in your life! They are perfect companions to one another; without the understanding of God's Word, you'll never understand the BOOK you're reading, and it won't make any sense!

To believe God, we must rest upon what He says, for there is not one jot or tittle of His Word that will fail until all be fulfilled. Paul tells us in Romans 4: 19-21, "And being not weak in faith, he considered not his own body now dead, when he was about an hundred years old, neither yet the deadness of Sara's womb: (20) He staggered not at the promise of God through unbelief; but was strong in faith, giving glory to God; (21) And being fully persuaded that, what He had promised, He was able also to perform. (22) And therefore it was imputed to him for righteousness."

Abraham wanted children, yet there was no way possible for this to come to pass without a miracle. Every child that you're blessed with is a miracle of life, a gift of precious value, and pages upon pages, upon pages of potential. Will you trust God, and believe God, that your children or your child will be everything that God has ordained them to be?

Zechariah 4:6 says, "Then he answered and spoke unto me, saying, this is the Word of the LORD unto Zerubbabel, saying, not by might, nor by power, but by my spirit, saith the LORD of hosts.

It's not you; it's not me; it's the Spirit of the Living God, who cannot lie that will fulfill His Word and His will concerning your child.

Chapter IV

For Whom the LORD Loves...He Corrects!

There's a battle that has been raging through the ages, and it's even made inroads within the body of Christ. To think that God's people have been roped into the theory that to spank or discipline your child is wrong is really amazing. According to Proverbs 13:24, "He that spareth his rod hateth his son; but he that loveth him chasteneth him early." I honestly don't believe that the answer to every discipline crisis is to spank your child; more often than not this is literally overkill. (Smile)

However, there are times when it's the only method left available to us as parents, and we must trust our LORD, and not fear this means of discipline, for the greater loss to us, may be in our not having used it.

There is no greater example for us to follow, than the LORD. If He has declared in Hebrews 12:6, "For whom the LORD loveth He chasteneth, and scourgeth every son whom He receiveth." Going down to verse 11 of this same chapter, "Now no chastening for the present seemeth to be joyous, but grievous; nevertheless, afterward it yieldeth the peaceable fruit of righteousness unto them who are exercised by it."

There was a popular commercial a few years ago that dealt with automobile owners and theirs cars. The basis of the commercial was that we as consumers needed to adhere to a very strict maintenance routine on our cars, and that by failing to do so the cost to us would be quite substantial, when it could have been very modest. As the commercial closed the repair man simply said; "Pay me now, or pay me later, but you will pay me!" This is more than true with our children; they will make us pay now, or pay later, but we will pay for not doing what the LORD says!

The scripture verse for this chapter title is found in Proverbs 3: 11-12. "My son, despise not the chastening of the LORD; neither be weary of His correction: (12) For whom the LORD loveth He correcteth; even as a father the son in whom he delighteth."

In the scripture we have the words, "whom the LORD loveth He correcteth."That absolutely says it all.

Checking out the dictionary for the meaning of two words *chastise* and *chasten*, we find them to be rather harsh and severe. (The word *chasten* means to punish either physically or morally. The word *chastise,* to punish, usually by beating.)

There is tremendous value in discipline. Endurance cannot be accomplished within your child's character, nor ours for that matter, without the adherence to strict discipline. The endurance Jesus suffered to accomplish redemption for mankind could not have been achieved without the determined focus of self-will that guided and strengthened each step He took towards Calvary.

Discipline is essential to the growth and character development of every child. Our children can never sustain the endurance necessary to obtain eternal life and the rewards earned for having fought the good fight of faith without concentrated effort on our part as their parents to train them up according to the Word and will of God. We're told in Mark 13:13, "And ye shall be hated of all men for my name's sake; but he that shall endure unto the end, the same shall be saved."

The crucial part in our lives that discipline plays has no measure. There is nothing more important to us as Christians and as parents; yes, I separated the two because the two are separate! We are first and foremost Christians. We belong to Christ; we were bought by His blood and redeemed by the same! Second, we are parents who are responsible for the salvation and training of our children loaned to us by God the Father.

Chastening, for someone we really love, is not an option if what we're seeking from God is His divine favor and absolute best for our children. In Hebrews chapter twelve the writer tells us again and again about the value of chastening according to God's purpose. The Christian Jews to whom he is writing this lesson were becoming disheartened and discouraged because of the severe challenges they were facing in their lives. It's natural to be frustrated and discouraged when things are happening to you and around you, and you have no clear understanding as to why. What they needed to understand, and some came to understand, was the opposition and difficulties in our lives are the tools or methods used by God to train His children.

In Hebrews there are several things that we as parents can learn, according to verses six through eight of this chapter. First, God's discipline is always loving! We should never reject God's love discipline nor His correction simply because it makes us uncomfortable.

Secondly, if we love our children, and are truly devoted to them, as our LORD is to us, they will have our complete concentration on everything that pertains to their lives. We'll know and understand their weaknesses, their strengths, even their fleshy tendencies to become lackadaisical in their studies, chores, or creative disciplines. The Word of God in your life, and conveyed to them whenever possible, will help shape their thoughts regarding their training and instruction.

Thirdly, a parent only accepts responsibility for the training of legitimate children! Let me explain what I mean. According to Hebrews 12:8, "But if ye be without chastisement, of which all are partakers, then are ye bastards, and not sons." Are they your children? Do you not just care for them…but care about them? Do love them, keep a watchful eye on them, participate with them, validate them, accept them by telling your community, neighbors, church, even your family, that your child does not only belong to you, but they are valuable to you, and that you hold in high regard God's love for you by entrusting this child to your care?

If so, use the means available to us by the Word of God to discipline them according to the same! If God's Word refers to us as bastards if we don't allow His discipline in our lives, then where does that place your child or children if you fail to discipline or correct those you say you love? To love them but fail to chasten them is to open them up for every harm, every foul attempt of Satan to eternally destroy God's investment for His kingdom.

When we understand that in a human environment where man has control, there will always be something wrong, wrong with us, our children, our finances, our health, etc.. That's why Jesus came and died: to redeem us, to not only save us but save us from ourselves. Not even Adam, in his perfect environment, could get it right! We were without hope, but for John 10:10, "The thief cometh not but to steal, and to kill, and to destroy; I am come that they might have life, and that they might have it more abundantly."

When you love your child so much that the thought of seeing them in pain renders you ineffective as their parent—that's not *love*, that's idol worship! And we all know God's point of reference on that issue can be found in Exodus 20:3-5, "Thou shalt have no other gods before me. (4) Thou shalt not make unto thee any carved image, or any likeness of anything that is in heaven above, or that is in the earth beneath, or that is in the water beneath. (5) Thou shalt not bow down thyself to them, nor serve them; for I, the LORD thy God, am a jealous God, visiting the iniquity of the fathers upon the children unto the third and fourth generation of them that hate me;"

According to the dictionary an idol is a person or thing that is *blindly or excessively* adored. Is this your child? Do you bow yourself to their will or demands? Do you sacrifice the needs of the entire family for their wants? Are they held responsible for poor or negative behavior? Are they allowed to kick, throw things, or destroy things, without consequences for this behavior? Is your child the first considered and the last refused?

Let's look at 1 Samuel 2:22-25. "Now Eli was very old and heard all that his sons did unto all Israel, and how they lay with the women who assembled at the door of the tabernacle of the congregation. (23) And he said unto them, why do ye such things? For I hear of your evil dealings by all this people. (24) Nay, my sons; for it is no good report that I hear: ye make the LORD's people to transgress. (25) If one man sin against another, the judge shall judge him; but if a man sin against the LORD, who shall mediate for him? Notwithstanding, they hearkened not unto the voice of their father, because the LORD would slay them."

We continue down to verses 28-29. "And did I choose him out of all the tribes of Israel to be my priest, to offer upon mine altar, to burn incense to wear an ephod before me? And did I give unto the house of thy father all the offerings made by fire of the children of Israel? (29) Why trample ye upon my sacrifice and upon mine offerings, which I have commanded in my habitation; and honorest thy sons above me, to make yourselves, [Eli was included in this stern chastisement] fat with the chiefest of all the offerings of Israel, my people? (30) Wherefore the LORD God of Israel saith, I said indeed that thy house, and the house of thy father should walk before me forever; but now the LORD saith, be it far from me; for them who honor me I will honor and they who despise me shall be lightly esteemed."

Is it strange that our LORD would compare honoring Him to the chastising our children? That He would compare this dishonor of Him to despising Him! That in the above scripture the condemnation of the parent, who is Eli, is held to the same accountability of his sons, even though he did not take part physically or spiritually? Do you think our LORD was just picking on Eli, and should have dealt with the sons only?

There can be no injustice to God's judgment! He never makes mistakes. Let's look at what the Psalmist David said in Psalms 89:14. "Righteousness and justice are the habitation of thy throne; mercy and truth shall go before thy face." According to the Word of God, our LORD lives in righteousness and justice!

Paul tells us in Romans 3:4-6, "God forbid: yea, let God be true, but every man a liar; as it is written, that thou mightest be justified in thy sayings, and mightest overcome when thou are judged. (5) But if our unrighteousness commend the righteousness of God, what shall we say? Is God unrighteous who taketh vengence? (I speak as a man.) (6) God forbid; for then how shall God judge the world?"

The Old Testament and The New Testament both uphold and sustain God's standards of what is right and wrong behavior in our lives, and make us aware of our sins.

Eli as a parent was obviously lax in his discipline and control of his two sons, Hophni and Phinehas, and they were to pay the price for this obscene affront to our LORD and the Law of God and the abuse of his people, Israel. God declared that He would destroy them, and in 1 Samuel 3:31 said, "Behold, the days come, that I will cut off, thine arm, and the arm of thy father's house, that there shall not be an old man in thine house. Reading at verse 34, "And this shall be a sign unto thee, that shall come upon thy two sons, on Hophni and Phinehas: in one day they shall die both of them."

The story continues, and God's prophesy is fulfilled with the death of the two sons of Eli and Eli himself. I know that this example is severe, but if God's Word is to be taught, understood, and lived according to His will, then all of it is if fit for instruction. (2 Timothy 3:16, "All scripture is given by inspiration of God, and is profitable for doctrine, for reproof, for correction, for instruction in righteousness. (17) That the man of God may be perfect thoroughly furnished unto good works.")

If Eli had obeyed the law and taught his sons to love and honor God, if he'd taught them to love and respect the office of the priesthood, if they had been taught of the great love God had for them, that freed them as a people and delivered them from bondage, if they were made to remember the cost and shedding of blood the sacrifices represented for their sin and the sins of Israel, if all of this and more had been kept before them, they would never have fallen from the grace and favor of God. I'm certain of this! But Eli didn't, and they became a stench in the nostrils of God, and of course, anything spoiled or rotten gets thrown out! Amen...Amen.

When we fail to discipline our children, we not only place their physical lives in peril, but their spiritual lives also. We see in Proverbs 10:11, "Even a child is known by his doings, whether his work be pure, and whether it be right." Also Proverbs 29:15, "The rod and reproof give wisdom, but a child left to himself bringeth his mother shame."

The Word of God is replete with both clear and rather painful scripture of the disciplining and failing to discipline our children. We find in Deuteronomy 21:18-21, "If a man have a stubborn and rebellious son, who will not obey the voice of his father or the voice of his mother, and that, when they have chastened him, will not hearken unto them, (19) then shall his father and his mother lay hold on him, and bring him out unto the elders of his city, and unto the gate of his place. (20) And they shall say unto the elders of his city, this our son is stubborn and rebellious. He will not obey our voice; he is a glutton, and a drunkard. (21) And all the men of his city shall stone him with stones, that he die. So shalt thou put evil away from among you, and all Israel shall hear and fear."

Now, believe it or not, what bothers me most about that scripture is not the fact that the LORD allowed for this type of discipline; I'm certain that cases of this magnitude were few and far between, more than likely because is was known throughout Israel that this option was available to parents. What catches my eye and heart is the fact that the LORD says in verse 21, "So shalt thou put evil away from among you." That the LORD considers stubbornness and rebellion in a son or daughter, to be evil, really shows His disapproval and intolerance for this type of behavior in our children.

It seems as though God was jealously guarding all His children, and establishing strict guidelines that would not only keep them focused on their responsibilities regarding the discipline of their children, but it would also act as a deterrent to any outside influences they would obviously encounter in the lands they were going out to possess according to God's covenant with them, lands and cultures that would, or could possibly take their eyes off their God, so the children had to be kept in line and on a short leash, as we see in the history of Israel. People by nature are of a stubborn will. God was constantly having to deal with parents, who at one time were children their parents failed to deal with. This was a generational tendency, and consequently, as time passed and years went by, Israel was taken captive by these foreign people again and again. They were killed and often enslaved, until they fell on their faces and repented to God for their sin.

If we give attention to proper parental discipline, rebellious and stubborn children will not bring shame to their parents and dishonor the LORD. The only slide rule available to us as parents is the Word of God; if we acknowledge Him in all our ways, He will direct our paths and our efforts when disciplining our children.

As we are God's children, He doesn't deal with all of us in the same manner; so it should be with your children. What worked with one may not work with another, and part of your effectiveness as a parent will depend on how soon and how accurate you are with this analysis, and this will most likely determine your success in disciplining your children.

I've been blessed with three children, and they are as different in all their needs as their names are. My daughter Toi was my first child, and needed to be disciplined often and with a strict no-tolerance approach to that discipline method. She was strong-willed then, and is today. This determined attitude was channeled, but not destroyed, and has become her most vital source of success, not only with her own family, that began when she was very young, but also in the powerful and anointed ministry she thrives in to this day. I'm so thankful that I listened to the LORD in regards to this spirit of "I must do it" that always seemed to envelop her actions, because without His will, this harnessed determination, she would not be used in the powerful way our LORD uses and depends on her in the ministry today, and can always rely on her faithfulness to Him, her ministry, and her family.

My second child, Jonathan, needed only to know that belts were invented before he got here! He was so afraid of being spanked that his answer to a spanking was to submit, while he still had breath in his body! If he knew that he'd drawn the last straw from the broom, so to speak, he'd simply on into his room and lay across the bed and wait. He'd just wait! He never ran or got hysterical; he just waited, and naturally I could never swat him more than two or three times because like the innocent child (he wanted me to think he was) that never kicks against authority, he made things easier on himself. He's sensitive, creative, artistic, sings beautifully, loves people, and he's loved by all. But all these beautiful and creative gifts placed in him by God could have been crushed if I'd destroyed His willingness to please and not make waves. Everything he touches, and everything he does turns to awe and wonder in our hearts.

Ethan, who is my youngest, has a sense of determination and survival that boggles the mind, and he will not be deterred. When you come to discipline Ethan, come fully armed, for the victory is given to "he that endureth to the end!" Don't get me wrong, it's not physical; he'd take his spanking with the best of us, only, prove it! He will talk and negotiate his way out of a sealed up bomb shelter. If I were not his mother who knew better, I'd declare he came from the womb talking! Only I forgot to ask the doctor if that was possible. Anyway, Ethan never gives up, and will always determine to prove it with words. Words: Ethan has a gift for writing that seems to amaze even his professors in college. His imagination at times is boundless, and what he imagines he writes. If I'd always, without even listening, just shut him up, and had not allowed his creativity to fully develop, (smile) would he love to write, to rap, do screen plays, etc., anything with words? Would he be able to do these things? Maybe, but God's Word tells us to train up a child in the way he should go. Because of this, with my children I had to use different methods and different measures in their discipline. Our LORD was always faithful. They turned out great, loving and serving their LORD with all their hearts. And also being more than just gifted, they are able to provide spiritual encouragement for themselves and their families whenever it is necessary.

The liberty we have in training our children does not allow for them to never have consequences for their negative behavior. As with grace, because it affords us so much liberty, we are held in closer check, as it were. As it is written in Luke 12:48, "But he that knew not, and did commit things worthy of stripes, shall be beaten with few stripes. For unto whosoever much is given, of him shall be much required; and to whom men have committed much, of him they will ask the more."

The beautiful bonsai plant is nurtured and pruned with almost an obsessive discipline. However, this art of creating such beauty is also dwarfing beauty. The creator takes a normal tree, plants it in a small restrictive pot, and cuts into it the shape and design he thinks it should have. This constant cutting and pruning back does not allow the plant to grow in a way that is natural for it, but the natural growth is blocked, hindered to achieve a certain look and certain quality. Bonsai plants, or trees, are beautiful to look at, only they serve no purpose! Although it's a tree, it cannot offer shade, rest, fruit, protection, shelter for the birds, etc.

We cannot allow Satan to distort the growth of our children with fear, pride, and a false sense of purpose on our part. We can't dwarf or inhibit what is natural and healthy in their make-up. We must train it and channel it, but not cut it away! We cannot destroy what they are intended to provide to the world, the church, and their families, because of what we see them to be. Our LORD has already programmed into our children the purpose and design they are destined for and He doesn't want His plans altered to fit our image of what's right for them, according to us or anyone else!

Every mother comes equipped with a built-in bag of tricks that is more than effective in disciplining our children, when properly applied. One item in this bag of tricks is as effective as the Clint Eastwood line, "Go ahead...make my day!" It's called the "Mother's Look." It's actually the Clint Eastwood statement translated! (Smile)

This Mother's Look doesn't work if there isn't a more severe consequence that follows. You have to back up this look with something more severe or painful if it's to have the desired effect. When they get the Look, they must know without a doubt, the best is still to come if they're not careful! (Smile)

The Mother's Look says, "Do you really want to do that?" Or "I will kill you, then call for the Elders of the church!" Or as one famous comedian as said, "Let the beatings begin!" (Smile)

It's a look that's cultivated with much devotion, staring, and spending countless hours practicing the look in the mirror. "Ya gotta get it right!" I love the way Webster defines the word *stare*, (to look with a steady, wide-eyed gaze…as though amazed). That's so funny, and so true! The operative word in this definition is steady; don't cower, mothers! Stare 'em down; the Sorority of Motherhood is depending on you!

What I enjoy about the Mother's Look is its practicality. Because it's so compact, it goes with you everywhere. No one, other than your child, needs to know that you're about to lose your mind at this very moment. It works in church, restaurants, malls, when you're out visiting with friends and you don't want to be overly demonstrative, and it's really effective when they're among their friends.

When the look is in place, your children will appear to be normal and well behaved, even to the most discerning eye. Only you and the LORD will know, that this I *far* from the truth, and that at that very moment, they are under the power and control of an unseen vise that has gripped them tightly about their shoulders and given them a stern shake. (Smile) Another plus, is that the look is so user-friendly mothers of all ages can quickly learn and adapt themselves to its use. (Smile)

Another point of importance regarding the discipline of your children, never allow your children to make a liar out of you! What you say you're going to do, if they don't comply with your wishes, do it, even if it does hurt you more than it hurts them!

In the Bible we read in 2 Peter 3:9, "The LORD is not slack concerning His promise, as some men count slackness, but is long-suffering toward us, not willing that any should perish, but that all should come to repentance." Another scripture in Galatians 6:7, "Be not deceived, God is not mocked, for whatever a man soweth, that shall he also reap."

These scriptures are used in two different contexts. The first applies to the second coming of our LORD, and the other applies to good stewardship, yet because all scripture is good for instruction and reproof, they also work and apply to the disciplining of our children.

We can be patient and long-suffering, but once you put your foot down, so to speak, about a matter, whatever you have determined to do...do it! If your child is aware that a certain behavior will guarantee a certain response from you, don't shirk your responsibility, do it! If they discover inconsistencies in your discipline and weakness in your resolve, they will probe this imperfection and destroy the whole of your effort to train and discipline them according to the Word and will of God.

Children are no mystery; nor are they complicated to understand or predict. Our problems come when we refuse to read the obvious signs of rebellion and territorial struggles.

The moment your child resists your words of instruction or correction, some form of discipline should take place immediately. There is no need to debate the issue. There's a difference between your child trying to manipulate you, and trying to offer an explanation, especially if one is warranted. Listen to them, and try to understand their point of view; however, if they're blatant in their attempt to defy you, then act accordingly.

Never discipline your child when you're hurt or angry. Whether you're angry because of them or someone else, don't allow Satan to cloud the issue. You'll only do more damage than good, and it could be very harmful to your child physically and emotionally if you've allowed your emotions about something else to blur the lines of your disciplining them fairly.

Separate yourselves by sending them to their room. You sit down and calm yourself before the LORD, listen to what He tells you, then when He has released you to discipline, go and do as He has instructed you to do: no more, no less.

Inconsistent behavior on your part will only confuse your child, and send messages you'd rather not have to deal with at a later date. Children need and desire to have boundaries in their lives; it gives them comfort (believe it or not) in knowing you love them, and that you're concerned about them, and also about what others think about them. Have you ever frowned at the thought of a certain child, or children, coming to an event at church or a birthday party your children are invited to? Well, that's because they bring only trouble and confusion with them. Their parents have failed to do for them what any good parent should always want to do: make them the best they can be!

This takes work and effort and patience. It doesn't happen overnight, but the benefits will last a lifetime. Every effort you make to train up your child, even when you make mistakes, and you will make mistakes, our LORD will reward your sincere effort as, His child, to be obedient.

If the occasion demands a harsh method of discipline, never, never use your hand to discipline your child. Your hand should not hold fear for them, nor should your hands bring them pain.

Your hands are meant to heal, caress, bind up, encourage, comfort and bring peace. They should not be used to inflict pain or hurt on your child. In James 3:10, "Out of the same mouth proceed blessing and cursing. My brethren, these things ought not so to be." This scripture explains what I'm trying to say about your hands more clearly than I can.

You say, what should I use? Well, that depends on the child and the age of the child. If the child is young to very young, you shouldn't need anything more forceful than their own little hair brush used on the inside of their hand, lightly once or twice. As they get older, you may need to switch to some other paddle or implement you and the LORD will determine, but please, don't use your hands to spank them, slap them, or shake them. It's too confusing for them to understand where to go for comfort and reassurance. When God said, *rod* God meant that you should put something in your hands.

The hand of discipline upon your children is simply preparing them for the voice of God. The older your children become, the less they should need your hand of discipline. Your desire for your child is that their will, their heart, and their mind would be so centered in Christ, that He only needs to whisper and they will obey.

As Christians our children will need to become as comfortable in the presence of their God, as we are. Growing up means growing away. They will need to be able see His eyes, hear His voice, and know His touch. Wise and consistent discipline, is a huge factor in the molding and shaping of their will.

Our will is like a precious coin given to us by the LORD. It can take us anywhere we want to go, and open doors once locked to us. Our will is something that most of us clutch tightly in our little paws until we see the benefit in spending it; only what can our eyes really see? The same is true with our children. They are also limited by what they can really see.

Let's talk a little bit about this word *will* and maybe our LORD will open up our understanding to the importance of sound and wise discipline for our children. That they may become all He has ordained for their lives, and that His favor will always rest upon them.

To put it simply, we're talking about our wishing, our desiring, or choosing, especially in reference to the will of God. The LORD tells us in John 5:30, "I can of mine own self do nothing. As I hear, I judge; and my judgment is just, because I seek not mine own will, but the will of the Father who hath sent me."

We see and understand that Jesus is not acting on His own, but according to the will of His Father. The LORD tells us in John 4:34, "Jesus saith unto them, my food is to do the will of Him that sent me, and to finish His work."

Jesus is telling us that to obey the Father and to do His will is like food...like meat! He finds His nourishment and strength in doing the will of God.

A child carried within the womb of his mother has a life source that binds them together before the child takes their first breath of oxygen. The umbilical cord is that hidden tie that binds! It's there doing exactly what it's meant to do, yet hidden from the natural eye. But, does the fact that we cannot see this cord with our eyes, make its use and purpose of less value and importance? Of course not! It provides for the child the means of life: nourishment and strength to grow. After their arrival, the mother must still provide life, nourishment, and strength to grow by a more visible or tangible means.

The umbilical cord not only provides an invaluable source of nourishment to the child, but it also dispenses of its waste, protecting the baby from himself. Imagine, God provided for our children a way to not only nourish them, but also protect them from themselves through one source: a cord. This cord, upon birth, is severed from the child and discarded because it is no longer needed. The child is then placed in its mother's arms, and she becomes the first link he will have to the God that gave him life.

What you want for her and desire to deposit within her is not only a will to serve and obey our LORD, but a need and a hunger to do His will.

Life will always offer them choices, the wisdom and knowledge necessary to make the right choices come from the discipline, training, and instruction you've instilled in them. These tools will give them the ability to judge correctly and follow the best course of action, based on this knowledge and understanding.

If the love for your child has hampered your judgment and caused you to not only be ineffective in your discipline, but maybe, in the eyes of our LORD, disobedient, it also gives opportunity for Satan to bargain for that valuable coin in their hands: your child's will.

For our children to have the ear of God, they must want the will of God for their lives. When they are willing they will also be obedient. If they've learned obedience when it comes to your will, this instruction will help them to also submit to the will of God.

No one wants to be around disobedient children for long…no one. They not only destroy the environment of the occasion, but they often hinder its success. Another thing about disobedient children is that they can't be trusted; you never know from one minute to the next what they will do, what they will say, where they will go, or how they will act when they get there. They keep everyone, including their parents, off balance. This has to be heartbreaking for everyone involved, sometimes even life threatening. No loving parent wants this for his child.

When you've raised obedient children you've given them the ability to carry out the word and will of other people, i.e., teachers, neighbors, doctors, law enforcement officers, and especially the will of God.

The word obey in the Bible is related to the idea of hearing…hearing God! The only thing God asks of His people, of His children, is to hear and obey. When we fail to obey God is forced to act, and man's failure to obey God always results in His judgment. In the Old Testament man's obedience to God was the basis for knowing God's blessing and favor. In Exodus 19:5, "Now therefore, if ye will obey my voice indeed, and keep my covenant, then ye shall be a peculiar treasure unto me above all people; for all the earth is mine:" Also, in 1 Samuel 15:22, "And Samuel said, hath the LORD as great delight in burnt offerings and sacrifices, as in obeying the voice of the LORD? Behold, to obey is better than sacrifice, and to hearken, than the fat of rams."

Obedience tells us that your child not only heard what you said, but they were listening attentively, and with a compliant heart to submit their will to yours. For your child to walk around with her will, this precious coin, visible and accessible to God, allows for God's opened hand to be accessible to your child. His divine favor and blessings will always rest upon your child. What else could you possibly want from Him? And, what else could you possibly want…for them?

Chapter V

Adoption...Perfectly Placed, and Privileged

Christian parents are the most valuable gift God can give a child. Their position and responsibility cannot be determined in this lifetime. Only in eternity will we be able to ascertain the immeasurable value, responsibility, obligation, and gift of being blessed with Christian parents.

The birth of a child brings such joy and happiness to the hearts of the family. I think that the miracle of childbirth alone is enough to cause anyone in their right mind to stagger at the beauty and awesome majesty of God. After nine months of expectancy, preparations, parties, shopping, anticipation, decisions on names, nursery items, whether to nurse or not to nurse, will the mother work outside of the home and if so, who the day care provider will be, just a million and one things that must be decided, after all of this, finally the day arrives, and we're off to the hospital.

Waiting in nerve-racking anticipation is every member of the immediate families, i.e., expectant grandparents, aunts, uncles, older children, godparents, best friends, worse friends...just everybody. And why? Because what you've been waiting for praying for and believing God for is finally here! Finally, after nine, ten or eleven months, depending on the mother's perception (smile) little Jane, Paul, Mary, Johnny, Gilbert, Shadonda, Moniqqua, and Egg-settra, smile, are finally here! Father!

It's easy to be excited and to thank and praise God for this beautiful blessing; only what if bearing a child in your own womb is either not possible, or no matter how hard you try, is not successful? Modern medicine can literally work wonders in the effort of helping families to enjoy the entire process of childbirth, but sometimes this option is not available for you and your family. So now what? Does that mean you'd rather not have children, or that for you children are impossible? Please, why relegate yourself to this gloomy prospect! You, too, can be tormented day and night, night and day! (Smile) Seriously, our LORD has a marvelous option available to His children, whether they already have children, or desire to be a blessing to other children, or maybe you've never thought about it, or considered it. Adoption is a wonderful opportunity!

I mentioned earlier that Christian parents are a precious gift to their children, and that some of us will not know until we're in eternity just how special we were to have been blessed with Christian parents. Well, as far as I'm concerned, Christian adoptive parents are royalty!

There is nothing that compares to the generosity, the selflessness, and unconditional love of Christian adoptive parents! They're not only special in ways we will not understand in this life, but they're also in marvelous company! What better example can we have than God the Father, God the Son, and God the Holy Spirit! I mean, weren't we adopted into the Heavenly Family, and made joint heirs with Jesus Christ? In Galatians 4:6-7, "And because ye are sons, God hath sent forth the Spirit of His Son into your hearts, crying, Abba, Father. (7) Wherefore, thou are no more a servant, but a son; and if a son, then an heir of God through Christ." Also in Romans 8:15 and 17, "For ye have not received the spirit of bondage again to fear; but ye have received the spirit of adoption, whereby we cry, Abba Father. (17) And if children, then heir…heirs of God, and joint heirs with Christ, if so be that we suffer with Him, that we may be also glorified together."

To voluntarily assume the responsibility of another parent's child is one of the most beautiful, selfless acts one can give. When our LORD looks upon His children, knowing everything He knows about us, from the moment we began to the last that we will be, and when He smiles on you, and says…yes…they'll be perfect! What more could anyone want, especially, to have God smile on them. There is no greater trust than for God to add to your life a wonderful BOOK, that someone else has either put down and refused to read, or left at the door of someone else, never bothering to even read its introduction.

Every family or newlywed couple desires and looks forward to the day when the doctor says that the wife is pregnant, and that the much-anticipated birth of their child is soon to come. They're excited to find the mirror image of themselves, or their mother or his father's face, smiling back at them, they dream of the day when he'll take off down some football field and the father can proudly proclaim, "That's my son," and in some cases, "That's my daughter!"

Adoption is an opportunity and a privilege that often goes overlooked these days, maybe because medicine has done so much to provide the means for families to experience childbirth by conventional means. Believe me, this is understood, and it's natural, only why does it have to be the only answer? If you already have children and are planning a larger family, have you ever considered adopting?

This act of grace is made available to us from the LORD. When you can allow the LORD to use you in this very special way, the blessings and the rewards go not only to the child, but to you and your family. They will be phenomenal.

Granted, a child is God's gift to you. What that child becomes is your gift to God! When God places a child into your life He's transplanting a vital soul into your midst! This is an opportunity to take part in the development and nurturing of someone else's child, a child whose parent was not aware of the possible pain, sorrow, neglect, abuse, poverty, illness, and other trauma they were indirectly inflicting upon their child. Also, depending upon the age of the child that is adopted, these negative effects may already be in process.

It doesn't matter if the child is six months old, six years old, or a teenager. When God places the life and future of this child in your midst, everything negative, even things that have already happened to them, things they may have been exposed to, or things that may have caused them pain because of their environment, all of this and more, comes to a complete halt, because God has stepped into their life! Because of your family's selfless love, God could open wide the windows of heaven to alter the path that Satan may have planned for them. Also, God has stopped the assignment that their birth parent relegated them to, by removing every obstacle of doom and negative influence, and switched reels, so to speak, allowing for the healing and restoration necessary to give new beginnings and hope to everybody involved.

There are a myriad of reasons you may or may not choose adoption, but the only valid reason before God is love. Either you have lots of love to give, or you fear you don't have enough to give. Sometimes fear or unresolved prejudices factor their way into our choice. Everything we do as a child of God, however, is rooted in, or finds its main resolve in love, either more than enough, or not enough.

Many children who haven't experienced the security of a real family environment, who have either spent their lives in foster homes, or under some other form of guardianship, will be plagued or burdened by the shame that comes from not having their own parents. This can only be understood or explained by someone who has been there. These children may experience a stigma from being foster kids. They can be shuffled from one foster home to another every few months of their young lives. This is extremely damaging to their self-esteem. They don't feel wanted; they feel different, or maybe they believe that something was wrong with them! It destroys the beauty and innocence that's innate in all children. Imagine the horror of what Satan can do to the self-esteem of the child that feels unwanted or abandoned!

It's really too profound for us to imagine or grasp without the insight of the Holy Spirit. When a child is an infant, the love of a mother's arms cannot be replaced by anyone other than someone with a mother's heart. Motherhood is not defined by the womb, nor the hours spent in labor but by the heart that's filled with room and love. Adoptive parents are no longer measured by their financial status, social standing, whether they're married or single; not even their ethnic grouping can hinder them from adopting a child of another culture of ethnicity. Adoption is also a matter of the heart, a heart that always has room for one more!

A child can be forgotten by everyone and anyone but God! God's love, devotion, and commitment to His children never change. He's always there for us and behind us. His desire is to make us all a part of His glorious heritage. That's why He came and died, not only to give us life eternal with Him, but to provide an abundant life for each of His children right now, today, no matter what has transpired to hinder that process!

I think of adoption as not just a blessing, in the way we often think of a typical childbirth, but it's just as much a miracle, a miracle that transcends what some would call the natural law of things. Example, a mother makes the excellent and Godly choice of carrying her child for the nine months necessary to give birth. She goes through the challenges those nine months of pregnancy give her. She travails in labor and for an infinite number of reasons, some real, some perhaps imagined, she decides to give her child up. No human heart or intellect can judge the reasons why; that's our LORD's responsibility. What we do know is that a child is left needing the care and comfort of a home and family that will love him or her. It's not natural for a mother to give up her child, and in most cases, I'm certain it's a heart-wrenching struggle. It's a struggle and heartache that will follow her, most likely, the rest of her life. However, our LORD is right there, seeing, knowing, and providing a way out of no way for that vulnerable little life, and when the mother lets go…the heavenly Father catches them! "When my father and my mother forsake me, the LORD will take me up." (Psalms 27:10)

Adoption is really a spiritual connection between the adoptive parent(s) and the child. It's made real and solid by the hand of God who orchestrates this symphony of music and magic, as only He is capable of doing. We can always rest in the fact that what He begins He will finish, and whom He calls He equips, and what He does is always good! He makes no mistakes.

The Holy Spirit produces in our lives the fruit of the Spirit, and this spiritual fruit is all for His delight, His glory and His honor. The spirit of love or kindness to others is definitely a fruit of the spirit. In Galatians 5:22-23, "But the fruit of the Spirit is love, joy, peace, long-suffering, gentleness, goodness, faith. (23) meekness, self-control; against such there is no law." There is no other law that totally governs our lives, for the law of man must inevitably bow to the law and will of God.

When we consider the attributes of any good parent, Christian or non-Christian, the fruit of the Spirit must be evident in our lives, and certainly most beneficial to the parents who have chosen to not only give of themselves so unselfishly when they consider to adopt, but to impart to this young life the hope and security and destiny that this precious fruit will manifest unto them.

Sometimes in our life we will make a promise, or as the scriptures would say, a covenant with someone we love dearly. Young children will prick their fingers and touch them together so that the blood will mingle, and from that point on refer to themselves as Blood Brothers or Sisters. Well this is the type of arrangement that was made between David and Jonathan, the son of Saul. They swore to each other that no matter what separated them in the future, they would search out each other, and if one of them were dead, the one left alive would seek out the family of the other and take care of his family. Well, this is exactly what brought about the spiritual adoption and care of Jonathan's son…Mephibosheth.

Mephibosheth was only five years old when his father Jonathan, and his grandfather Saul were both killed in battle on Mount Gilboa. Because of their deaths, the family fell from the throne. In terror of that defeat in battle, and the death of the king and his son, the nurse picked up Mephibosheth and fled with the child in her arms. But in her haste, by accident, she let the little prince fall, and he was lame in both his feet for the rest of his life.

The complete story can be found in 2 Samuel, the 9th chapter, but to shorten the story, after David was established as king, he set about investigating to see if any of Saul's family was still alive because of the covenant made between him and Jonathan. David wanted to be able to fulfill this covenant if at all possible, because of his friend Jonathan, whom he loved. "And David said, is there yet any who is left of the house of Saul, that

I may show him kindness for Jonathan's sake?" (2 Samuel 9:1)

Well, the search turned up Mephibosheth. David not only made Jonathan's lame son a member of his household, but also deeded to him Saul's extensive estate. Suddenly Mephibosheth's status was transformed from the helpless and poor cripple he was at this point, to a wealthy and powerful man who enjoyed access to the king and ate at his table.

This is not only a beautiful picture of redemption, for us as saints, who were lost, crippled by sin, made poor by the act of our parents, Adam and Eve, separated from everything that our God had purposed and provided for us, but it also shows the power and beauty of adoption, and what God desires to take place in the lives of all those He chooses to place together. It's marvelous. It's just like God! Amen? Amen.

Adoption is one of the most beautiful pictures of restoration made between God and man. It not only allows for the dignity and security of being loved and covered by the name and heritage of someone that has chosen to choose; it affords God this most perfect answer to childlessness, loss, and heartache. Maybe neither of these is the case; perhaps you simply wanted to share and be a blessing to someone's child who, without any choice in the matter, has been made a victim or painful statistic. It's always better to choose than to loose!

Because of the generosity of David and his covenant faithfulness, Mephibosheth was now only a cripple physically; he was no longer a social cripple, an emotional cripple, a spiritual cripple, or crippled financially. Mephibosheth had been redeemed, restored, reclaimed, and relocated! This young man no longer lived in the valley of Lodebar that represented so many sad memories and painful mockings from those around him, especially as a child when he could not run and play with the others, Lodebar, the place that once closed him up and hid him away from the rest of the world, that place of limitations and futility, the place of constant reminders that you'll never be like everybody else, never quite good enough, where nothing really belongs to you, the place of tears that no one sees. Lodebar, because of David, was NO MORE!

Whenever a child is available for adoption it's due to circumstances that were not of his or her making, circumstances that without this possibility would render a child hopelessly trapped in a life of ignorance, pain, suffering, abuse, poverty and instability. A life so dysfunctional that it might produce the type of horror and violence that our society must contend with on a daily basis in epidemic proportions. Violent acts are perpetrated on our society that may have been avoided if someone simply cared enough to repair the breach that abandonment inflicted upon a child.

The definitions of the words *adopt* and *abandon* are so different from each other that it's as if they're not only different in their meaning, but in the action as well. The word *abandon* means to withdraw one's support or help; or surrender one's claim. The word *adopt* means to take or assume responsibility for someone or something. The words are not related, and neither are the deeds, not even the character of the person who decides to make the choice to do one or the other.

There is no greater love for man to give to another man than to give the gift of life and hope to those who have no hope.

When we're blessed with a child, by either giving birth to that child or by adoption, we're not just responsible for the nurturing and training of the child, we will also be held accountable to the LORD for our failure in not having successfully accomplished the task He placed in our trust.

Adoption is not something you do because "everybody else is doing it," or "it's just the thing to do," or "I felt so left out, not having a child like so-in-so!" Adoption, to be successful, must first take place in the heart. It cannot be for selfish or strictly personal reasons. There must be so much love bursting inside you that if you don't share it with someone who is in need of this love, you feel as if you'll just die! It's not because there's emptiness, although there might be emptiness. Neither can it be because you're lonely or have too much time on your hands, and this may very well be true. The one and only reason to adopt is love! No other reason is good enough, and no other reason will take you through the difficult times ahead, and be assured, there will be difficult times ahead.

What you have decided to do is accept full responsibility for someone whose long-term needs and care you may not be fully aware of. There are generational influences that may not be visible to anyone from the beginning. Sometimes there are illnesses or other challenges that will only be known to you and your family after the dust has settled around you and years have passed.

There are children born today with addictions and crippling disorders, even mental disorders that may not be instantly diagnosed. These disorders might create emotional and financial demands that you never imagined possible. Nothing will get you and your family through these difficult and demanding challenges but your love for God, and your love for your child, a child whose emotional structure may have been severely compromised, who is left without the tools or even the understanding of how to cope. Except for the wisdom, understanding, and knowledge that our LORD will give to you in his or her behalf, it will seem, at times, hopeless. Sometimes discovering how difficult things can or will be, may be heartbreaking! But, love…love really does conquer all!

Children deserve every chance and every advantage life has to offer; sometimes you and your child may have to work harder to accomplish your goals, but the rewards: o-o-oh the rewards, will be without measure.

I spoke about adoptive parents being also privileged, and I mean it. God has privileged us in Christ to live above the norm, above the ordinary. When we not only want to live, but expect to live the extraordinary, it usually happens. Exactly as one sense appears to sharpen at the loss of another, the possibilities of an adopted child will most often—in a healthy and nurturing environment, surpass even your dreams for them! You will give them all the strength they need to leap over every hurdle, but the privilege lies in that God chose you to join in the bows and the applause and the cheers when they succeed, and believe me, they will succeed!

We have all heard and been charmed by the adoption of Moses by the Pharaoh's daughter. Her adoption of him as her own son and his royal upbringing is always a joy to read or hear. We look at how God intervened in the history of His people and provided a way of deliverance for them from the least-expected way, and this deliverance that would also be the conduit, if you will, for God's pronounced judgment and retribution for His people, Israel.

If God had not placed Moses in the care of Pharaoh's daughter, the decree to kill every male child would have been a death sentence for him also. Everything that Moses gained in the way of privilege and education was made possible because of *whose* he was, not *who* he was. Because of this privilege, and his upbringing, he became a powerful leader, orator and patriot. But the greatest honor of all, he was known as the friend of God.

When we see Moses, we can also find similarities between Moses and our LORD. Both were preserved from the perils of infancy (Ex. 2:2-10 with Matt. 2:14, 15). They both knew what it was to fast for forty days (Ex. 34:28 with Matt. 4:2). Both were initially rejected by the hometown folk (smile) (Num 12:1 with John 7:5). They both performed miracles dealing with water (Ex. 14:21 with Matt. 8:26). Both fed multitudes (Ex 16:26 with Matt. 17:2). Also both dealt with murmurings (Ex 15:24 with Mark 7:2). They both were mighty intercessors (Ex. 32:32 with John 17). They both reappeared after death (Matt. 17:3 with Acts 1:3).

There are even more similarities, but none of these wonderful accomplishments would have been possible without the protection and adoption of Moses by Pharaoh's daughter. Moses was perfectly placed and privileged. This magnificent life that started out threatened and doubtful caused an entire nation of people to be delivered and given a powerful place in biblical history, and made a way for us in the adoption process through Jesus Christ.

God's two-fold purpose in adoption is not only to comfort the heart of a child and to provide for that child through the chosen parents, the life, stability and destiny that He has ordained. It is also that the parent(s) will gain a new and clearer understanding of ministry, purpose and self-sacrifice, to have hands-on knowledge of who God is and His will for our lives, and that these disciplines will not only focus us, but will strengthen and encourage our resolve to be everything He wants us to be, without hesitation.

Our willingness to be used by God, in this most special way, allows Him to show His might and His power, to undo the lie and assignments of Satan in the life of a child, no actually in the life of anyone. It offers Him the opportunity to show others that indeed we are all one flesh, one blood, and have only one hope of salvation!

We're never really aware of all we have to offer to someone else until we are placed in a position to draw on all our personal resources, to accomplish His desired will and purpose for our lives.

We always have our most perfect example in the LORD and our heavenly Father. God always reveals Himself as a Father who is tender, close to His children and sensitive to their needs, always teaching, encouraging, helping, and healing all their painful scars. Growing up is something He will never leave to chance. He is a Father who carefully nurtures His children.

As believers, having children is a response to the command, "Be fruitful and multiply;" fill the earth with hope, light, direction, and purpose. We are to subdue, not to allow this earth or this world to gain the territory bought and paid for by the sacrifice of our LORD. All children belong to God, those carried by us and those carried by others; there is no exception. Psalms 127:3-5 says, "Lo, children are an heritage from the LORD; and the fruit of the womb is His reward. (4) As arrows are in the hand of a mighty man, so are children of one's youth. (5) Happy is the man who hath his quiver full of them; they shall not be ashamed, but they shall speak with the enemies in the gate."

In the above scripture I don't see anything that reads: "Just your children, the ones you birth are a heritage from the LORD, " or "Only the fruit of your womb is His reward." All children are His gift to mankind; all children are His reward to us! We are to nurture and care for all children, because they all belong to us. They are loaned to us for a season. God blesses us by giving His children to parents…all parents, in the same way a man might entrust his fortune to his heirs. Jesus wants us not to despise even "one of these little ones." And our LORD holds up their faith, the faith children have in God, as an example for all adults to follow. Reading in Matthew 18: 1-5, "At the same time came the disciples unto Jesus, saying, who is the greatest in the kingdom of heaven? (2) And Jesus called a little child unto Him, and set him in the midst of them, (3) And said, verily I say unto you, except ye be converted, and become as little children, ye shall not enter into the kingdom of heaven. (4) Whosoever, therefore, shall humble himself as this little child, the same is greatest in the kingdom of heaven. (5) And whosoever shall receive one such little child in my name receiveth me."

In verse 5 of this chapter we have beautiful insight to the great value and purpose of a child, all children, and that when we receive a little child—those that come from us, and those that come to us— if we receive them in the name of Jesus, then we're accepting Jesus and His will for our lives and their lives.

No child should be left without the nurturing, loving arms of our LORD. We are our brother's keeper saints, even when they are pint sized! (Smile) In some families there may not be room. Maybe everything that surrounds you demands too much to include the special needs that may be inherent in an adoptive child. If this is the case, God truly knows this and will not demand of you or your family what might be too much for you and your family. However, if there is not just room in your heart, but room in your family and home, and resources in your income that are more than enough, then maybe, just maybe, this wonderful ministry is tailored made for you. The cost of a lost child, a lost soul, and a lost opportunity is just too great.

There is a responsibility that belongs to parents only, and that is the raising of our children. Responsibility might be shared by grandparents, schools, youth groups, churches, other family, and friends. But the final duty rests with the parents and particularly with the father, whom God has appointed head to lead and serve the family.

There are two essential things necessary for the care and nurturing of all children, especially those children God has placed by His divine appointment in our midst and in our lives: a right attitude and a right foundation. We must guard against an atmosphere that reeks with destructive criticism, condemnation, unrealistic expectations, sarcasm, intimidation, and fear. These conditions in our home will only provoke our children to wrath, but in such an atmosphere, no productive and beneficial teaching can take place.

When the LORD entrusts us with the life and nurturing of a child He's chosen to place in our lives, the last thing the child needs to further complicate his or her life is this type of acidic environment. What He's asking from us is to provide what they've either never experienced or are in dire need of, and that is an atmosphere rich in encouragement, tenderness, patience, listening, affection, and love. These priceless gifts to every child, especially a child that has never known what it is to be cared for and cared about in such a way, is exactly what the LORD has ordered.

Sometimes roots of pain and sorrow, even abuse, have grown so strong in them because of the years of neglect, and waiting for the impossible, someone to love and adopt them. In instances like this you must allow the LORD to equip you with every tool necessary to establish the trust and confidence needed for your child to prosper and be in health.

We must understand that love is measured by hugs, kisses, and discipline. Discipline is the other side of teaching and nurturing every child. To develop a teachable spirit within a child, (and some adults have not developed this discipline yet!) cannot be accomplished without your willingness to listen intently to what God is telling you about who they really are, what they've seen, where they've been, and what they've been told. If you've adopted a younger child, or even an older child, many knots in their emotional make-up and development will have to be untied by the wisdom of God. This will take patience, and the opportunity to try to experiment with what is most needed and most effective, but also allowing your child the right to fail and to learn by failure.

Many walls and perhaps strongholds of stubbornness, harsh temperaments, and unwillingness to initially trust you, or willful disobedience may be the result of protective safeguards and survival techniques necessary for them to preserve their own sanity! If these traits are allowed to remain and only grow in strength, they will destroy effective teaching and disrupt the harmony of the family. God's answer to this is firm and loving discipline. We're told in 1 Samuel 15:23, "For rebellion is as the sin of witchcraft, and stubbornness is as iniquity and idolatry. Because thou hast rejected the Word of the LORD, He hath also rejected thee from being king." This word of rebuke was given to King Saul by Samuel because of his unwillingness to obey God, no matter what. Yet, it also cautions us against allowing rebellion and stubbornness to remain a part of our child's character without doing those things necessary to subdue them. Why? Because we want the destiny that God has ordained for our children to come to pass; we don't want them dethroned by Him.

The Bible makes a clear distinction between discipline and physical abuse. Discipline may be painful but not injurious. We are never to inflict harm on a child. "Withhold not correction from the child; for if thou beatest him with the rod, he shall not die. (14) Thou shalt beat him with the rod, and shalt deliver his soul from hell." (Proverbs 23:13-14). At times, dear friends, pain may be part of effective correction. Remember in our earlier chapter, God describes Himself as a strict disciplinarian. Although He always disciplines us out of love and for our own benefit, His correction may cause us pain.

Your child's eternal destiny may hinge upon the godly discipline provided by you as their parent. There is no need to fear if you discipline according to the Word and will of God, and with the sincere love of a parent for your child abiding in your heart.

We sometimes speak about difficult circumstance into which people are born as "an accident of birth." Viewed from a divine perspective, however, our placement in a human family is not accident; it is a divine appointment, and God establishes the solitary unit of the family. The protection and care that one receives in a family is so essential to human life and development that God says He will personally intervene on the behalf of widows and orphans who lose the normal protection of a husband and father. Exodus 22:22-24 says, "Ye shall not afflict any widow or fatherless child. (23) If thou afflict them in any way, and they cry at all unto me, I will surely hear their cry; (24) and my wrath shall burn, and I will kill you with the sword; and your wives shall be widows, and your children fatherless." Whew! That's so deep! Imagine the love, concern, and empathy our Father has for His own! He's a wonderful father, a wonderful LORD and Savior and a wonderful God...Amen? Amen.

When we are tempted to complain about our family, or suppose that our birth circumstances would be better somewhere else, we need to back up, take another look at what might have been had it not been for the LORD, who was on our side, and regain His divine perspective. To an adopted infant, child, young-adult, or the adopted child who is now an adult and on your own: God's placement and the circumstances of your birth can never deter His destiny for your life; it will only enhance it. We are encouraged to remember that the ultimate well being of our families rests upon the promise and care of our Father in heaven, and that His sovereign and loving purpose will always intervene for our benefit.

If we really are to honor God as parents, we are to do so by loving and caring for His children. As a family there isn't a better example of the Christian life, or the church, than the Christian family. As Christians, and ministers of His gospel, we are to live according to 1 Corinthians 13:4-8 and 13: "Love suffereth long, and is kind; love envieth not; love vaunteth not itself, is not puffed up, (5) Doth not behave itself unseemly, seeketh not its own, is not easily provoked, thinketh no evil, (6) Rejoiceth not in iniquity, but rejoiceth in the truth; (7) beareth all things, believeth all things, hopeth all things, endureth all things. (8) Love never faileth; but whether there be prophecies, they shall be done away; whether there be tongues, they shall cease; whether there be knowledge, it shall vanish away...(13) And now abideth faith, hope, love, these three; but the greatest of these is love."

When these precious gifts flourish within the family setting, any foul thing, whether it's of man or of Satan, will not take root and choke out the abundant life that God has ordained for your child. The sheer beauty and strength of these gifts will enable you to not only complete the task that lies ahead, but you will do it with the gladness of heart and spirit that only our LORD can provide.

Never allow the enemy to cause an exaggerated feeling of inadequacies, or to sow suspicion about your child, or the parents that gave him birth. Don't allow yourself to indulge any attitudes of self-pity for you or for your child. Know that God has done a good thing, a perfect thing; don't be anxious or fearful but rejoice in your newly-found wealth and opportunity, for the blessings that shall unfold before you, you cannot imagine. You're blessed, and great is your reward in the earth and in heaven. God will always provide all the help and wisdom needed for you to give the love, nurturing, instruction, and discipline necessary to provide Him with a more-than-willing and yielding vessel for the gospel's sake.

As the father of your adopted child, there is much that you need to understand and again, your perfect example is our heavenly Father. In Psalms 68:5, "A father of the fatherless, and a judge of the widows, is God in His holy habitation." We are taught by the Holy Spirit to call God "Abba." A very simple form of the word *Abba* is *Ab* and many claim it is the first words a baby can speak. When you get the opportunity, check it out. See if other relatives or friends have ever noticed this. I confess I never really noticed or paid attention, although I have heard them sort of babble; "Ah,ba,ba,ba," or something to that effect. Most of us are listening for "Da Da" or "Ma Ma." What is beautiful is that Jesus applied this toddler's word to His divine Father in Mark 14:36: "And He said, Abba, Father, all things are possible unto thee. Take away this cup from me; nevertheless, not what I will, but what thou wilt."

When we research this word *Abba,* which means *daddy* and its prefix *Ab,* we find it used as the prefix to many names in the Bible, for example, Abraham, "Father of a Multitude;" "Abimelech, "My Father Is King;" Yoab (Joab), "Yahweh Is a Father;" and Abshalom (Absalom), "Father of Peace."

As a father your value and input cannot be calculated, and just as our heavenly Father wants an up-close and personal relationship with each of His children, so should be your desire with your children. I wanted to place this information in your heart to maybe reinforce the importance of the father's role to any family unit, and that it's even more essential when you've decided to adopt. It's easy for the mother to form close attachments to her baby beginning at the point when she discovers she's pregnant. It usually happens at the first doctor's visit, and this feeling of pride and joy becomes even more intense with each month that passes. So for nine months, or ten, eleven, or twelve, depending upon the mother's size and discomfort, (smile), she's already bonded with her child. It's birth that makes that bonding visible to all that see them together for the first time. However, the father has not been able to really take part in a way that makes him feel a part of this new addition, so the mother must allow for the infant to bond with the father by including him in on everything she can that pertains to its care.

Having said that, imagine how much more the father of an adopted child might have a tendency to feel left out if he's not immediately included in on everything that involves the adoption of your child, from the deciding upon which child, to what name she is to be given if this is necessary, to when she is picked up and introduced to the rest of the family—just everything. The decision to adopt must be everyone's decision, including other children if this applies. Only a father can give a child the kind of assurance and security she needs, along with the strength and comfort of having him hold her tight as they laugh and play together. Everything he can contribute to ease any fears or even the slightest misgivings will be invaluable. A mother's love and a father's love are separate emotions, and are most effective and beneficial when they operate in concert with one another. It will take both parents to accomplish what the LORD desires for your brand new family.

Love is an emotion that needs no explanation; when it's there everyone will be aware of its presence. Love for a child cannot be faked. It will manifest itself like a counterfeit dollar bill, and not just to those on the outside looking in, but to those who are on the inside, trying to get out! (Smile). Let God's love flow through you and give shape and meaning to the lives of your children, to all your children. If the people around us do not see the love of God in us, they will not seek, or find it anywhere else. All believers are called to demonstrate God's love to our community, neighbors, and church family, but most of all our immediate families. Our homes are a field of harvest that must be cultivated by the love of Christ. It's our children we want to win to Christ, and we do this by allowing the love of God to shine through us.

A child who has been adopted by you, and placed in your home has been given a new lease on life! He's been given an opportunity to become all that he can be, through Christ Jesus. Your willingness to be used of God has given him a hope and a sense of permanence that even he will not be aware of until eternity. When God planted him in the soil of your home, soil that has been made rich by His love, by the compassion of the Holy Spirit, and by the unfailing tenderness of our LORD and Savior, Jesus Christ, anyone, I mean anyone, would flourish and grow like a beautiful vine, stretching and reaching for the glory and majesty of God! It's an awesome opportunity to take part is such a beautiful thing. Adoption is an opportunity of ordained placement, and high privilege!

The love we give them will cause them to hunger and thirst after the God you love and serve. They will be drawn to Christ and ministry with little effort on your part, for it will all be Him. As Jesus is lifted up in your home and introduced to their hearts, they will fall in worship and adoration before His presence with hearts filled with thanksgiving for what He's done and made possible because of His love and concern for them.

God has never changed in His commitment to us, to His children, and He never will. It's our commitment to Him and the ministry He's placed in our care that we must be determined to complete for the gospel's sake. I guess I've said that often, or referred to raising our children as a ministry more than once. (Smile). There is no better pulpit than your living room, or family room, and no better altar than the bedside of your child. No better time for teaching and instruction than every day, all day, Monday through Sunday, and no time off for holidays, or good behavior smile. It is ministry...your children may be your most difficult converts, because they know the real you, (smile) also...maybe your only converts, believe me...they will also be your most important!

Knowing that you are in excellent company, if they are your only converts, it might help to remember Noah…Noah preached to the known world at that time, as he warned of God's judgment, and when the rains came, as he warned the people they would, only Noah and his family: his three sons, their wives and Noah's wife, a total of eight people, along with the animals that God had chosen to preserve the animal kingdom, were saved in the Ark. So you see…you're in excellent company. (Smile). Keep living, preaching and teaching this gospel, they will hear.

As adopted parents there are qualities that the LORD has either seen in you, or qualities that He is establishing in you. God is going to stretch you in ways you never thought possible, or never experienced up to this point, but it will be worth every spiritual sore muscle you'll feel.

Always remember, when God speaks to you in regards to your child, obedience is a must. Obedience is the premier quality of a Christian. Hebrews 5: 8 says, "Though He were a son, yet learned He obedience by the things which He suffered; (9) And being made perfect, He became the author of eternal salvation unto all them that obey Him." Also in 1 Samuel 15: 21-22, "But the people took of the spoil, sheep and oxen, the chief of the things which should have been utterly destroyed, to sacrifice unto the LORD thy God in Gilgal. (22) And Samuel said, hath the LORD as great delight in burnt offerings and sacrifices, as in obeying the voice of the LORD? Behold, to obey is better than sacrifice, and to hearken than the fat of rams."

In the first scripture our LORD learns obedience and is made perfect because of that obedience to the fulfilling of the scriptures, and becoming our eternal Savior. Saul, on the other hand, refused to obey God, and not only placed himself in sin, but also the children of Israel were made to sin, and they thought this to be okay because they attempted to cover this sin with a spiritual act.

When God demands our obedience it's for a purpose. It requires faith to obey God when all the facts regarding a matter may be unknown to you! To successfully carry out this day-to-day trust, this no-matter-what belief and confidence, and this total reliance upon God is probably the most difficult task you'll accomplish for God and for your child.

I think the most frightening things about being obedient are the uncertainties which come with it, and being afraid of the possible consequences, especially those that Satan implants in our vivid imaginations. Obedience sometimes causes real pain that is generated through conflict, whether human or circumstantial. However, God has called His children to obedience. If you don't resist this call, you will experience miraculous and glorious results and enjoy the evidence of your devotion to God and your child.

Your life has become a blank canvas for the hand of God to paint, creating a beautiful future of hope and purpose for you and your family, and you must allow Him free reign in every area of your life. Self-discipline is another must for your life. Any lack of resolve and focus in Christian living primarily stems from hesitation to apply the spiritual principles of self-discipline. In Daniel 6: 4-5, "Then the presidents and princes sought to find occasion against Daniel concerning the kingdom; but they could find no occasion nor fault, forasmuch as he was faithful, neither was there any error or fault found in him. (5) Then said these men, we shall not find any occasion against this Daniel except we find it against him concerning the law of his God."

Quite often, biblical principles and society's standards for right living do not match up. Living out biblical principles will inevitably cause confrontational assaults by those who reject the Bible's mandates. Therefore, if we are to be the parents God expects us to be and has ordained us to be, we must discipline ourselves in thought and deed to stand firm in our commitment to God.

As we discipline ourselves to stand in right relationship with God, we'll find that God will provide the strength necessary to move forward in our Christian life, and will reward our courageous efforts as we continue to draw and drink from His Spirit and the resources He has provided. Finally, spiritual discipline can only be achieved by the deliberate and conscientious yielding of our will to the spirit and the power of God.

The true worth of Christians is defined not by how much they have acquired, but how much they are willing to share and give of what they have acquired. In Acts 2:44-45, "And all that believed were together, and had all things common; (45) And sold their possessions and goods, and parted them to all men, as every man had need."

When we sincerely share and give of ourselves without thought of what we'll receive in return, this is known as selflessness, another quality that all Christian parents should possess, especially those who are or have considered adoption. Selfishness shrivels the soul and lessens its capacity to demonstrate the true nature of God, which is love. We are never diminished by giving ourselves away, and nothing produces more harmony and beauty in our lives than giving of one's self.

Only the spirit of fear produces selfishness. The need to have and keep everything to yourself, or to keep everything undisturbed by outside influence and demands is selfish and creates a total breakdown in the spirit realm of God's purpose for you and your family. There is a boundless joy and satisfaction that comes from self-giving, an openness before God and man, that comes from love.

As a salmon that swims upstream, is a family that desires to be a family of integrity. Ecclesiastes 7:28-29 says, "Which yet my soul seeketh, but I find not: one man among a thousand have I found, but a woman among all those have I not found. (29) Lo, this only have I found, that God hath made man upright; but they have sought out many devices."

A world that's not only influenced, but controlled by the ever-mounting ills of humanistic philosophies and situation ethics fights against integrity. No child of God can possibly doubt that today's moral values derive their source from the human experience with little or no regard for God. We may attain worldly acclaim, social standing, and even financial prominence through honest means, but if our emotions, mind, and will are not submitted to the Holy Spirit, we risk being pulled away from the wholeness and wholesomeness our LORD desires for His children. It's a risk we cannot afford.

We must say as Joshua said in Joshua 24:15, "And if it seem evil unto you to serve the LORD, choose you this day whom ye will serve, whether the gods which your fathers served that were on the other side of the river, or the gods of the Amorites, in whose land ye dwell; but as for me and my house, we will serve the LORD."

Friends, the spiritual lines have been drawn: if children of God are to prosper in everything they do, and be complete in all they seek after, we must walk with God in total integrity of heart. It's a *must do*…no exceptions.

I think one of the most difficult qualities of human nature, even for the child of God, is humility. Matthew 11:29 says, "Take my yoke upon you, and learn of me; for I am meek and lowly in heart, and ye shall find rest unto your souls."

This is also a rather remarkable yet perplexing quality, sort of like a two-edged sword. One side will develop the soul and character of our lives, and the other will make us feel almost weak and puny before others. And yet, humility is a quality that our LORD zealously seeks in us, and guards it jealously when He develops it in us. Why? So that you will not only be *blessed*, but will be a *blessing*!

From the world's perspective any show of humility, or a yielding attitude, is not only a show of weakness, but like blood in the water to a shark, is the ringing of the dinner bell. It might, also before man, create an eating frenzy (smile), as they cry out, "Fresh meat, go get 'em!" (Smile). Only as Christians, if there's nothing else we've found out about our LORD, is that when we say, "Up," He moves down; if we think left, He moves back and around! If we believe the situation calls for aggressiveness, He whisper to us, "Stand ye still and see the salvation of the LORD!" Amen...Amen. (Smile).

This is also true of His view of humility. To show our true strength as Christians we must sometimes submit ourselves to another's will in order that God will be glorified. And we're also given Christ's perfect example. In John 13: 13-17 he says, "Ye call me Master and LORD; and ye say well; for so I am. (14) If, then, your LORD and Master have washed your feet, ye also ought to wash one another's feet. (15) For I have given you an example that ye should do as I have done to you. (16) Verily, verily, I say unto you, the servant is not greater than his lord; neither He that is sent greater than He that sent him. (17) If ye know these things, happy are ye if ye do them."

God needs His children to be humble, so that He can use us to touch, change, and restore lives...even the lives of our children. And for their sakes...no request of Him...is too much to ask. Amen? Amen.

There may be no greater challenge, no greater privilege, and no greater ministry than being an adoptive parent. If you're wrestling with this decision or maybe you've even decided to adopt, fear not!

Sure, it's our nature to want to know all, see all, and be prepared for all! We want and need to be in control, to know what God is doing, or going to do next. But, it's a funny thing about our Father; we want to know everything ahead of time, and He loves surprise packages! What wonderful surprise do you have in your package? Do you have the cure for cancer in your care, the next Billy Graham, or maybe even the first female president? Who knows? God knows!

When the time comes and all the tape has been cut away, the ribbon and bows untied, the wrapping paper removed, and all the protective tissue paper taken away, you'll see! God doeth all things well! Fear not! Praise His glorious name. Hallelujah!

Chapter VI

TEEN…A Great Four-Letter Word!

A teenager brings to light the cliché…"God must have a sense of humor!" I mean after all, they're equipped with just enough of everything to get them into trouble, and they have a way of doing it that will either break your heart or make you crack up laughing!

It's my opinion that teenagers should be recognized as a separate culture. When we look up the definition of the word *culture* we have: The totality of socially transmitted behavior patterns, arts, music, beliefs, institutions, and all other products of human work and thought characteristics of community or population. I mean, really. Don't they qualify under this definition? They have their own dialect, way of dress, music, hair, make-up, social and moral guidelines, and economic base. Us! Do I really need to say more? I believe that all parents should draw up a contract with no small print or hidden clauses explaining to their thirteen-year-old that they will be out of their mind for about seven years—God's number of completion! Then things should return to normal. (Smile)

Seriously, our teenagers are one of our most precious natural resources. They are blessed with an inexhaustible treasure source of hope, courage, energy, and commitment to those they hold dear. They possess a flawless beauty, a fearless devotion to what they believe in, and a daring that causes them to believe they can leap tall buildings at a single bound. They're absolutely wonderful, and a tremendous gift to humanity.

What God wants us to realize is not only *who* they are, but also, *whose* they are that we are fully aware of the special guidelines He's established in our hearts that the Word of God might abound in them. We are to do our part to establish and fix their hearts upon the living Word of God, thus, enabling them to leap spiritual mountains in a single bound!

They are not going to be the church of tomorrow, they are the church of tomorrow. The church of tomorrow is here right now! Friends, this is it! What we are going to do for Christ, for the gospel, we must do it now and instill that same desire in our children, especially our teens, for they are nearest to adulthood, families, career choices, and ministry commitments.

In the earlier chapters we've talked about knowing your children, blessing your children, praying for them, calling the gifts forth in them, and providing a healthy and proper form of discipline that will fully equip them for the gospel's sake. Now that some of these issues and needs or concerns have been addressed, let's try, with the help of the Holy Spirit, to continue building, molding, and shaping the lives and destinies that God has ordained for our children who are now teenagers.

I asked the LORD in prayer, "Father what makes a teenager different?" "What makes them so special?" "Why are they such a crucial part to the body of Christ?" It's my hope and prayer that we will learn together what His Spirit will convey to all our hearts about this very special and precious resource to the church, and the body of Christ.

With the help of the Holy Spirit, we are to prepare them, and make them ready for every perfect work, equip them in such a way that every opportunity for them, whether at school, at play, in a friend's car, or even just chillin' among other young saints, would be an instant opportunity to lift up to Christ. They will not be able to do this unless they've seen it in you. That's the difference with a teenager: you can't really lecture or preach to them. Your best means of communication is your life! How you live and handle life's challenges and opportunities and its stress will speak louder to them than any words!

I know you've heard the old adage: "Do as I say, not as I do!" Well, that's the ultimate in hypocrisy! This might possibly be one of the greatest stumbling blocks to any children, especially teenagers; they watch and take mental notes on almost everything any adult may say or do. Remember, anyone, over the age of twenty-one, even parents, is the enemy (smile). Teenagers above almost everyone else hate a hypocrite. They can spot one wearing sunglasses with a hood over their head on a foggy day! (Smile)

As their parent, your life is under the powerful scrutiny and discernment of their watchful eyes. Satan will always do his best to give them cause to defy you and your disciplines. Remember, they're getting pressures from every side. Satan is bidding high for control of their lives. He never has played fair and never will play fair. He'll use their friends, teachers, talents, gifts, goals, ambitions—just about everything, including the never-to-be-forgotten kitchen sink! Therefore, remember the scripture in Matthew 10:16, "Behold,

I send you forth as sheep in the midst of wolves; be ye therefore wise as serpents, and harmless as doves."

Everything about your life must point to Christ, allowing the Holy Spirit to make their hearts pliable in His hands.

Remember when I was saying earlier that one of the characteristics that makes our teenagers different is that they will not tolerate our preaching to them or lecturing them. The same is true of comparing them or their behavior to anyone else. Never tell them that if they don't obey, "The same thing that happened to Jerry will happen them," or "See, Betsy? That happened because you don't listen, the way Martha never did!"

Our teens may look and act similar to each other, they may even be related, but the last thing that they need is your trying to intimidate them, or embarrass them into feeling bad about something they do that irritates you. That's not the way to hold them accountable for their actions or to gain the trust and respect you will definitely need.

By now I know you're tempted to shake your head wondering, "Well, what do I do?" The answer to that is: nothing. It must be done by the Holy Spirit. Remember, according to 2 Corinthians 10:4, "For the weapons of our warfare are not carnal, but mighty through God to the pulling down of strongholds."

Pray! And when you've done all you can do, fast and pray! If we want our teenagers to turn away from the gods of their friends, i.e., alcohol, permissive sexual behavior profanity, smoking, rebellion, stubbornness, and the like, to the one and only True God, our Father, it will take prayer and fasting, not your lecturing and preaching. Without a changed heart and attitude, they will be turned off, and you never want to turn off communication with your teenager.

I know that some may think that's a little too passive for them, but for those that do, I refer you again to the above scripture in 2 Corinthians 10:4. We're also told in Acts 2: 17, "And it shall come to pass in the last days, saith God, I will pour out of my Spirit upon all flesh; and your sons and your daughters shall prophesy, and your young men shall see visions and your old men shall dream dreams." Your prayers for your children will bring about whatever changes need to take place in their lives; fasting and prayer are your weapons!

This generation of young people, of teenagers, will bring about revival to this present generation. I declare it, by the Word of God that says, in Malachi 4:5-6, "Behold, I will send you Elijah the prophet, before the coming of the great and terrible day of the LORD; (6) And he shall turn the heart of the father to the children, and the heart of the children to their fathers, lest I come and smite the earth with a curse."

This scripture is an exhortation, a promise to the church to remember the law and Word of God, while we wait for the promise of His coming! The promise of His coming will be borne on the backs and hearts of our children, our teenagers and young people!

Only God can turn the hearts of the fathers and mothers to their children, and the children to their fathers and mothers. Only when our young people, our teenagers tire of Satan's liberty in their lives, and the lives of their friends and peers, only then can God do "exceedingly abundantly above all we ask or think" in regards to their lives and ministries. They must fight and regain the territory the enemy has stolen. They are a new warrior. This is the Josiah Generation!

Josiah, whose name means: "The fire of the LORD" or "Jehovah supports!" became king at the age of eight years old for the people of Judah. His mother was named Jedidah, meaning, "God's darling." Her only dream was that her son would be the holy man of God that He desired.

At the age of sixteen, Josiah turned from the ways of his father Amon and his grandfather Manasseh, and took his nobler and remoter ancestor King David, as his model. Josiah set his heart to seek the LORD. Youth didn't deter Josiah from turning things around; he took down every idol, and he swept away groves of abominations. With the same zeal and righteousness and determination, he led the people of God to repentance. In 2 Kings 23:3, "And the king stood by a pillar, and made a covenant before the LORD, to walk after the LORD, and to keep His commandments and His testimonies and His statutes with all his heart and all his soul, to perform the Words of this covenant that were written in this book, and all the people joined in the covenant!" Hallelujah! Praise God!

Our youth need to know and understand that it's God, their God, that will change their lives and hearts. Whenever God wanted to change man's history, He raised up an extremist. God's revival is always stronger than rebellion. Your sons and daughters will go beyond your dreams if you dare to trust God in fasting and prayer.

Let's look at another extremist, another revolutionary: David. His name means *Beloved*. He was the youngest son of the eight sons of Jesse, and the second greatest of Israel's kings, a young man of integrity, and a man after God's own heart.

David was chosen to be king over Israel, by God himself. As with many of our young people, they have a tendency to be overlooked by others. David was overlooked by Samuel, as he went from one tall, dark, and handsome son to the other, just certain they were the right age, had the right experience, and looked the part! The LORD had to tell Samuel, back up."Arise anoint him, this is he." His father must have thought David too young to be used of God, or too young and insignificant to be effective for God, and neither concern was true. There are many in the church today that also believe that the youth are out of control and they seem to have a mind of their own, and that they're not normal! Well, this is true, but it was also true of David.

Friends, we're usually sidetracked because we look on the outward appearance; we trust what we see, and God knows what He sees within the heart of a man. 1 Samuel 17:7, "But the LORD said unto Samuel, look not on his countenance, or on the height of his stature; because I have refused him: for the LORD seeth not as man seeth; for man looketh on the outward appearance, but the LORD looketh on the heart."

When the LORD looks on your teenager what does He see that you don't see? What behavior is Satan trying to wash your face with so that you'll give up, and stop interceding with fasting and prayer for your son or daughter? We talked earlier about fasting and prayer, and that these spiritual weapons will harness the very qualities that Satan and our LORD want to use. Satan, for destruction, and the LORD, for His glory! It's your refusing to be "moved by what *you* see," and allowing God to develop what He sees that will give you and your child the true victory!

Now, back to David. David was a young shepherd who tended his father's flock. He was nothing like his brothers. He was courageous, had a mind of his own, and was not afraid to speak up. Does that sound like somebody you know? I thought so. When his flock was faced with the threat of "Lions and tigers, and bears, oh my!" (smile) David fought, and eliminated the threat, without the help or knowing of anyone else.

How many threats and fears have your son or daughter faced on a daily basis, and you were never told or made aware of it, unless the LORD told you, or made it known to you? The more information you want to know from your teenager, the less they are willing to tell you. Pray and wait. They will eventually come and tell you all. Only allow them the space of determining when and where that will be. At this age privacy seems to be key in their lives.

Teenagers will not fit into the mold we live in, nor should we want that for them. Allow them the comfort and mobility to walk, play, and live according to the shape and mold God has prepared for them.

David was sent by his father Jesse to bring food to his brothers, and to see how things were going for them, and also to give a gift to the captain who was in charge of them. In 1 Samuel 17: 17-18, "Jesse said unto David his son, take now for thy brethren an ephah of this parched corn, and these ten loaves, and run to the camp of thy brethren; (18) And carry these ten cheeses unto the captain of their thousand, and look how thy brethren fare, and take their pledge."

When David arrived at the battle site and saw and heard the calls and taunting of Goliath, he was incensed! When he saw the fear and shame on the faces of the army and King Saul he was indignant, and like most teenagers he was like a bull in a china shop! He couldn't believe that this was happening, not only to Israel, but in the face of the Almighty God, and that this uncircumcised Philistine had the gall to insult His God, the armies of Israel, and the king with his loud and wrong ranting!

Now his brothers, on the other hand, were just as afraid as everyone else, but were even more embarrassed by their brother. We have their opinion in 1 Samuel 17:28, "And Eliab his eldest brother heard when he spake unto the men; and Eliab's anger was kindled against David, and he said, why camest thou down hither? And with whom hast thou left those few sheep in the wilderness? I know thy pride, and the naughtiness of thine heart; for thou art come down that thou mightest see the battle." Translation: what are you doing here, and who's doing your chores while you're being so nosey? This is none of your business! You're a conceited brat, and as usual, up to no good! How's that? (Smile)

Like most young people, David totally ignored what he said about him, and added his two cents. "And David said, what have I now done? Is there not a cause? (1 Samuel 17:29) Translation: Now what have I done, and what does that have to do with the price of tea in China? (Smile)

David continues talking and asking what's going on, and why isn't someone doing something about this Philistine, and what will be the reward if I do something? As with most teens, "Show him the money!" After a while the men go to Saul and tell him what David is saying, and Saul tells them to bring David to him. When Saul gets a really good look at David, he puts on his royal, are-you-crazy? expression.

After further discussion, however, David sort of convinces Saul he can do this thing, only Saul, again like most adults, wants him to use the traditional means of warfare. Let me switch reels a little bit here and bring up another matter that really coincides with this, and that is: worship. Our young people need something fresh, and alive. We know there's nothing new about the gospel, for it is the same yesterday today and forever, only they need a freshness to draw them unto Christ. God never changes, and this is the truth, but He does update!

There is a beautiful method and truth to ministry of what every child of God must develop within their hearts, and it's found in 1 Corinthians 9:19-22. "For though I be free from all men, yet have I made myself servant unto all, that I might gain the more, (20) And unto the Jews I became as a Jew, that I might gain the Jews; to them that are under the law, as under the law, that I might gain them that are under the law; (21) To them that are without law, as without law, (being not without law to God, but under the law to Christ) that I might gain them that are without law. (22) To the weak became I as weak, that I might gain the weak: I am made all things to all men, that I might by all means save some."

That's such a beautiful insight to our LORD, who became mortal that we might be immortal. He died that we might live. Became poor that we might be made rich. Became sin that we might become the righteousness of God. And rose from His death that we might have resurrection unto eternal life! He too became all things to all men, that He might win *all*! Hallelujah!

Our young people thrive on life…they want to live, and life to them is anything that's bright, beautiful, full of energy, different, always changing, never restricting or binding. I've heard some pastors say that anything dead needs burying, and that's true, so why would we resent our young people when they show us a brighter and fresher way to worship God with their music, their songs of praise, their way of communicating or rapping out the gospel, if it's the gospel, if it's the Word of God? What does it matter if the method of ministry is a little different? Don't look on the outward appearance, allow the LORD to look on their hearts. Their gifts are from Him, as it is written in Romans 11:28-29, "As concerning the gospel, they are enemies for your sakes: but as touching the election, they are beloved for the Father's sake. (29) For the gifts and calling of God are without repentance."

In that verse Paul is talking about Israel. They are not really looking the part right now, but God's rejection is only temporary. That God has opened the door for the gentiles and the world, but that Israel will be saved, they will be grafted into the original vine. When it's time, Israel will be totally restored. When it's time…your young man or daughter will be serving the LORD, with everything that's within them, and maybe serving Him a little more…like you! Give them time, God's time.

Saul was worried and concerned for David because he was looking on the outward appearance, that's all he could see. So we are told in 1 Samuel 17:33, "And Saul said to David, thou art not able to go against this Philistine to fight with him: for thou art but a youth, and he a man of war from his youth."

David tells Saul of his exploits and victories about the challenges he faced when caring for his father's flock, and convinces Saul that he was at least brave enough to try. Saul tries to put his battle gear on David, and David refuses to wear it because it just wasn't him! It was the mold Saul was used to! David could not fight in someone else's armor! And neither can your teens, they will not be successful in ministry doing what you do the way you do it, and really, not even for the reasons you do it. They must fight in their own armor. They must discover who God is to them and for them!

Moving down in the story, David comes face to face with Goliath with only a slingshot and five smooth stones. And when Goliath saw David, this kid, he was thoroughly insulted. "And the Philistine said unto David, am I a dog that thou comest to me with staves? And the Philistine cursed David by his gods." (1 Samuel 17:43) Goliath is typical of any bully who's been given too much rope, and now he was about to hang himself.

David tells Goliath in 1 Samuel 17:46-47, "This day will the LORD deliver thee into mine hand; and I will smite thee, and take thine head from thee; and I will give the carcases of the host of the Philistines this day unto the fowls of the air, and to the wild beast of the earth, that all the earth may know that there is a God in Israel. (47) And all this assembly shall know that the LORD saveth not with sword and spear: for the battle is the LORD's, and He will give you into our hands." Translation: Man, you've lost it! I'm not only going to thrash you, but I'll do it with all your homies looking on; not only that, I'm going to bring your hat to you, only your head won't be there to receive it! Furthermore, the God I serve is an awesome God, and He doesn't need the stuff you use, to get a job done! Dude, you and your homies will be grub for the birds and the beasts of the field! Smile!

We know the rest of the story, everything David said he would do, God did through him, and Israel was given a mighty victory that day. And David was promoted in the heart of our LORD, and in the heart of the people, and Saul, well, "Saul said to him, whose son art thou, thou young man? And David answered, I am the son of thy servant Jesse the Bethlehemite." (1 Samuel 17:58)

Saul was still preoccupied with the age of this young man, never considering the fact that the LORD had used this young man to deliver His people, not only from the armies of the Philistine, but also from the bondage of slavery that Goliath had pronounced upon them if they lost to him. Saul, like many of us, allowed the fact that he was young and his means of fighting was different, to steal the spiritual and physical victory that he achieved.

Because of David's valor and willingness to be used by God, even when those around him didn't understand the "method to his madness," God blessed and used him mightily. As a king for his people, a mighty warrior in battle, marvelous musician and worshiper, prophet, and a man with a heart that was always willing to repent before His God.

David was an extremist used by God during a crucial time in the history of Israel. David was a man that God who could not only trust, but a man God could depend on to swim upstream, and to not be deterred from ministry and doing the will of God simply because he was young when first anointed by God.

Most young people swim upstream. We should not allow their way of doing things, or their motivations for doing it to frustrate and keep us off balance. It's their differences that not only please our LORD, but that He depends on. As adults we've learned from years of living to do things by the book, yet I've personally heard more pastors than I can even remember say,"You can't put God in a box!" Or "God is too huge to confine." There have been times when we've prayed and waited for the LORD to do a new thing in our churches and homes, and in our families, yet we keep our young people in the strait jackets of religious tradition!

May I attempt to use another example? In the Old Testament and the New Testament our Bible tells us about wine when and how it was to be used. We know that the first recorded miracle of our LORD was turning water into wine at a wedding they were all attending.

If wine wasn't kept in jars or other vessels, it was kept in wineskins. Wineskins were containers made from animal hides to preserve the wine. Now, the thing is that new wine cannot be put in old wineskins but must be put in new wineskins because when the new wine ferments and expands, it will break the old wineskins and spill out. New wine must be put into new wineskins, so that they will be preserved.

When are LORD came on the scene as our Savior as the *new way* to the Father, the only way to God, everything that was done in the past, according to Old Testament law, was done away with. Jesus came with a new and better way. He brought with Him new teachings and a new kind of spiritual life. And this new life, this new wine could not be put into old Judaism...or old wineskins. The new wine would and did destroy the old wineskins, or the law, the "learned" thinking and theology of the day.

These men or adults, we'll call them—let's see, what shall we call them? I've got it; let's call them Pharisees (smile). These men didn't want this young man shaking the boat, and undoing years of futile human effort that only supported their self-righteous and superior image among the people. When Jesus came on the scene with His long hair uncovered, plain and almost drab clothing, speaking in a new way and declaring He was everything, could do anything, and that His Father could beat up their father, and hanging out with just everybody they were incensed!

They couldn't stand Him! Who was this young upstart! How dare He tell them how to live their lives and instruct the people, after all, we're the adults here; we've been doing this longer than He's been alive! Sound familiar?

Jesus is the new wine, and the church…is the new wineskin! The old ways are passed away, and all things have become new. Old wineskins cannot support the highly-charged fermenting of the Holy Spirit. His people require new containers, namely, the Living Church!

You might say that Jesus was no teenager. I know this, but He was a young man by their standards. Don't forget, He was a boy of twelve years old when He was at the temple on His very first Passover trip. Jesus sat in the midst of these teachers of the law, the Pharisees of that day, and they marveled at His wisdom and His understanding of spiritual truth.

I believe that the LORD wants us to understand that wisdom and knowledge is not unique to the aged or the adult. That what He's blessed us with through our children, is a way to keep the Church young and current to the needs of the day. To not allow tradition and religious trappings to destroy the truth of who He is. What He wants accomplished in the earth, is for everyone, young and old, to come to the knowledge of Him as LORD and Savior.

It takes innovative thought to draw generations to Christ. If you consider our young people a little extreme and little too bold and maybe even a little too unconventional, it sounds to me like that's exactly what Jesus Christ was to the Pharisees of His day!

Let's try not to destroy this wonderful new wine we have in our young people by forcing them into old wineskins that can never really contain them but will cause them to spill out of our grasp. Whatever year your child was born, speaking as the wine experts would speak, "It was a very good year!"

Another issue that seems to distinguish the teenagers from the rest of us "normal" people is their emotional make-up. It's like trying to handle a powerful two-edged sword. On one hand they are fearless and seemingly invincible, and feeling like nothing will bring them down but Kyrptonite! (Smile) How do they run all day, play all night, eat nothing but carbs, sugar, and grease, get two hours of rest, awaken to a brand new day looking and feeling better than the day before? Beats me! And what about this tendency to blindly leap into anything without the slightest thought to the negative consequences, never stopping to realize that this leap so to speak, might be hazardous to their heath and to yours?

The other side to this emotional two-edged sword is their sensitivity! It's like having a wound that never seems to really heal. At times they have this raw place that causes them to overreact to even the slightest question about someone or something, that they choose to keep to themselves, a hurt that you thought to be over or healed, and the mentioning of it brings tears or tantrums. Like pulling the scab off a wound, they begin to bleed and hurt all over again.

On one hand they appear fearless and seemingly full of faith and all grown up. On the other hand there's this little child that seems to need cuddling and holding again! As parents we're swinging from such an emotional pendulum, that we may sometimes feel as if we're losing our minds! Well, a word of comfort: you are! It's true. You're losing your mind! For reasons of pure survival, the only life raft available is grabbing hold of their mind, their thoughts and their feelings. You have to go back to when you were their age and recall the days of yesteryear!

With everything that we have to contend with on a daily basis, we sometimes forget (probably for sanity sake) what it was like to be where they are, caught between two worlds and two bodies. On the outside you see your lovely daughter with her beautiful bright eyes and grown-up figure, or your son, this masculine athlete needing to shave. On the inside is this quiet storm of trying to deal with all this new equipment, with Satan and their peers encouraging them to go for broke, all of this while working hard to not forget they have their parents and God to answer to!

The youth of today are faced with challenges on every side. Issues and temptations we didn't understand until we'd been married for at least ten to fifteen years! (Smile). Issues like what to do with all these new feelings and emotions? What about my skin and my hair? And, why can't I do this or that? Or I'm almost old enough to vote! Oh yes, we can't forget the, "Good grief, what's the *big deal?* Everybody else is doing it!" Whew! LORD, help us! (Smile)

Another issue they must deal with and that we've hinted at, is peer pressure, this having to dress, to act like, look and smell like everybody else. The stress of trying to belong to, or to be a part of the "in-crowd," the need to be accepted as being as good as, not wanting to stand out, or to draw unwanted attention to yourself. Trying out for all the important clubs and teams at school just to be respected and looked up to. All of this and so much more that pressures and vies for their attention. It's hard, and very difficult, for them to manage all this without our help and understanding. This peer pressure is at the top of the list for every teenager in the world today. It's item number one or two, on their list of fears and concerns. It's also very real and painful, and when dealing with them, we must do so with a heart of compassion and understanding.

I say to handle with understanding because we as adults know where they're coming from, don't we? It's called, "Keeping up with the Joneses," where we live, how we dress, what people think about our children. Did our child walk soon enough to be considered bright, and how soon do we want them reading and mastering the gifted toys? When trying out for the school play, did they get the leading role, or do they have a solo part in the choir? Oh, and your husband, what does he do? Do you tell people he's a teller, which is the truth, or that he's in high finance, a stretch of the truth? Do you drive this huge utility vehicle that requires a stepladder or a leg up to get into because you love riding above sea level, or because everybody else has one? Get the picture? Of course you do. Oh, and one more thing: living beyond your financial means, so that you and your children can look, dress, and be like everybody else. You're so over extended that your credit cards have a metal detector attached them to keep you from entering the department stores without a reliable and disciplined companion!

It's crazy, and yet we are responsible. If our children and our teenagers give in to peer pressure, it's because they've seen us do exactly the same thing. Only the pressure they deal with can take them from us. For this reason, we must deal with them according to wisdom. Helping them to understand that peer pressure is something that we all deal with, and that it's a real struggle, even for you. Explain to them that there will always be consequences for the choices they make, and that you only want to be there to assist them in making these choices, not to dictate your choice to them.

It will be touchy because teenagers hate being lectured to, so be certain to seek the LORD for the words that will best instruct your young person. We want whatever decision they finally make to be made according to God's wisdom, not ours.

Remember friends, we're guardians, or an even better word is stewards. We're stewards over God's priceless resource. We have many guidelines given to us for the wise and careful use of the blessed gifts God has bestowed upon us. "Lo children are an heritage of the LORD: and the fruit of the womb is His reward. (4) As arrows are in the hand of the mighty man; so are children of the youth." (Psalm 127: 3 and 4)

A steward is someone who manages another's finances, household or estate. As parents we are to be disciplined in all areas of our lives, and this most certainly includes our children. The time we have with them in our care is so very, very short, and the last thing we want to do, and the last thing our LORD wants to see happen, is a severing of the relationship we should cultivate with our children. As He remains our clearest and best example of all things, keep in mind that the one and only thing He has determined not to touch is our will. It's left intact for us to do with as we see fit. What He does trust and depends on, is that our love for Him will guide us in the decisions we make, and that our desire to please and not bring Him shame, will over-ride any attempt of Satan to destroy us and our relationship Him.

In the Word of God we read about Job, about the severe testing and challenges he suffered. Satan was attempting to use every means possible, i.e., children, material gains, reputation, and status, health, and his marriage—he just took everything! But the Bible tells us, "In all this Job sinned not, nor charged God foolishly." (Job 1:22)

Be comforted in the knowledge that our LORD will not allow Satan to put on you or your family more than you can bear. If you're in prayer and fasting for your teenager, and have earnestly represented yourself and your God before them, it may take a little effort, but they will always do the right thing eventually (smile). I know that sounds scary to you, but rest in the knowledge that you may be biting *your* nails, but God isn't!

As God's steward you must never waste time, and always be willing to stop what you're doing or where you're going to be available when they need you. The one thing you can depend upon with any teenager is that they're not dependable. What they told you yesterday doesn't apply for today. Better yet, what they told you this morning about something may change by the afternoon. It's foolish to not be there for them. No matter what, you can't buy back lost years and opportunities. If you have their confidence and their trust today, take advantage of it and use it; it may be weeks before the opportunity presents itself again. When you can actually talk to them about the things that matter or that concern you, do so by the wisdom of the Holy Spirit, remembering that God has made us stewards over His most irreplaceable possessions, our children.

Allow that the time you have together is spent wisely, constructively, and in the worship, service, and lifting up of our LORD and Savior, Jesus Christ.

The last advice I can suggest to you regarding your young person is found in 1 Peter 4: 7-8, "But the end of all things is at hand; be ye therefore, sober minded, and watch unto prayer. (8) And above all things have fervent love among yourselves; for love shall cover the multitude of sins."

As parents, especially of teenagers, we must be clear headed in our motives and attitudes, never be moved by what we see, but watch and pray about everything we do see, resting in the knowledge that the love for our children, and God's love for all of us, will support and protect us until He comes again.

God Bless You!

Chapter VII

Stop…Drop…and Roll It Over

Almost every school campus in the United States has some form of emergency or safety measure in place to ensure the safety and welfare of our children.

The rash of violent outbreaks on our campuses has stunned our lives, terrified our children, and baffled our law enforcement agencies. This destruction to property, the devastation and heartbreak to homes and families has wreaked havoc throughout our communities and left us reeling from the impact.

We spend hours telling our children not talk to strangers, to come straight home after school, and never get into the car of someone they don't know, no matter how friendly they may seem, or what they may tell them. If they study after school at the home of a friend, we ask them to call us when they arrive and when they leave, and if it's late, we'll pick them up. We do all of this, and more depending on the routine of each family.

The one thing most homes and parents seem to neglect doing is preparing our children for the attack and challenges of Satan, the archenemy of their eternal souls. We don't mean to neglect this training, but we seem to think we have plenty time. After all, they're just children, right? But, in today's environment of violence, this is a literal life-and-death issue we must not neglect!

It's not my intent to frighten you, but to put you on alert. The struggle and battles we face daily will also affect our children. It's irresponsible as parents to not understand that whatever spiritual attacks we face will also impact their lives.

In the book of 1 John, he often refers to us as "Beloved," which means that God has placed His love upon us. He wants us to listen to what He has to say to us, because when we listen, we cannot be taken unawares. His Word cautions us, as His children, to watch and pray instructing us to know our enemy. Psalm 37:32 says, "The wicked watcheth the righteous, and seeketh to slay him." We're told in 1 Peter 5:8, "Be sober, be vigilant; because your adversary the devil, as a roaring lion, walketh about, seeking whom he may devour:" We're cautioned to choose our friends carefully: 2 Corinthians 6:17, "Wherefore come out from among them, and be ye separate, saith the LORD, and touch not the unclean thing; and I will receive you," and John 15:18-19, "If the world hate you, ye know that it hated me before it hated you. (19) If ye were of the world, the world would love his own; but because ye are not of the world, but I have chosen you out of the world, therefore the world hateth you."

The Word of God is replete with God's instruction to us, as His children, to guard against those that are antichrist, to not just go everywhere, and do anything. We're told to live our lives as examples of Christ, to hear His voice and trust His will and concern for our lives, to be careful of strangers, those who don't believe as we do. 2 Corinthians 6:14 says, "Be ye not unequally yoked together with unbelievers: for what fellowship hath righteousness with unrighteousness? And what communion hath light with darkness?" Isn't this is exactly what a good father, and parent should do? And if He is our most excellent example on how to live and raise our children, then we are responsible as His children, to be obedient, and to do the same for our children.

Our schools will disrupt the regularly scheduled routine to sound the alarm for fire drills, yellow alert, extreme weather changes, and now we even have to deal with foreign and domestic terrorist activity! Everyone is making a concerted effort to keep our children safe and free from harm when they're away from home and in their care. But are we dealing with issues far more reaching than just the welfare and safety of their physical bodies?

In this chapter we will talk about teaching are children what the fire department teaches them during fire drill instruction: *stop, drop, and roll over*!

That is to *stop* whatever they are doing that is not like Christ, or to *stop* Satan's attack or ambush against them...or to just *stop* and wait on the LORD to fight the battle. They've committed themselves into His care.

We want to teach them to *drop* everything they're doing, and fall to their knees and seek His will in a matter. To *drop*-kick Satan to his knees with the Word of God and to *drop* their plans for God's plans.

They need to *roll* over every care and concern they may have onto Christ. To steam*roll* the plans and agenda of the enemy, and to rest and *roll* along in life, being anxious about nothing!

As we touch on these aspects of training our children, it's my prayer for you that you'll not only hear what I'm saying, but that you'll listen to the tone the Holy Spirit is speaking in, because as with all children, they will understand the tone of your voice, clearer than the words of your voice. When we determine to use a no-holds-barred attack on Satan, by thoroughly preparing our children to be all that they can be through Christ Jesus, victory on every level belongs to them, and to us!

First, we want our children to know the voice of God. It's impossible for them to *stop* what they are doing wrong if they don't know the voice of the Father. As in John 10:3-4, "To him the porter openeth; and the sheep hear His voice: and He calleth His own sheep by name: for they know His voice. (4) And a stranger will they not follow, but will flee from him: for they know not the voice of strangers."

The great need before us today is to have the Word of God in our hearts, and to press this Word into the hearts of our children. The voice of the LORD, to our children, as well as to all of us, *is* and will always be in complete alignment with His written or spoken Word; there are *no exceptions*. The Word of God will not only give them a strong and sound foundation, but it will support and place them in position to hear and receive from God. It will not only enable them to stand during spiritual battles, but will keep them standing after every battle.

As God's children, we are to take on the complete character of our Father. We are called Christians, which means little Christs. Originally is was most likely a term of mocking and derision, but the name became a badge of honor for the early church, and not one of shame and mocking as Satan had intended it to be. Another point to make is that before we adopted the name of Christian the early church referred to themselves as *believers*, *brothers*, or *saints*.

All of these names are very positive, and carry with them a tremendous responsibility, a responsibility that we cannot take lightly. Our Savior would not be pleased about how our name, Christian, has been diluted to such an extent that a disciple of Christ, or a Christian is now a political issue totally void of His love, a religious tradition, again, void of His love and compassion. We have in many instances become a lukewarm church, with almost no voice at all. The world doesn't want to hear what we have to say any longer, because of what they have seen, and read, and yes, even experienced, from a Christian.

It can be difficult to win the confidence of your child in a world that they are forced to live, work and play in on a daily basis, when your time with them is limited or scarce by comparison, a world that speak volumes about the hypocrisy they've experienced in our churches, and by those Christians.

Don't be dismayed; it's not your tasked to challenge what people say or think about us. Our only task is to be the example of Christ in our homes and among our families that our LORD expects us to be. The home is the most important arena we have for the voice of God to be heard in us. There is nowhere on this earth where the listening audience is more favorable for His Word. Remember, we don't save the world one step at a time, but one child at a time and it must begin with your child.

Until their voice is strong enough to speak the Word of God, and hear the Word of God, faith comes by hearing, and hearing by the Word of God, (Romans 10:17-18, "So then faith cometh by hearing, and hearing by the Word of God. (18) But I say, have they not heard? Yes, verily, their sound went into all the earth, and their words unto the ends of the world.") Until then you must speak aloud for them. Be the voice of God when you pray His Word, be His voice as you instruct them according to His Word. When you're challenged by Satan, and blind-sided by him, whenever possible let them hear your voice as you *stop* everything and seek God for direction, wisdom, and strength.

As they listen to you, and your praise and worship, their voice will become stronger, thereby increasing their ability to also hear the voice of God!

When our children come with their concerns and their pain, usually inflicted by someone else, never allow yourself to be tempted to take matters into your own hands. I know this is a hard thing, when our children hurt and are in pain, our first response is to kill (Smile)! and then cry out, Lazarus, come forth (Smile)! But we can't; God will never honor such behavior and we will have lost the opportunity to teach our child a better and more perfect way. Amen? Amen.

When the school routinely schedules emergency drills for our children, it's so that they won't panic in times of emergency or crisis. They don't give the children any idea about when the drill is coming, what time of day, or anything that allows them to prepare themselves. What they are trying to achieve is quick and accurate response at a moment's notice. This type of training enables them to react quickly, and quietly, and to do so without fear.

If they are to *stop* the enemy, they must not be afraid. They must have a confidence in your teaching, and the Word of God you've placed into their hearts. It's condition and response! It's also a willingness to experience a little discomfort and maybe even some pain. But it's the kind of pain or discomfort that produces experience and growth or maturity. It builds an alertness, and awareness for the many ways Satan can attack, and the different directions he can come from.

One great example of this discipline is when we taught our children to ride their first bike. We didn't go out a purchase a Harley Davidson in miniature, of course not! Most likely you did exactly what we did as parents, we started with a tricycle. Why? Because it gives the child the comfort and feeling of balance beneath them. They would ride for hours doing all sorts of little tricks, and feeling so proud of themselves because they could ride alongside their older brother or sister. They felt safe, secure, and a part of all the fun, but you watched to keep them safe, because they were still so young.

Although a tricycle doesn't appear to be dangerous for them because of the way it's made, it's the outside influences that can be dangerous. The older children, on larger bikes, who are riding faster, are darting in and out among their friends, even small pets that may run after them and frighten them perhaps even causing them to topple over.

So when using the tricycle example, explain to your children appearances can be deceiving. What seems safe, what may give you the impression you are in control, will only make you more susceptible to the enemy's attack. Teach them to never take anything for granted, and to always ask the LORD for His protection and guidance.

When the tricycle is mastered, children will most likely graduate to the two-wheeler with…training wheels. This bike gives your children a grown-up feeling, security and the opportunity to do a little more handling of the bike itself, on their own. They must learn to keep their bodies in the center of the bike for balance, or it would lean to the left or right, but it won't topple over too easily, because the training wheels will keep the bike with enough balance for them to correct themselves. You're there, watching and instructing them on how to be safe, watch for cars, and not to go too fast, etc.

Tell them that while this bike is a little bigger, and a little more grownup in it's appearance and ability, still, if they lean too far to the left away from God, or too far to the right, they will fall. Tell them that the little wheels are like the presence of the Holy Spirit; it will help keep them from falling, but He will also show them…when they're leaning too far in one direction or the other for safety or good balance.

Now as they ride alongside their friends they really feel grown up. Not becoming too distracted, so the bike wouldn't lean to the extreme left or right, they stay alert and stay prepared. Trying to remember all the things you told them about safety.

After they mastered the two-wheeler with training wheels, we remove the training wheels, and now they had to depend upon all that they learned from us. Here is where everything you've taught them must now be allowed to develop, and here is where they may experience a little pain. They have their helmets on, and their kneepads, and elbow pads, they look as if they're going to do battle with Shaq O'Neil rather than simply learn how to really ride their bike.

Now let's look at this from the spiritual aspect. As your children are learning to ride this bike, with no other source for balance but what they've learned from you, tell them that just as their earthly father runs alongside with his hand on the seat to help when needed, that their heavenly Father is also always by their side, and that He will never leave or forsake them, nor steer him wrong! No matter who else, or what else fails them, their heavenly Father never fails!

Explain to them that their LORD is standing right alongside them telling them exactly what to do. They must listen to Him but can't turn to watch for Him. We must simply trust that He's there and that His instruction is perfect. He will always caution them against leaning to the left, because they may fall off, and also against leaning to the right, again, because they may fall off. The Father will tell us to sit firmly in the seat, or in the palm of His hand, resting in His ability to keep us from falling, holding the handle bars tightly, which is the Word of God, looking not to the left or to the right, but unto "the hills, from which cometh our help," to go slowly and not move ahead of His will for their lives.

Then you let go of this spiritual bike, and let them ride on their own. As long as they concentrate on what they are doing, they are just fine. Every child feels the need to experiment. They want to try doing it all alone for themselves. This is good...but painful, and sometimes it will delay their progress. So when they fall, not if they fall, be there with tissue in hand, and apply the antibacterial medication, which is the Holy Spirit, and a nice clean bandage: the Word of God. Put them back on the bike immediately, and off they must go.

The only thing that matters is that you're there for them, the way our heavenly Father is always there for us. You wipe the tears, tell them what they did wrong, and put them right back on that bike. They cannot be allowed to give up; they must keep trying or they'll never learn to ride that bike or *stop* the attacks of Satan!

When they begin to speak to themselves the Word of God concerning anything they're dealing with, Satan will flee. Maybe not at first; be certain to tell them this. Let them know that they must do as you do, consistently resist the Devil and he will flee, he has to go! So if at first they feel doubtful, tell them to remain steadfast in their confession of faith, concerning God's Word and will for their lives, and Satan must go! "Submit yourselves therefore to God. Resist the devil, and he will flee from you." (James 4:7)

Teach your child that God's love for us and His willingness to fight in their behalf, to protect them and stand with them, is undisputable. If they learn at an early age to submit to God in word and spirit, there will be no room for Satan to gain control over anything that pertains to them. Teach them to stand for God, and do so on a daily basis, listening to His Word and being obedient to the same.

Satan doesn't need to be feared; he needs to be recognized for who he is. When they feel the tug from their friends to participate in something that's not only against the law of their parents, but against the law of God, they must learn to choose. And after they have decided what they will do, they are to rest in the decision they've made, knowing that there are always consequences for wrong decisions. Parents, they will not always do what's right; they will make mistakes, and this is where the compassion and long-suffering shown to us by the Father must also be shown to them. We must love them to righteousness, because Satan is counting on us pushing them to failure!

Comfort them with the knowledge that all of us, even as their parents, have sinned and fallen short of the glory of God. The LORD holds tomorrow in His hands. And as we seek Him today tomorrow will be a better day for them in Christ! Every day is another day to get it right!

Secondly, teach them to *drop* to their knees and seek God's direction and answers for their lives. Our children cannot be afraid to pray! They must be able to reach God for themselves. The ability to pray is not for adults only!

Adults always seem to want another adult to pray, whether we're at church or even in the home. When it's time to pray, the adult or the parent is always expected to lead the group in prayer. So our children get to the place in their lives, and spiritual walk, that they feel uncomfortable at the thought of praying before others, or even worse, that God only hears and answers the prayers of adults or their parents! What a trick and wicked device of the enemy! If our children are afraid to pray at home, they will never pray in the field, or away from home. Because of this, they are now wearing a bright red sign on their foreheads declaring to Satan, "Open Season on this child!" Even the thought of this is just too dangerous to even contemplate!

Friends, this is not an option. Teach your child to pray, not just for themselves, but for others, never to be ashamed of the fact that they are a Child of God, and that they not only pray, but they are expected to pray as a daily discipline.

Prayer is the only weapon other than the Word of God that will destroy the work of Satan without question. There is no man-made scale of measure that can calculate the value of this weapon, and the younger our children become proficient in its use, the sooner and more effective they will be in the work of their LORD, and His gospel.

There are many Saints that are under the absurd and utterly mistaken opinion that children cannot pray. They fear God too much to say that they should not pray, so they rationalize that they're too young, too inexperienced. My opinion is that if they can talk they can pray, and when they do pray, God hears them!

Prayer is simply asking of God, or inquiring, or desiring of God, something that you want only from Him. The battleground our children stand on, that they must fight on, is much too fierce to take anything for granted. It's not only frightening, it's also irresponsible to not instruct them in one of the most powerful gifts our LORD has paid for by the shedding of His blood, and that is access to His throne. When they pray, when they cry out to Him from their hearts, He will not only answer them, but will also deliver them.

God desires a people that will walk with Him in prayer, march with Him in praise, and give thanks and worship to Him out of their sincere love and willingness to please Him.

Look at it like this: if you as their parent were royalty, complete with throne room, crown, scepter, and all the other trappings of royalty, what would be your heart's desire for your child? To run to this servant or that servant asking of them for whatever they needed? Or to do without rather than disturb their father who is much to busy with the affairs of state? Wouldn't you rather that they simply come running into your throne room, with no regard for those around you, or for what you're doing right then, because they must ask Daddy to help them, to intervene in a matter for them, or better yet, to just say, "I love you, Daddy"? (Smile) And, just as quickly as they came in, they smiled, kissed the father on the cheek, and left! What love would burst in your heart for this gentle, unreserved love and admiration? Why can't we believe that our heavenly Father wants this from us, that He desires this of all His children? Why?

Prayer should not be thought of by our children as some mystical experience that only parents and adults can do right. That as their parents, you are the only one they need ever talk to about what concerns them. Never give them the impression that "You can do no wrong!" Or that as their mother or father "Your word is law!" Teach them early, that our LORD is our only complete source, and that He and only He is the answer to whatever we have need of. Impress upon them the need to trust and depend only on Him, and that you do exactly the same thing, because He is your father, too.

Always keep in mind that you'll not always be with them, and that even though your prayers are a covering for them, and that God is ever watchful and present to meet their need, that they have to know how to reach God for themselves, exactly the same way any child must be taught how to ask for something from their father. Teach them how to be polite, giving reverence for who He is. To respect the wishes of others and rejoice also with them, for there may be times when God will bless another with something that you've asked for and have not received. Only God knows what's best for His kids. Help them to also understand that sometimes His answer is, "Wait…not now," or Yes," and at times His answer will be "No," that every answer from God is the right answer for His child, and it is their best interest He has in His heart.

When Satan comes to tempt, challenge, or even cause them harm, and they *drop* to their knees; they must have faith. The most meaningful prayer will always come from the heart. Tell them prayer is the sincere desire of our heart, and comes from a child who places his complete trust in the LORD, that it's not the words they may utter; it's the heart that only He can see.

You may ask, how do I teach my child to pray? It's simple; tell them it's just conversation, that they're talking to their Father, and that their prayer does not need to sound like your prayer to be heard by Him. Also, that He's anxious to hear from them; in fact He's waiting right now, right this very minute to hear from them!

Take them to the Word of God where His disciples are asking our LORD to teach them to pray. Luke 11:1, "And it came to pass, that, as He was praying in a certain place, when He ceased, one of His disciples said unto Him, LORD, teach us to pray, as John also taught His disciples."

This will accomplish several things; it will show them that even adults must learn to pray, and that even the disciples, that walked with Jesus, needed help to know how to pray, and that the LORD didn't get angry, but gave them exactly what they asked for. He taught them how to pray. Using the "Disciples' Prayer," as I choose to call it. Others may frown on this, but it was given to His disciples as a gift from Him personally. I see nothing wrong with referring to it this way, but to each his own.

The Disciples' Prayer, is a marvelous teaching tool and is based on seven major topics, each one representing a basic human need: 1) "Our Father," the need for a parent, someone to instruct you, to guide you. A parent has unconditional love for their children; a parent never gives up, and is always available to them. Tell them the same applies to our heavenly Father. All our needs are met by Him. That He will always be there, and in Him there is no condemnation. That when Satan comes, like the bully on the block, that our big brother Jesus will kick his teeth in if they call on Him.

This prayer will teach your children 2) that our LORD and our Father, are holy, and to be in His presence is a holy thing. That all of this was made possible because of the blood of Jesus who died in our place, that we might have the right, once again, as we did when our first parents Adam and Eve lost it, to come before our God without fear and without hesitating. That because is this 3) we can call Him "Abba" Father, or Daddy!

Teach that even as children 4) they must realize that He knows what's best, and we must allow for His will, or His judgment to always be done exactly the way it is done in heaven. That what He wants; for all of us he wants the very best. That when we say 5) "Give us" this day, our daily bread." We're asking for Him to provide when there is no other source of provision, not our food only, but whatever we are in need of, i.e., healing, help in learning a particular lesson, the skill to do well enough to make the team, or even that a friend might come to know Him as LORD and Savior.

We're to 6) always ask for His forgiveness because as the Bible says in Romans 3:23-24: (23) "For all have sinned, and come short of the glory of God; (24) being justified free by His grace through the redemption that is in Christ Jesus." And that's why we pray, "Forgive us our sins, as we forgive those who have sinned against us." When a friend hurts them and mistreats them, or maybe doesn't include them in something, explain to them that it isn't their friend, but Satan using their friend to hurt them. They should always be ready to forgive, as our heavenly Father is always ready to forgive us.

They should always be ready to love and lead others to Jesus, by the life they live. All of their friends will see and notice that they are different, and someday they will ask why. That's when they may have an opportunity to invite them to church or to Christ, whatever door our LORD will open.

When the Disciple's Prayer, asks the Father 7) "And do not lead us…deliver us from the evil one," that means, "Father please protect us from Satan's vicious attacks and painful challenges, and help me to make you proud of me by not doing or saying what does not please You, or give You glory. Help me to love those that are not lovely. To forgive everyone…that may mistreat me."

Lastly, for "Thine is the kingdom, and the power and the glory," LORD…everything, including me, belongs to you; use me, LORD, for your glory. Do what pleases you, for my trust is in you!

There are no shortcuts in good teaching and training. I know your child will be a little uncertain initially, but as you continue to carefully urge them on as you're lead by the Holy Spirit, they will make you proud of them, and the LORD will be proud of you.

Quality time with our children is so precious, and every contribution we make towards their spiritual strength and trust in the LORD, will reap bountifully for the kingdom of God.

Now that we've talked about teaching our children to *stop*…what they are doing, *drop*…to their knees in prayer, it's time for them to learn at an early age, how to *roll* every care and concern over onto the LORD.

This, dear friends, is very difficult, even for us as adults. Perhaps with our help, it may be easier for our children.

There seems to be something innate within us that causes us want to keep a portion of our life in what we think of as our control. It's very difficult, and for some impossible, to "Let go…and let God!"

What it really boils down to is trust. It's just that simple. What you must develop within your child is trust. Trust in what you tell them is right. And trust that their heavenly Father is never wrong! That no matter how difficult things may be for them, or how hard it is to trust someone else, that they can always, without exception, trust God!

For our children to learn this most important discipline of a child of God, they will have to see it in you. They will follow your example. When you're challenged, or tested by the enemy, what is your immediate response? This is the key. Our one and only response is to immediately give it to the LORD in prayer, and walk away different!

We must walk away without fear, without stress or concern. When the question or matters arise again, whatever the reason, we must declare in faith and say something like this aloud: "Oh, that…I've given it to the LORD, and He will work it out!" Maybe, "I prayed about it yesterday; my trust is in the LORD." There are some of us who would dare to say, "Satan is a liar! My God will not fail!"

If your response is always *rolling* it over on the LORD, and that it's no longer your problem, but His, your child will listen, and learn!

The Bible tells us in Psalm 57:1-2, "Be merciful unto me, O God, be merciful unto me: for my soul trusted in thee: yea, in the shadow of thy wings will I make my refuge, until these calamities be over past. (2) I will cry unto God most high; unto God that performeth all things for me." Thank you, Father!

The younger your children are when they fully understand and accept that God has privileged us in Christ Jesus to live above the ordinary, and that the decision to do so belongs to us, the better. We must determine within ourselves what we will do and how we will live on a daily basis before them. Will we live ordinary, "so-so" lives, or will we choose to live like Christ, and that's anything but ordinary!

For them to fully trust in our LORD, and to ROLL every care upon Him, they must see Him for who He is and that He is anything but ordinary! Tell them about Jesus! Show them from the Word of God, who He is!

Introduce them to Him as their Savior. According to John 3:16, "For God so loved the world, that He gave His only begotten Son, that whosoever believeth in Him should not perish, but have everlasting life." God's love was for His children, and the world He created with a passionate love. That the world may refuse to receive Him, but His love for us continues forever and without reservation.

The Father had just one Son, and He gave that Son to us...to all mankind. He gave His only son, and allowed for Him to die that we would live forever with Him. Explain to them that Adam and Eve, our very first parents, failed to obey God, that Satan lied to them and they believed his lie, and Eve ate from the tree that God told them they could not eat from, lest they die.

Genesis 3:1-3 says, "Now the serpent was more subtil than any beast of the field which the LORD God had made. And he said unto the woman, Yea, hath God said, ye shall not eat of every tree of the garden? (2) And the woman said unto the serpent, we may eat of the fruit of the trees of the garden: (3) But of the fruit of the tree which is in the midst of the garden, God hath said, ye shall not eat of it neither shall ye touch it lest ye die."

So what Adam and Eve did was to sin against God by eating from the tree. The sin that caused them to listen to Satan was the sin of pride, pride that always wants more, and then more, is never enough! Pride was also the sin that God found in Lucifer, known to us as Satan, and that sin got him kicked out of heaven. For this disobedience, God had to banish Adam and Eve from the Garden of Eden. All children whose parent really loves them, will always have to be disciplined when they are disobedient. This must have been extremely painful to the Father, for He loved them so.

The Father, from the beginning, desired to have fellowship and communion with His creation. Adam and Eve were surrounded and blessed by the beauty of every tree, and flower, animal, bird and, every other creature created by God, but they wanted more! They could walk, talk, and laugh with the God of the entire Universe, but they wanted more! Their bodies, were beautiful, healthy and strong, and would live forever, but they wanted more! Adam was so brilliant that he named every animal and bird and beast of the field, but they wanted more!

Right here I must add that pride was not only the original sin, but it is the foundation of all sin. Search your heart honestly before God. Every sin you or I have ever committed was somehow, or someway self serving, self-gratifying, or just plain selfish. Really search your heart, and God will prove what He's given me in that *pride*, is at the core of all sin.

This separation brought mankind under the penalty of death. We were made to live forever, in perfect peace and harmony with all of God's creation, but because of sin we were sentenced to physical and spiritual death, or separation. God had to bring us back to Himself, to the way of holiness.

Despite God's effort to have eternal fellowship with His creation, mankind, our sin separated us. Imagine looking at the Grand Canyon, with its deep, steep, never-ending walls and valleys. That's just a tiny glimpse of the breach that separated us from the Father. His love for us would not allow Him to remain separated from those He loved, and He found a way, the only way possible: His son, Jesus Christ.

God's perfect love found the very best gift He could give, the ultimate gift of love…the life of His only Son. Jesus had to come and use himself to close the gaping canyon between mankind, and the Father. So God the Father…*rolled* all of our sin upon the sinless Christ. It was like Jesus taking the only body He had, and stretching it across the Grand Canyon, using Himself as the bridge for us to walk across to safety, the safety of the Father.

We know that Jesus died on the cross, with nails in His hands and feet, and a crown of ugly, sharp, long thorns placed into His head, that He was beaten, tortured and spat upon, cursed and mistreated by those He loved, and that the heavenly Father *rolled* all of our sin upon Him, that we might have redemption from our sin. He *rolled* all of our sickness and disease upon Him that we might be well. The Father *rolled* all of His anger for all the sins we will ever commit on His Son, that we might be able to repent and be forgiven. He *rolled* all of our weaknesses on Him, that we might be made strong. He *rolled* our eternal death upon Him that we might have eternal life! It was our disobedience, all of our ugliness *rolled* onto His only Son, who was perfect, and in Him, there was no sin, no sickness, no weakness, no poverty, no lack. He bore it all. Why?

Because, "God so loved the world" that through the death of His son, God the Father has chosen to give us eternal life and so much more than that! We are not just redeemed, not just restored to the Father; we are also joint heirs to everything that Jesus has in heaven. We share it with Him in all of His glory! All of this because the Father said, "I know who I can trust, someone who will never fail me, someone who will not listen to Satan or anyone else but me: my Son, Jesus Christ!" I will just *roll* the weight and the sin of all mankind upon my Son. He will never fail me!

Every one of God's children, including your child, can make a decision to listen to what we're told in the Word of God regarding the love of our Father and our LORD and His Holy Spirit, or we can like our first parents Adam and Eve, and follow the will and words of Satan, who has always lied to God's children.

If the Father loved us so much that He *rolled* all of our sin, sickness, and disease, all of our weaknesses, pain, sorrow, and frustrations on His only son, what is left for us to bear, except those things we choose to *pick up* again.

Your children should understand that they never have to face anything that has not already been rolled over onto our LORD. When Satan comes with a lie, with sickness, with a challenge, with anything that causes them discomfort or pain, they are to *roll* it back onto Jesus! That's exactly where it belongs. Because of Calvary, we are to travel very lightly; in fact, our backpack or our suitcase, should be empty!

Surely, if God the Father could trust His son with our eternal souls, and His Word and will for our lives, surely we can trust Him!

I believe that Satan has many devices and that they are worse today than ever before. I also know, and have an absolute confidence in the fact that, "Ye are of God, little children, and have overcome them: because greater is He that is in you, than he that is in the world." (1 John 4:4)

Our LORD has already paid for and carried everything, and anything that will ever concern us. Furthermore, in Isaiah 54:17, "No weapon that is formed against thee shall prosper; and every tongue that shall rise against thee in judgment thou shalt condemn. This is the heritage of the servants of the LORD, and their righteousness is of me saith the LORD." Teach your children today to *roll* it over!

Look at that verse again. Satan cannot attack us with anything that will work! Whatever he attempts to use, whether it be of man, or from himself, it's *broken* because of Jesus. It's *broken*, and he can't fix it! Jesus *Broke* all of his little toys at Calvary! Tell them that whatever Satan brings, *roll* it over! *Roll* it over! Hallelujah! *Roll* it over!

Thank you, Father, for everything that you've given to us, that we might have life, and life, more abundantly! Thank you, Jesus, that you came and died to fulfill what was necessary to bring us back to the Father. And thank you, sweet Holy Spirit, for Your comfort, help, and guidance and keeping power until He comes again!

God bless you, my friends!

Chapter VIII

Fragile...Handle With Care!

I imagine that the most difficult, or the heaviest piece of the mantle worn by our pastors, other than their congregations, is the weight they bear because of their families, specifically their children.

Pastors are continuously under the microscope of: "We can, but you and your family, shall *not*!" I don't know where this ever came from, that our pastors are somehow gifted beyond all other of God's children, to live without the slightest hint of spot or wrinkle!

Isn't it enough that God weighs and judges everything that they say or do that might affect His sheep for all eternity! Is it not enough that the Word declares in Jeremiah 23:1-2, "Woe be unto the shepherds who destroy and scatter the sheep of my pasture! Saith the LORD. (2) Therefore, thus saith the LORD God of Israel against the shepherds who feed my people, ye have scattered my flock, and driven them away, and have not visited them; behold, I will visit upon you the evil of your doings, saith the LORD."

If God held Israel's leaders and the judges over His people to such strict mandates because of His children, I don't think He's changed much today. In fact I'm almost certain that "Jesus Christ is the same, yesterday and today and forever," as it says in Hebrews 13:8!

We're always declaring our love and devotion to our pastors and their wives. We'll celebrate their anniversaries and birthdays, and always remember them on holidays. We're so proud and confident when we introduce them to our families and friends, always inviting others to share in the joy and blessings that God has given us, through those He has placed over us as His pastors. This is all just great, just wonderful, but what about the children!

Why are we so unyielding when it comes to their children? I'm not saying it occurs in every congregation, but I've seen it enough, and pretty close to home, too close for comfort.

Our LORD is impartial and shows the same love, grace, blessing and benefits to all of His children. He is no respecter of persons. He neither favors one more than the other, nor expects from some, more than He does of others. We must follow His example and never allow our own perception of what things are or should be to influence our actions or behaviors, especially when it comes to our pastor's children. If anything the pastor's children may need more from us in the way of love, patience and gentle instruction than the other children. The other children are not always under so much pressure to be on their best behavior at all times, or even expected to perform better than everyone else's children. We watch how they're dressed. Is it more appropriate, and are their manners always the best? Even when it comes to their knowledge of God's Word, they may not be Bible scholars, or maybe they will be. A child is still a child, and a parent, a parent; all of our children grow and are nurtured under the exact same slide rule of the Holy Spirit, and His influence is the only common denominator we should all hold to.

The pastor's family lives in the proverbial fish bowl. We know they are only children, just like our children or teens. However, we seem to have this intolerance when it comes to the pastor's children, expecting from them what no other child is expected to do, just because they belong to our pastors.

When we correct them it's so stern. "You know better than that; you're the pastor's son [or daughter]!" or "You should be ashamed of yourself; remember, you're the pastor's daughter [or son]!" Can you imagine being told as a child, "That you're not like other children…you're the pastor's son [or daughter!]" Even being told that, "You shouldn't embarrass or shame your parents, remember you're the pastor's daughter [or son]!"

I've seen them snatched without mercy by ushers, by elders, and other members of the congregation, even the so-called, "mothers of the church!" They're pulled on and yanked about, as if they're rag dolls, with no concern of embarrassing them before their peers or friends that are standing near.

When they get older, they either talk too much, or not enough. The skirt is too short, or his hair too long. They either walk around with their noses in the air, or they're just too stuck-up for their own good. We either push them forward all the time to do everything, or deny them the right to say or do anything!

It's an absolute sin the way some churches treat the pastor's children, and God does not hold them guiltless for this abuse, and it is abuse!

If our pastors are gifts to us from God, if they are truly sent and called by God to proclaim the gospel and God's saving grace through Jesus Christ, then we should guard and care for their children as special treasures entrusted to our care. They should be free to minister to our families in great time of sorrow, testing, and challenges.

The only way for the gospel to reach the multitude and draw souls to Christ is for our pastors to be free to preach at home or away, without the slightest care or concern that their families will be care for and cared about, not because we want the praise and glory or admiration of man, but because the Word tells us. Luke 18:16 says, "But Jesus called them unto Him and said, permit the little children to come unto me, and forbid them not; for of such is the kingdom of God."

The only example of Christ seen by our children, and all children for that matter, is through us. It's not just what we say that makes a lasting impression upon their hearts, it's also what we do. With that thought in mind, we are never to mistreat or misjudge any child, to include the pastor's children. They will never forget how they were treated, whether it was in love or is condemnation, whether they were abused or sincerely mentored in the things of Christ. They will never forget. And sometimes it's the treatment from the congregation that does more to draw them to Christ or push them away.

You may ask why it is our responsibility to nurture and instruct the pastor's children more than their responsibility. It's not, only we cannot negate the influence we do have with them. What children do you know that always listens to their parents first, even if they are the pastors? Children will always love and respond to others faster than to their own parents. Amen, Amen.

If our hands, our words or our instructions are harsh and without the balance of God's love, or His charity, they will know it, and they'll see it, and they'll refuse the Christ you *claim* to love and serve, the very Christ who you *claim* is always so gentle and understanding.

You may still be wondering why our pastor's children are also our responsibility, well, because most of the time our pastors are dealing with *us*! They're either burying our loved ones, visiting our sick ones, or marrying our silly ones (smile—just teasing). Seriously though, if they are to be available for us and the needs of our families, twenty-four-seven, and we all expect this, why can't we help them by seeing after, loving, and encouraging their children to righteousness?

Can't we lift some of their burden by allowing them to see in us a sincere love, not only for Christ, but also for them and their children? Why can't we free them up to minister to every need in our communities, so that others may come to know Christ?

How often have we just picked the kids up and allowed them to play with our children, maybe even spend the night, so that our pastor and his wife might have rest, and have a little quiet time alone, or just to quiet the house down for them to study and prepare the messages for us? How often have we suggested to the pastor's wife that we be allowed to babysit if necessary, so that she can rest and be available to minister to the congregation? Most pastors would think of this as an imposition, but we should at least attempt to lessen their stress.

I've been blessed to be very close to my pastors and their wives, and have benefitted greatly from their ministries. My first pastor went home to be with our LORD after years of service; my second retired, and the third we are blessed to have with us. We love and enjoy them so much, and we do our very best to not add to their burden of ministering, by being thoughtless and unkind to their children, young or old.

Their children are always in the home of my daughter, and my granddaughter is always in their home. Because of this closeness, we see and hear so much of the pain that seems to touch their lives, and the last thing they need to concern themselves with is whether or not their children are being treated unkindly by their members!

It's difficult to raise our children alone, especially without the input and concern of others, but it's nearly impossible for pastors who must be everywhere at the same time, attempting to do everything for us, except leaping tall buildings at a single bound! They spend so much of their time smoothing our feathers, wiping our tears, healing our wounds and fixing our messes, they don't have time the quality time they need for their own children! That's the reason they need their members to really understand their children, and to understand that they miss the attention of their parents. Satan is doing everything he can possibly do to direct their attention away from Christ and towards the things of this world!

Satan barters so highly for the children of our pastor the reason being that some part of that mantle our pastors wear belongs to them. They will someday either be pastors themselves, missionaries, elders, husbands or wives of the same. Satan knows that the call of God is on the life of all our children, especially…the pastor's children! Not to mention the influence they will have on the lives of their peers…Satan needs to gain control, and to derail the plans of God for their lives, as soon as possible.

As members of the church, we must stand in the gap, and stand guard over our pastor's children, being ever watchful and diligent in our task!

Ever reminded that the Bible tells us in 1 Peter 5: 8:9, "Be sober, be vigilant, because your adversary, the devil like a roaring lion walketh about, seeking whom he may devour; (9) Whom resist steadfast in the faith, knowing that the same afflictions are accomplished in your brethren that are in the world."

We won't know until we get to glory the effect that preachers children have had on the world, for the positive, and for the negative. How many have hindered others from coming to Christ, because of the pain and hypocrisy they themselves saw and received from the church. One of Satan's biggest weapons against the church are those who either once knew the LORD, or whose parents were ministers of the gospel!

Satan attacks every Christian because we're bought with such a high price, but he also attacks the head or the leaders, of everything that belongs to God, and that God loves. Remember the havoc Satan caused between God's people Israel, King David, and his son...Absalom! David was not a pastor but he was king, and all the people depended upon him for protection, guidance, for their prosperity, and safety in times of trouble and war, also that his powerful influence would insulate them from any threat or outside influence. This sounds exactly like a pastor's responsibility to his congregation.

Absalom was the third son of King David, by his wife Maacah. The story of Absalom is fascinating. And what he lacked in integrity and character is certainly made up for in charm. The story of Absalom is as intriguing as any modern day Soap Opera, and just about as heart wrenching. He was the apple of his father's eye, and quite literally, well, eventually anyway...was all wrapped up in himself. We'll talk about that a little later. What I want to deal with now is the character and the conduct of this young man that brought such pain and heartache to Israel, and to his father King David.

Absalom was of royal descent on both sides, because his mother, Maacha, was a king's daughter. Undoubtedly he was heir to the throne, and he was David's favorite, the pride and joy of his father.

David's children shared his weaknesses, but very few demonstrated his redeeming character, that quality that allowed him to always be opened and responsive to the correction and instruction of God.

We know of how David refused to lay one finger on Saul, as long as he held the office of God's anointed, and king over God's people Israel. David was hunted and tracked like a wild animal, but his respect for the office, and the man who stood in that office, never allowed him to dishonor his God by seeking revenge upon the people's choice of king. Saul was not God's choice, but He allowed for the people's choice. David on the other hand, was God's chosen one, His anointed one, also God's choice for replacing Saul.

This will help to show the two most distinctive traits about David, especially when comparing him to his son Absalom. 1) He was a man of great integrity and character; 2) his love and fear of God was always uppermost in his thoughts and efforts. David never allowed sin, or his desires to keep him separated from the God he loved and served. The operative word here is keep him separated from his God. Yes, David sinned greatly, but there is no better portrait of the repentant heart, than what we find in Psalms 51: 1-15.

David realized that only a heart willing to repent before God would renew his spirit for service and wholeness before God and his people Israel. David wanted to remain God's anointed, God's choice; he couldn't bear the thought of separation from God, nor from the service of his people, as their king.

Absalom, on the other hand, was self-seeking, vindictive and dishonorable, but…gorgeous! In 2 Samuel 14: 25, "But in all Israel there was none to be so much praised as Absalom for his beauty: from the sole of his foot even to the crown of his head there was not blemish in him."

The people absolutely loved him. They didn't honor their king, by instructing his beloved son according to wisdom, they allowed his good looks to destroy not only the life of Absalom, but to break the heart of David.

I know that Absalom was an adult, and obviously was lacking in the training and proper instruction necessary for leadership. Where was David's help when Absalom was younger, and needed the love, and the firm hand, of someone like Nathan, to mentor him, before it was too late. The people were obviously only in awe of his beauty, so much so, they refused to take part in properly nurturing and directing this young man, whose father, their king, would spend days and weeks fighting and attending to the needs of the people.

To make a long story short, Satan took the love Absalom had for his beautiful sister Tamar, and the injustice that befell her by her half brother Amnon, and used it to destroy an already fragile home environment. Satan split the family and the nation in one felt swoop, simply because no one saw him coming. There was no one really standing in the gap for David, his throne, or his family. Amnon the half brother of Absalom fell in love.

When Amnon fell in love with his own sister, and forced himself on her, he brought shame and extreme anger upon the family. And Absalom was determined seek revenge. What's so amazing about Amnon is that he was as repulsed by her afterwards, as he was totally obsessed by her in the beginning. This entire scenario smelled of brimstone! It was a tool he used to spread hatred, murder, and confusion among the family and people of God, and his anointed...David, and it worked, just like a charm! Satan destroyed and alienated the entire family and nation with this one sick act by Amnon, and the vengeful act of Absalom against him, to avenge his sister Tamar.

Absalom's vengeance for Tamar's outrage, was justified, but handled poorly by all parties involved. The breech created by this act was never healed, and was only worsened by feelings no one bothered or sincerely attempted to mend. David had on his I'm-the-king! How-dare-you? face! Then there was Absalom with his..."I had a right to do what you wouldn't do...face!" Let's not forget, there was Tamar who was Amnon's victim, Absalom's victim, and her father's victim! Tamar was honestly the only real victim, caught in the middle of such chaos, and probably felt responsible for it all!

When Absalom fled to Geshur for safety, David was caught between two straights. On the one hand, we have a son who murdered a brother for the violation of his sister. And on the other hand, the act against Tamar was too extreme to justify. David wouldn't really forgive Absalom, and wouldn't really go after him...he was just a weeping mess!

When Absalom does eventually return, and is sort of forgiven by his father, he shows his gratitude by stealing the love of the people of Israel. His charm and eloquence and persuasiveness gave the people such hope in this, their new champion. How could this traitor be trusted by anyone? Why would the people dare to believe or even attempt to follow this young man so eager to over-throw their king...his own father!

Well, let's see what we have; 1) A rape; 2) A murder 3) An indecisive father, who happens to be king, 4) A murderer and traitor who happens to be the king's son! Where were the people? Where was the congregation? Why was Satan given such a free hand in the lives and hearts of all Israel? Was there no one willing to stand in the gap, and seek God...where was everybody?

How with all of this in Absalom's sight, did he not succeed? He had a throne ready made for him, and a nation bowing at his feet to give him exactly everything he wanted, and yet his life ended in a tragedy. Brilliant in its beginning, but buried like an animal in the woods. How do you lose what yours at birth? How is it that so many of our young people get off track, and lose everything that God has planned for them...how?

How is it that our Absalom's fail to get turned around and placed on the straight path of good success and great depths in the LORD? How can people sit idly by and watch our promising, talented, beautiful children, become nothing, simply because they don't belong to us, or better yet tell themselves…"I'm certain the pastor sees, or knows these things are happening." No, sometimes our pastors are like David, so busy taking care of our needs and the needs of so many others, they just don't see…until it's too late.

Try to realize how very weary and sometimes just plain tired they must get, both physically, and emotionally, not to mention being spiritually drained, because of the mantle they wear for all of us. Where are all the Aarons and Hurs of the church?

In Exodus 17:10-13, " Joshua did as Moses had said to him, and fought with Amalek: and Moses, Aaron, and Hur went up to the top of the hill. (11) And it came to pass, when Moses held up his hand, that Israel prevailed, and when he let down his hand, Amalek prevailed (12) but Moses' hands were heavy; and they took a stone, and put it under him, and he sat thereon; and Aaron and Hur held up his hands, the one on the one side, and the other on the other side, and his hands were steady until the going down of the sun. (13) And Joshua vanquished Amalek and his people with the edge of the sword."

Now do you really think that the LORD needed Moses, Aaron, Hur, or even Joshua, to defeat the Amalek? Of course not. What he needed was for them to realize that teamwork, working together, is always better than standing or attempting to do it alone. What God always needs and desires of His children, is for us to work together, to be of one mind, and of one spirit for the gospel's sake.

You have those like Joshua who do physical battle, and those like Aaron who are the priests that stand in the gap interceding for those who do battle. You have the pastor or those like Moses, who give the orders as God gives the purpose and vision. And then you have the Hurs, those who are the lay persons that fill gaps, just doing what needs to be done, whenever it is needed, the strongest and most necessary part of any congregation: the supporters, the backbone, the very fiber of every congregation!

Without the Hurs, without the Aarons and Joshuas, without those that are willing to carry out the vision that God has given the pastor the church, the congregation, the body of Christ will die.

You are the very people I'm speaking to, those who can look around and see what needs to be done, and just do it. You can see the pastor's children getting a little out of hand, or needing a little one-on-one attention and love. You notice that they are also getting a little weary of dealing with everything that's expected of them, and that maybe they need someone (other than their parents) to talk to.

Like in all families, there's always that one, maybe the middle child, or the oldest, (seldom the baby…smile) that get sort of lost in the shuffle. You see them and know that what they need is some time alone with someone who really loves them, who really cares about them, and who will give to them their undivided attention.

Sometimes the pressure is too great on the pastor's kids to be the most popular, the tallest, the best athlete or the most spiritual of all of children. How can we possibly expect them to be healthy and spiritually sound, if no one ever allows them to just be kids, or teens, or even young adults? Why is it that we expect that everything they say or do, should make them little evangelists in our sight?

One trait about Absalom, David's son, was his Godlessness. Those around Absalom recognized God, and had a religious faith in God that gave them some restraint and principle to their conduct. But the handsome, selfish, scheming Absalom had none of these qualities. His own will was his only law. He was destitute of principle and destitute of faith. His lack of love, tenderness, and pity, were his only traits. He had no reverence for God.

He was able to divide the people of Israel, much like Lucifer drew a third of the angels in heaven to his way of thinking, by his beauty, charm and sheer presence. That's why prayer, and fasting is sometimes the only thing that will keep a congregation and a people in tact. If you notice that one of the pastor's children, and there is usually at least one, is particularly gifted and talented beyond even their parents' comprehension and ability to deal with, it's really time to pray! That child will be a huge target of the enemy, just too valuable to leave alone. Some may even confuse them, by showering them with constant praise and compliments they are not equipped to handle.

As in the case of Absalom, our pride and joy, like beauty and the hair of Absalom, can become the cause of our greatest shame. Our choicest endowments and most cherished gifts can become our greatest temptations. Gifts, need to be washed and rewashed daily in the fountain of God's truth, and guarded and sanctified by prayer if they are to be fit for the highest service in Christ.

Who better to stand in the spiritual gap, to stand in prayer watching after the souls of our pastor's children, than the congregation they have chosen to serve and pour their lives out for? We're their extended family, and they'll be as fit for service and spiritual warfare as our prayers and intercession allows them to be.

Whatever they carry in the way of concern and unnecessary burdens, will always follow them to the pulpit. That's why we are our brother's keeper! I know it's difficult to ever fully understand what a difference "I" can make; after all, "I'm just one person!" But, when we stand for Christ, and for the gospel, we're never standing alone!

Remember when Elijah ran from Jezebel after he challenged Ahab, and the gods of Baal? After his magnificent victory before all the priest of Baal and the people of Israel, he runs, fearing Jezebel! Anyway, the LORD has to encourage him and protect him as he flees for safety. "And he said, I have been very jealous for the LORD God of hosts, because the children of Israel have forsaken thy covenant, thrown down thine altars, and slain thy prophets with the sword; and I, even I only, am left, and they seek my life, to take it away." (1 Kings 19: 14) Moving down to verses 17 and 18 of the same chapter, "And it shall come to pass, that him that escapeth the sword of Hazael, shall Jehu slay; and him that escapeth from the sword of Jehu, shall Elisha slay. (18) Yet I have left me seven thousand in Israel, all the knees which have not bowed unto Baal, and every mouth which hath not kissed him."

God had prepared those who would fight with Elijah, and even seven thousand that had not bowed to Baal. When Satan comes in and attempts to attack God's children, or the LORD has placed a special burden on your heart for the pastor and his family, and for his children, believe me, you are not alone! He has also prepared the hearts of others to do just as He's told you to do. You may find each other, or you may not; it's all up to Him. You just be faithful and stand in the gap, and it will be more than enough! Our LORD is faithful to show you the fruit of your effort and your labor being confident that His Word declares in Matthew 6:3-4, "But when thou doest alms, let not thy left hand know what they right hand doeth, (4) that thine alms may be in secret; and thy Father who seeth in secret, shall reward thee openly."

Most parents are grateful for whatever we can do to lessen the stress that's involved in parenting, so why wouldn't our pastors feel exactly the same way? After all, they are people too. (Smile)

Some may feel as if they are stretched enough with their own homes and families, and I really understand this point of view, only I've never given anything to our LORD, and had less in my economy or effort for having done so.

In man's economy, the law of supply and demand regulates the price paid for the goods and services we use on a daily basis. In times of plenty, the prices go down; in times of little or shortage, the prices rise. Man's economy fluctuates with the times and the seasons.

However, in God's economy, there are no shortages. God's supply always equals our need. He does not want His people in lack, but rather, to increase more and more. If you have a burden for your pastors and their children, and you feel you don't have the resources or energy to really undertake anything extra, in the way of that type of responsibility, then please feel free not to. Only, if you know they need help, you know they're tired and stretched, and you know that every time you see them, the LORD touches your heart to help out, and you don't, then that is sin. "Therefore, to him that knoweth to do good, and doeth it not, to Him it is sin." (James 4:17)

This is indeed a good thing. Do you really think that if you give something to God, you will have less? Less for yourself in the way of energy, time, patience, even monies after having taken them out to eat with you and yours, every now and then? No way! You will never give to God and lose on your end. If you spend time and fasting in prayer for them and their children, our LORD has your back!

If the pastor's anniversary is coming up, and groups of members want to divide the children among them so that they can have some time alone for a week or so, believe me, your meal barrel will not go empty. We can never out-give God. No matter what we give to Him, He will always multiply it back to us in an amount greater than we gave!

Our ability to receive the harvest of our giving is not automatic. Expecting to receive, not from the person to whom we give, but from God our total source, is an act of our faith. Whenever we invest in our church, or in the family of our pastor changes take place in our life, and in their lives. As other members begin to see the blessings of God in your life, simply because you're willing to give of yourself to lessen the weight of someone else, they will be encouraged to do the same thing.

What is it that you need from God in your life, or in the life of your family? As you begin to pray, intercede and stand in the gap for your pastor and his children. Your family will reap the blessings and benefit of this commitment. You'll find that your children will need less discipline than before. Your home will become more peaceful, and the plans of Satan halted immediately.

The time spent with your spouse will also increase in quality and quantity. It works and works absolutely.

Notice that when our LORD said to give, He also said, "Give and it will be given to you." Giving and receiving belong together! It's only when we give, when we share, are we in position to expect to reach out and receive a harvest. And Jesus said the harvest from our giving, will be "good measure, pressed down, shaken together, and running over."

We don't give only to receive, but isn't it really a wonderful thought that what we do for God does not go unnoticed? When we're giving, our hearts should not be focused on what we receive, but rather on what we can do for our LORD to lessen the weight and strain on those He placed over us, those who guard over our eternal souls and the souls of those we love.

Whenever you feel as if you have absolutely nothing to give God, you will always have a seed to plant for Him to multiply when you invest in a faith-believing, love-motivated prayer in another person's life!

When something is out of alignment in our families, we always want someone to please pray, and no matter what time of day or night you call the pastor's home, they will answer and be there for you and your family. If you've called in the middle of their mealtime, and it's urgent, they will leave the table, and go to wherever they are needed just because you called. Do you remember the time(s) that they visited you or someone you loved to pray with them and encourage them while in the hospital, and kept calling to be certain of your progress or theirs? That's love and devotion, and it comes without measure. You cannot put a price on that kind of devotion to you and your family.

Some may say, well, he's the pastor and that's his job; that's what we pay him for. My reply to that is, *repent*, for the coming of the LORD is at hand! (Smile)

Did our LORD have to come and die for our sins? Did He have to take upon Himself the weight and sin of the entire world, especially a world that wanted nothing to do with Him? Did He have to become sickness that we would be well, or become poor that we might be rich? Did He have to leave everything that He loved, including His own Father, all the glory and beauty of heaven, to come down in weak flesh, be spat upon, cursed, beaten, shamed and nailed to a cross of shame? Of course not! Then why did He? "For God so loved the world that He gave…" (John 3:16)

Our LORD is revealed to us as the Good Shepherd who gave His life for His sheep. When He said, "I am the good shepherd," Jesus linked His own divine nature with one of the most ordinary occupations in Israel. Now, our

New Testament pastors are called shepherds, accountable for their flocks to Jesus, the Chief Shepherd.

A trusted shepherd also provides loving protection for his flock. He stands guard in the midst of danger and threats to their safety. Our LORD used sheep, I believe, because they so epitomize man's rather curious but helpless ability to attend to their own needs. A sheep will clear the area right in front of him, eat it bare, and if the shepherd doesn't take his rod to steer him to another patch of grass, would literally stand there and die (smile).

What I'm really trying to say is that when we are blessed with a pastor that has a true shepherd's heart for his congregation, a pastor who is willing to give all that he has to complete the task God has placed before him, not because he's paid to, but because he fears and reverences God enough to deal with every challenge that comes his way, whether in the church or in the field, if we are blessed with such pastors, our responsibility is to protect them and their families with our prayers and our help. To guard after their welfare and the welfare of their children, as they guard after ours.

If God has blessed you with pastors that are diligent in their quest to be the very best they can be for you, if they are willing to "Study to show themselves approved unto God, a workman that needeth not to be ashamed, rightly dividing the word of truth." (2 Timothy 2:15), then we are to honor them, according to Romans 13:7. "Render, therefore, to all their dues: tribute to whom tribute is due; custom to whom custom; fear to whom fear; and honor to whom honor."

I'll share with you my own personal experience regarding this particular issue. Our first pastors had two small children. The oldest was their son who was almost exactly the age of our son. In fact, the only thing they didn't share was the actual birth dates. Anyway, when they were old enough to start junior high, they attended the same school together. Now the school was on our pastor's end of town, but still several miles from them.

My husband and I both worked outside the home, so when we took Jonathan to school we decided to pass by and see if Paul needed or wanted us to take him, and naturally to be with his best friend was sheer joy, so that's how it started. Every morning we'd come by and pick up Paul, and our pastors were able to have breakfast in a quiet house, share coffee, or just sleep in! This little simple thought was such a gift to them and cost us nothing but the willingness to do it!

After several services through the week, late night phone calls and counseling sessions at the church, a weekend jam-packed with weddings, funerals, church anniversaries, council meetings, women and men's ministries, etc., their mornings became such a treasure to their hearts, they actually looked forward to it like a mini vacation! How very simple to please them, and what a joy it was to the heart of my husband and me, and I know our LORD was also pleased.

Another example is a little far upstream from the spiritual aspect, still quite effective in its analogy. My husband told me of several instances known to him because he grew up the only son of his parents, with two extremely popular and attractive sisters. The story was rather sad but true.

The school would plan certain affairs and dances that allowed the students who attended to bring a date. They would dress up, and have an evening of games, dancing, and food. He would sometimes wonder why a certain girl or certain beautiful girls were not there when everyone else was. His sisters told him that because the girls were so pretty, everyone else thought that someone else had already invited them, so many of the young men never bothered to ask. I mean, why ask such a silly question, i.e., do you have a date to the dance, and would you like to go with me?

Why ask this of someone you were certain already had a date weeks ago, right? Well, it turned out, the young ladies ended up staying home because no one had asked them. Everyone assumed they'd been asked. My husband said this happen to several girl friends of his sisters before the word got around, spread by him to his friends. So then they began to ask everybody, even the most beautiful girls, because you never knew; you might arrive at the dance with the future Miss America on your arm!

That's probably what happens in our churches. Everyone thinks that someone else has thought to ask, or to do, or to help the pastor and his family, and they end up with no one helping at all. You see, when programs or special events go on at the church, everybody helps, everybody is involved, and nothing is left undone, except we forget our pastors and that their children may need some special help and attention, especially during these crazy, whirlwind occasions. And yet, they may never feel comfortable in asking for help even though they might be sorely in need of it.

If we give of ourselves, not just of our means, as we do with our tithes and offerings, but of ourselves, then we ourselves will reap the benefit of these seeds. God will bless what we've planted into the lives and hearts of our pastors by being attentive, aware, and also accountable for their children. This isn't something that must be done by us and us alone; it should be a shared responsibility belonging to the entire congregation.

What better way to show our LORD and our pastors that we are not only grateful for the blessings we have in them and for the gift we have in them, but that we're also aware of our need to take part in preserving and protecting this precious gift, and are willing to do so with great joy and love? Also, what better way to show that we desire God's continual presence in our church, realizing that nothing can touch our lives without His presence and His knowledge, and what else touches His heart, more than our love one for the other?

Chapter IX

Now...Who Made a Mess?

Probably one of the most difficult things for us as parents to do is admit that we were wrong about something, or having to say, I'm sorry. It's not that we think of ourselves as perfect, it's simply that one of the most common human frailties is admitting that we're wrong about anything!

Years ago there was a movie out entitled *Love Story*, and the underlying theme, stated by the star, was simply, "Love means never having to say I'm sorry!" It's sounds so perfect, so right but I really disagree. When you really love someone, it should be easy, almost a relief to say, "I'm sorry," or "I was wrong!"

The time we have together cannot be spent hiding the fact that as parents, we cannot only be wrong, but we may not be right either! (Smile)

It's been said that the best teaching on being a good parent, is simply applying what it is to be a good Christian. To be the kind of parents we need to be for our children, one of the main qualities you want to teach them is acceptance. They must be able to accept and like who they are, who others are, and who their parents are. Out of this acceptance will come love, a love wrapped in all the frailties of human flesh, but empowered by the strength and purpose of the Holy Spirit, which is love!

Their measure of success will be based primarily on how they are perceived by others, and how others perceive them. If our children are accepting of the weaknesses and disappointments they see or find in themselves and in others, they will have a healthy, well-rounded emotional make-up, and outlook on life. If they stumble and fall or become shocked at what others do, their lives may remain in a state of unbalance and perhaps be a little shaky. Their moods may swing up and down, or to and fro, all because of something someone else may have said or done, perhaps something they didn't see coming from a friend they trusted and depended upon.

Well, let's get one thing straight, our homes are the boot-camp of life, and as the master sergeants of our troops, we must never allow ourselves to become the dispatcher of mixed messages. For an example: "Do as I say do, not as I do!" We should never allow ourselves the "escape route" of, "Because I'm your mother…that's why!" Or to give that look that tells the world, "I'm never wrong!"

Whenever a sergeant's character is depicted in the movies, he stands before his brand new troops, Spic 'N Span, shining like a brand new penny, his hat sitting just right on his head at that just-so angle, shoes that are so shiny you can see your face, and hair cut so neatly that not one strand of hair is out of place. He has medals that run from his time of service spent in the Garden of Eden, to the very first Star Wars battles! And he's in your face! He shouts to these young impressionable men and women that they no longer have a mother, that he's their mother, that from now on what they wear, what they eat, when they sleep, and for how long they sleep, rests with him, that your sons (or daughters) no longer has to worry themselves with the trivia of life, they need only to concern themselves with inhaling and exhaling, unless they accidentally forget one day, and then he'll even breathe for them if necessary! Get the picture? It's the wrong picture! (Smile)

We are parents who not only make mistakes, we make them often, and the ones that suffer the most are our children, especially our first children.

My daughter Toi is my best example. She was such a precious little thing. I couldn't believe that her father and I created such a beauty, despite what we had going for us. She was just perfect! I was so young and so eager and wanted to do everything just right, so I started with breast-feeding; well at least I thought it was breast-feeding! Toi was crying and crying for several days. Finally my mother said, honey…she's hungry! I was insulted. How could she be hungry, when my breasts were larger than they'd ever been? My mother insisted she was hungry and suggested that I call the doctor's office, so I did.

When I talked with the doctor I found out that because I was so young he assumed I wouldn't want to nurse my baby, so he gave me a shot to dry up my milk. My daughter was starving, and me with such huge breasts, too! (Smile) I mean, I couldn't believe it! Yet, as much as I loved her and wanted the very best for her, I was starving her. It's funny now, when you really think about it. There I was thinking I was nursing her and providing the very best for her, when in actuality, I was starving her, making her vulnerable to illness, and other problems due to vitamin deprivation.

All of my best intentions, all of my baby-book dreams for her were derailed for a short time, because *I was wrong!* Not intentionally…yet wrong all the same, and the cost to her was painful. What matters is that she was too young to suffer any lasting effects from my mistake, and my good intentions. My mother, God bless her, found it necessary to tell her this when she was not only old enough to understand, but to hold it against me personally, forever! (Smile)

This example is simple when you look at it, but it tells us how easily Satan can use us to bring harm and possibly severe damage to our children, by our not realizing that we are fallible and more than capable of making mistakes. The sooner we realize this and are willing to accept it, and take responsibility for it, the sooner our children will benefit from this knowledge and will desire to be more like us, especially when they see that even their parents don't always get it right the first time.

In the first part of Genesis, God is dealing with all of mankind as a whole, from creation to Abraham. What I want to talk about is Abraham and Sarah, about how their mistake in judgment and in their trust as to who God was, and what He was capable of doing for them, is still impacting our lives today.

The very heart of Genesis is the covenant that God makes with Abraham, as found in Genesis 15:3-6, "And Abram said, behold, to me thou hast given no seed: and lo, one born in my house is mine heir. (4) And, behold, the word of the LORD came unto him saying, this shall not be thine heir; but he that shall come forth out of thine own lions shall be thine heir. (5) And He brought him forth abroad, and said, look now toward heaven, and count the stars, if thou be able to number them: and He said unto him, so shall thy seed be. (6) And he believed in the LORD; and He counted it to him for righteousness."

After Abraham and Sarah waited on the LORD, and waited on the LORD…and waited on the LORD, they determined to take matters into their own hands. Now, we all know the story, but the ones who suffered from their actions were not only Hagar, the mother of Ishmael, but Abraham, Sarah, Isaac, and yes, we have even paid a price for their impatience. We have only to look at Israel to see the bitterness, struggle and bloodshed that is the result of brothers striving against brothers for boundaries of land to know that this to be true.

Abraham and Sarah were sincere, but…sincerely wrong! We're always wrong when we move ahead of God, and we are *sin*-cerely wrong. It's not only the moving ahead of God that may cause us to error in our judgment and actions when it comes to our children, but everything that we are seems to get in the way, and cause us to error. The sin of omission is simply omitting to wait and trust in the judgment and wisdom of God, to know and do what's best for all those involved. The sin of commission is ignoring all the signs and alarms sent to us by God, and going head-long into disaster!

It's our own pre-programming about our children and what they need, and what it will take for us to help them in arriving at whatever plans we may have for their lives, that derails God's program. We as parents are usually so bogged down with our own shortcomings, our own misfortunes of childhood, even our own glorious days of youth, that we somehow forget that our children are composed of two entire family histories, histories that entail physiological backgrounds, emotional backgrounds and tendencies, even the traits that are inherit in them from parents, grandparents and even great grandparents. We have no idea of how to bring all of these factors into balance when it comes to God's will for their lives.

How do they create something from nothing, with a formula they cannot possibly decipher, when the only thing available to them are the smoke and mirrors of their own experiences? It is impossible! They will always make mistakes in judgment, without the help of the LORD, and the wisdom of His Holy Spirit...they'll never get it right!

It's so amazing that Abraham, without any supporting evidence discounting the physical circumstances, could believe God for the fulfillment of His covenant! This so pleased our LORD that He counted the act of his faith as righteousness!

Our trust in God and that He will do what He has promised to do, produces the quiet assurance within us, that nothing is impossible with God, and that without Him...nothing is possible. So...what happened with Abraham and Sarah? Well, it took God too long to do what He'd promised, so they thought they would give Him the help He so obviously needed (Smile). Big mistake!

The last thing we ever want to create in the lives of our children, and their future is what I will call for this chapter an Ishmael Result! Let's try to hone in on who Ishmael was, and what his birth meant to the people and children of Israel.

We know that Ishmael was the son of Abraham, by Hagar, Sarah's Egyptian maid. That Ishmael was born when Abraham was eighty-six years of age, and was circumcised when he was thirteen years of age, along with his father and his father's male servants. He received the divine promise that he would beget twelve princes and become a great nation. Ishmael dies at the age of 137. What we really need to understand is that Ishmael was the founder of the tribal family called Ishmaelites, sometimes referred to as Midianites.

Which we find in Genesis 37:27-28, "Come, and let us sell him to the Ishmaelites, and let not our hand be upon him; for he is our brother and our flesh. And his brethren were content. (28) Then there passed by Midianites merchantmen; and they drew and lifted up Joseph out of the pit, and sold Joseph to the Ishmaelites for twenty pieces pf silver: and they brought Joseph into Egypt."

Abraham and Sarah did what we so often do as parents when it comes to our children, and the plans we have for them don't seem to be happening fast enough. When we'd rather act than wait for the ordained plan God has for them, and as with Ishmael…it can cause great harm and confusion. Firstly, Abraham and Sarah overestimated the importance of Ishmael in God's plan by mistaking him for the heir of covenant promises. Then, they underrated God's intentions for him by excluding him altogether from inheritance with Isaac! This was a mistake!

God will always balance our wishes with His plans, especially if they are honorable. Our children should never think that what we desire for them outweighs God's plans for them. When we allow them to think like this, they will also think that their own plans for themselves are more important than God's plans for them.

What Abraham and Sarah forgot to factor into their plans was the incomparable sovereignty of God, and that He will never bless His children with a life, or lifestyle, that makes Him unnecessary! All our plans and dreams regarding our children (and I use the term our children) must first pass the scrutiny of His divine will and purpose, for their lives.

The birth of Ishmael created some extremely painful problems for him, his mother, and as stated earlier, for Abraham, Sarah, Isaac, and modern day Israel. Ishmael became an outcast (one who has been excluded from society). Ishmael, who was fourteen years older than Isaac, was not his father's heir, and did not share in his father's property. Imagine…imagine, how this would make you feel!

I believe that most parents feel that because they are Christians that it's a forgone conclusion that their children will also be Christians. Well, more than likely this is so, but unless you've personally led them to Christ, or have witnessed their personal confession of Christ as their Savior I wouldn't take anything for granted. Their eternal souls are in your hands. We must never make the mistake of assuming our child knows and lives for Christ.

The blessings and the promises of God are written in His Word, but also written in His Word are the requirements necessary to become joint heirs with Christ, thereby being partakers of the blood-bought covenant through Jesus Christ our LORD. Romans 8:16-17 says, "The Spirit itself beareth witness with our spirit, that we are the children of God: (17) And if children, then heirs, heirs of God, and joint-heirs with Christ; if so be that we suffer with him, that we may be also glorified together." Galatians 3:29 says, "And if ye be Christ's then are ye Abraham's seed, and heirs according to the promise."

Our Father wishes that no man should perish. Just as the casting out of Ishmael brought great grief to Abraham, so will it grieve our LORD, if our children cannot partake of all the plans and blessings He has ordained for their lives.

You might wonder, how could I dare make a mistake with my child in this area of their lives, I could never willingly see them without Christ? I know this, and it's usually that kind of assurance about what we're doing, or think we've done correctly, that leads to trouble. Do you talk with your child on a regular basis about Christ? Are you listening to their conversation, their music, do you know friends they associate with? Have you bothered to talk with their teachers about their behavior at school? Are they really involved in church, or do they appear to be on the outside, looking in? Have you ever really noticed them praying or reading their Bible, or do you simply assume that they are? Has the LORD been tugging at your heart to sit down and talk with them about certain things you're beginning to notice, as they get older, and you can't seem to find the time?

All of these things and so many more can be the beginning of heartache, and trouble for you and your family. Our young people have so many things pulling on them, and bidding for their attention and what they want most in life, is to not be different. And what we want for them is for them to not become outcasts! Amen? Amen.

Like with Hagar, when she felt so deserted and abandoned, she cried to the LORD and He heard her. He heard the moaning of Hagar's broken heart, and God declared that he would make her son a great nation. There won't be any mistakes if you seek Him, and when He speaks...listen with an attentive heart.

Little did Sarah know that when she persuaded Abraham to go unto Hagar, that she was originating a rivalry, a family feud, and bloodshed that would run through the ages. And oceans of blood have not stopped this feud! The casting out of Ishmael has been productive, but...it has also produced a bitter fruit. The wild heart beats on in the bosoms of those who form the Arab world. In Genesis 16: 11-12, "And the angel of the LORD said unto her, behold, thou art with child, and shalt bear a son, and shalt call his name Ishmael; because the LORD hath heard thy affliction, (12) And he will be a wild man; his hand will be against every man, and every man's hand against him; and he shall dwell in the presence of all his brethren."

If we don't guard against making eternal and spiritual mistakes with our children, the by-product will be a bitterness and pain that we don't want to be responsible for. We must listen to God, and be willing to change directions in mid-stream, if need be. Sarah and Abraham never wanted to cause this pain, they were wonderful people, full of faith, but they were…p-e-o-p-l-e!

Part of the Ishmael Result is untold pain and heartache! The pain that comes from not reading the signs and signals that the Holy Spirit always sends us, those little signals that become cries for help and attention that only we as parents can give our children, the kind of pain that usually causes such injury, that only God…Himself, can mend and restore the brokenness. To be honest, it could cause the kind of pain and destruction your family may never really recover from.

Everything we say and do will mold and shape the character of our children. Some things we do can affect their lives and ours, for the rest of our lives. That's why we must be willing to listen to God.

When we see the life of Ishmael, and really, the best intentions of Sarah, it's like having a small speck on the mirror and we use a greasy cloth to clean it. What happens…the speck now blurs our vision entirely of what we initially thought we were doing. Not every child born to us will be the perfect little angel we'd hope for and it's this child I'm talking about.

Some children, like some Christians, require all that we can do in life to keep them saved and us sane! (Smile) Seriously, we may have a child that will literally kick, and kick…all the way to heaven! (Smile) I don't hold with the thought of…"Every family has one…" or that…"I'm the black sheep, of the family…." It's my thought that every child requires every effort to bring them to Christ; it's just that some require so-o-o much more! (Smile)

What we can't allow to happen is the utter destruction that Satan has planned for the lives of our children. Isaac and Ishmael had to be separated because the concept of how they were to be raised, what god they were to serve, and how he would be served, just about everything involving the background of their parents, was different. There were two extreme differences with the mothers, one a Jewess, and the other a Gentile, not to mention their religious and moral convictions. Also Ishmael…being the eldest son, would probably have influenced Isaac in a negative way and that God just couldn't have. As I was saying earlier, there are generations that influence the growth and development of your child. We shouldn't add insult to injury by not consulting God, and then resting in His answer.

Just as we have two entirely different illustrations for the types of mistakes parents make, from the potentially damaging or really just inconvenient that later become the family joke, to the severe, life-altering mistakes, that only God can correct, and bring about the result that we are all praying and believing Him for. Except, let's face it, most of us live right there in the middle, and that's what we have to deal with on a daily basis.

Most parents get into trouble when the line between parent and that of friend becomes blurred. Now let me help with the definition of parent: a father or mother, a guardian, or protector one who causes to come into existence (don't forget this one...smile!). A friend is: a person whom one knows, likes, and trusts, one who supports or sympathizes with a group or cause or movement.

Although these two definitions are similar in meaning, what separates them is *one who causes to come into existence*! This factor is fundamental in its meaning. A friend can make a mess, or cause a mess, and leave never to be seen again. A parent can make a mess, or cause a mess, and must remain to clean up the mess!

A friend can promise you everything, and then tell you I'm sorry, but I can't do what I promise. A parent can promise something, and if they attempt to forget it, or get out of it, their in deep trouble, and might kill their child, then cry out, Lazarus, come forth! Or run the risk of being seen on News at Eleven!

A friend can pick the battles she chooses to fight in, and the enemy she chooses to fight, and how long she chooses to fight, but, a parent has to fight in every battle, all the time, no matter the enemy, and no matter how long the war!

It's always a *big mistake* to allow your child to confuse your relationship. Being the parent is not a popularity contest, and you're not running for office. The position was filled when the doctor said, "Congratulations, it's a boy," or "it's a girl." No matter how hard you try, disguises don't work. I've tried them! (Smile) You're stuck...oops...sorry, you're blessed!

The authority given to us as parents is a divine authority, and to ever relinquish our rights as parents is *sin* and *dangerous*! The only thing to do when you become parents is to take your position seriously and earnestly, just jump in, step up to the bat, and do all that your can do to clear Satan's bases!

Never allow him the upper hand, and never allow him to frighten you into thinking that if I'm too severe, or too strict I'll lose them; it's a lie! The prayers you've prayed and the times you've spent in training and teaching your children will not return void. When you've done all that you can do cast the whole of your care upon the LORD, He'll definitely do the rest!

When are children become a certain age, they begin to try pulling strings and attempting to make us march to their drum beat, but don't you dare allow them to bully you, and that's exactly what they are attempting to do—get your bluff!

Today's environment is filled with runaway teens and young adults, and children who seem to do everything possible to provoke an argument so that they can have a tantrum! You even see it in the markets or malls: this poor (seemingly helpless) parent, whispering to this toddler, begging them to not cry or strike out in public and cause them embarrassment. Well, my response to that is to "Do unto them before they can *do* unto you!" Just pop that little bottom with a little wooden spoon, the diapers make such a loud noise today, it usually shuts them right up! (Smile)

Sometimes our children, especially the older ones, attempt to hold their parents in emotional terror by threatening to leave home or to run away. In such severe instances of rebellion, please read, Deuteronomy 21: 18-21, "If a man have a stubborn and rebellions son, which will not obey the voice of his father, or the voice of his mother, and that, when they have chastened him, will not hearken unto them: (19) Then shall his father and his mother lay hold on him, [I like that part, lay hold on him, smile] and bring him out unto the elders of his city, and unto the gate of his place; (20) And they shall say unto the elders of his city, this our son is stubborn and rebellious, he will not obey our voice; he is a glutton, and a drunkard. (21) And all the men of his city shall stone him with stones, that he die: so shalt thou put evil away from among you; and all Israel shall bear, and fear."

Israel won't be the only ones frightened by this scripture. After you've read this scripture with them, and then you've prayed together, telling them you're turning them over to the God that wrote that scripture, then ask if you can help them pack. Afterwards, don't say another word! It's now between them and the Holy Spirit, and of course, your silent, but fervent prayers. (Smile) For some strange reason, this has always worked with me and my kids. I can't imagine why; it just does! (Smile)

Then you have the child who wants to pout. This I never allowed. In fact, after disciplining my children, I'd always ask them for the biggest hug, and tell them how very much I loved them. Discipline without love, without the sincerest understanding of whom the struggle is really with, is not only dangerous but totally ineffective. There is a place that the Word of God can reach within your child…that your words will never reach and that's the heart. Remind them of Ephesians 6:1-3, "Children, obey your parents in the LORD; for this is right. (2) Honor thy father and mother (which is the first commandment with promise), (3) that it may be well with thee, and thou mayest live long on the earth." It's also a pretty good idea to remind them of they how difficult they make your life, and that you were so much younger, stronger, and healthier, BTKC (Before The Kids Came!). (Smile)

When a child pouts it seem rather benign in its message, but the opposite is actually true. When your child pouts they are telling you that they feel as if they are on your level, and like one adult to another. They just don't have to talk to you. It also gives Satan too much quiet time to run thoughts through their little heads. It's a mistake to allow your child this much power! Pouting is simply a more quiet, but effective way for your child to throw a tantrum. Don't allow it!

I've given several examples of how a child will attempt to manipulate or control you; all are different, and all have been tried. We want so very much to be accepted that we don't really consider these attempts at manipulation to be too dangerous, and that's a mistake.

What you must understand is that for us, as Christians, and as parents, all things are spiritual. There is nothing that comes into our lives that is not, or cannot become either a spiritual blessing, or a spiritual attack. All children are reaching for power, trying to gain a foothold on the situation, or the petition they've placed before you. Whenever territory is lost, it's just too difficult to regain control without causing unnecessary pain. Handle the branch or the twig, so that you don't have to deal with the oak tree!

Being a parent is difficult enough, without your having to deal with unnecessary damage control from either over reacting, or not reacting at all. The love we have for our children should not lessen our responsibility to be good parents. As parents we must never relinquish our parental authority. As they were tiny infants we were needed and loved for different reasons. As they become older the job description may expand, but the end result must be the same. We should be molding and shaping their lives in such a way that they are a joy to be known by all, and a pleasure for everyone to work with, whether a teacher, coach, or babysitter, and also invaluable asset to the body of Christ. It all depends upon us; don't make the mistake of not taking your responsibility as a parent seriously enough, and don't forget, you're the parent, not their friend. But you can be both if it's done with wisdom and love, and embraced by the Holy Spirit.

When you tell your child you're sorry, you're accomplishing two goals. First, you're acknowledging that you are not infallible, that you either made a mistake in judgment, or you were just plain out of order. Secondly, you're also showing them that apologizing is not the same thing as repentance.

Explain to them that an apology, while difficult to give, can be sheer joy to receive, and yet it does nothing towards our relationship with the LORD. That an apology can be given all day long to the same person and never change the outcome of their lives, or the life of the one offended. But, repentance on the other hand, can do both! True repentance is not just saying you're sorry about something, but you're also turning your back on that thing and literally walking away from ever doing it again, if at all possible!

When you apologize to your child, please be sincere; a child can always sense a lie, whether it's spoken of unspoken, and this will be insulting to them and to God. When you find yourself in error of judgment, or in opinion, be quick to say that you're sorry. If you've judged your child wrongly in the presence of others, it's in their presence; you must apologize, even if it's only their friends that are witnesses.

Be explicit in your apology, don't just say "I'm sorry." Tell your child what you're sorry about. The spiritual implications are tremendous if this is not done. Every day we are blessed with our children is a day for us to instruct them in the things of God, and we must use every tool available, even if it's our own pride. A child will never learn the importance of confession from the heart, if they've never witnessed it in their parents.

Repentance, comes from the heart, and is made clear by our actions, and our mouth, and requires willingness. An apology comes from the heart and is made clear by our actions, and our mouth, but requires will.

To apologize you must want or *will* to say I'm sorry. To repent you not only have a *will* to say I'm sorry, but have a *willingness* to change! This is why your commitment to teach you child, even when you're admitting you were wrong, or admitting to shortcoming in yourself or your judgment, is a priceless opportunity.

King David had two beautiful traits in his character going for him. First, a heart quick to repent, second, a heart to worship! These two qualities are almost, if not utterly, inseparable! When your child has learned, not only to say "I'm sorry," but to also repent to his LORD, the worship and serving of Him is guaranteed!

You're telling your child that life has a way of causing us to *sin* against God. We may hurt and offend others, but what they choose to do with the frailties of human error and mistake, will either destroy or cause to develop within them, the character and integrity that God will not only delight in, but that will also be invaluable to Him.

A tantrum is a tantrum whether your child is six years old or sixteen years old. They will always try to intimidate you into relinquishing your parental authority, attempting to make you an ally rather than the parent you are ordained by God to be for them. Don't make the mistake of giving up your rights and obligations as their parent; you will certainly live to regret it. I've used this before, but will make another quick reference to it in 1 Samuel 2: 34-35, "And this shall be a sign unto thee, that shall come upon thy two sons, on Hophni and Phinehas: in one day they shall die, both of them. (35) And I will raise up for myself a faithful priest, who shall do according to that which is in mine heart and in my mind; and I will build him a sure house, and he shall walk before mine anointed forever." This was God's judgment upon Eli and his sons!

Never bargain with Satan for the spiritual well being of your children. For it is indeed Satan you are fighting, and don't think otherwise. Satan doesn't want part of your testimony, some of your children's future, some of your confession of faith. He wants it all! Satan wants us, as he tried so desperately to get Job to do, to curse God and die! Your child doesn't understand the spiritual warfare we're in, nor the consequences that would result if you allowed him to take from you, the scepter that God has placed in your hands. You are to rule and govern according to the Word and will of God.

Every gift that God has placed within your children, every gift, will vanish, will simply perish, unless these gifts are used for the glory of our LORD. Your children are the most valuable gift God has entrusted into your care, and without the proper balance of love and discipline, nurturing and restraining, laughter and tears, they will never reach the potential God has destined them to reach.

The mistakes you make with your child and in their raising are expected, by God, by family, friends, by everyone, well...almost everyone. You and your child are probably the only ones that will be in state of shock! (Smile) Don't allow the enemy to make you feel as if you've failed, or have committed some unpardonable sin, when you're faced with having to apologize to your child, or repent before God. Do what needs to be done. Say what needs to be said. Learn what needs to be learned! And move on!

If you refuse to show your child that side of you that is weak and subject to mistakes in judgment and error it translates into "I am perfect, and I can do no wrong! You too, must be the same!" This is a big mistake!

We must be careful. If our bodies are indeed the temples of the Holy Spirit, and He has to dwell in these bodies, and they are to be for His purpose in the world, we are not working and living, and doing for ourselves. God must always be gloried. He cannot get the glory from a life that apparently doesn't need Him! I mean, if you're perfect, then why do you need Him? Better yet, if you're perfect, then your child gets the impression that he too can be just like you…perfect! With this thought process, how can the LORD ever reach the heart and will of your child? On the other hand, when you show your child that, "All have sinned and fallen short, of the glory of God," (Romans 3:23), they see humanity and will reverence the sovereignty of God. (See also, 1 John 1:9, "If we confess our sins, He is faithful and just to forgive us our sins, and to cleanse us from all unrighteousness. (10) If we say that we have not sinned, we make Him a liar, and His Word is not in us.")

When we operate in the frailties of this flesh, in sin God is not in it! However, when we allow God to take this flesh, manifest Himself through us, we then become the light effective enough to be used by Him to change lives, all lives, including the lives of our children.

A life of righteousness insists on obedience, obedience to God's Word, wholesome relationships, and a shunning, or avoidance of the filth and pollution of the world by staying close to Jesus. If God's Word ensures our being perfected in love, and that love is based on our love and knowledge of Christ, the only example our children have of this love, this willingness to repent, this willingness to humble ourselves, even before them when we've been wrong, is the best and truest example of the faithfulness and mercy of God they will ever see. Again, don't allow Satan to cheat you out of the opportunity to show the character of Christ in your life, every day of your life, even when it hurts.

You are an evangelist, and as I've stated before, the mission field, the harvest field, is your family, your children. Give your children the confidence and comfort of knowing that the door of parenting swings back and forth. Sometimes it may swing and hit them, but there will also be times when that same door will swing and hit you!

It's not difficult to own up to a mess, and certainly not difficult to clean a mess up if we realize that God's work of love in the human heart is a precious gift, and a tremendous investment. Disappointing things happen to all believers. But we cannot be disappointed with our effort and willingness to be the Christian parents we want to be. We don't want to be a stumbling block to our children, but for them to become the best, we must give to them our very best, and trust the LORD to give us the increase!

Keep your head out of God's way, and allow Him to encourage your heart! After all, He's doing the work; we're only the vessels. There are no social, cultural, physical or spiritual circumstances severe enough to separate the believer from God's love and from His own commitment to the children He's loaned to us! The attitude we show our children towards Christ and towards the mistakes, we will make will either be stepping stones or stumbling blocks.

Our children are not the church of tomorrow. It sounds really spiritual and very profound. But our children are the church of today! Our investment into their lives and how we live our lives before them, will either make them fit to do the work of the gospel for their generation, or unfit to carry the gospel to them.

The battles they contend with today, right now, can kill them right now! The peers they minister to by their lives today can be here today, gone today! Friends, please don't make a mess, and not be willing to do whatever needs to be done, even in your life to clean it up!

What I want from for my life, and I pray that God will deposit in all our lives, is a desire to earnestly be in God's will. That whenever and wherever we are, our God and our LORD, with the help of the Holy Spirit, will come and make Their will known in our lives, and we will not be failures, nor fail to be effective in cleaning up behind ourselves.

It's my desire to give God the very best of my children, not something that He'll have to break down and tear down to get his attention, not children so stubborn that they'll literally have to be broken before God can use them. He doesn't want children so full of pride (this, He truly hates) that He can't even bless their lives to touch and bless other lives.

How many children do you know personally that the only thing they understand or respond to is either a harsh word or severe punishment? The idea of simply doing what their parent asks of them, without them screaming or yelling at the top of their voice, will just never occur.

What about a child that must be told to do something again and again and again, and maybe still not respond? The parent promises, makes weak or almost benign attempts to discipline the child, and they still don't do what they've been told to do, and the parent is left standing there looking ridiculous! Never allow your child to make a liar out of you! What you tell them you're going to do, if they don't do this or that, do it! Don't wait until tomorrow, (what does the sports slogan say? Just do it!)

Please answer me this. What God can do with a child, or adult for that matter, who's like this, a child or adult who will never listen and obey, but must be told again and again, or threatened, or spoken harshly to? What can He do with them? Right, nothing! If you make a mess, clean it up! None of us wants God taking us out to the woodshed, but believe me, He won't come after the child, without first dealing with the parent!

Amen? Amen!

Chapter X

To Be...Or Not to Be!

In this chapter, we'll be dealing with a subject that really shouldn't be an issue at all for those of us who have given their hearts to the LORD. So, you may wonder, why write it? Well, because the Holy Spirit pressed it into my heart; so if it's not for you, then maybe it's been written for someone who our LORD may either lead you to, or that may cross your path.

No life is futile. This chapter is written with all the sincerity, and straightforwardness I can muster. Please accept the fact that I'm not writing in judgment of anyone in my life, or in the life of others that I may know. It's only because this issue is so close to the heart of God, and to the hearts of so many; consequently, keep an open heart and an open mind.

There are so many factors that cross the mind of parents in respect to their children, and because no one has all the pieces to the puzzle, judgment is irresponsible, and condemnation, sinful. The very first stage where thoughts, either positive or negative, enter in to terminate a pregnancy is when the tests results from the doctor's visit is positive. The doctor and the nurse may be smiling when they give the news, but your heart has dropped. We can't afford another child, LORD; we were so careful. Perhaps you've had children before, and this pregnancy is not an unhappy prospect; however, two or three months into your pregnancy, it's discovered your baby will be either severely retarded, or physically deformed, or some other tremendous challenge you don't feel up to. Maybe there was rape, or incest, or a million and one other legitimate concerns for you and your family.

What about none of the above? You have your home, a good job, financial security, two cars in the garage and even CDs in the bank. By everyone's opinion, you should be pleased. Only, you just don't want another baby because we finally do have our home almost paid for because the kids are finally independent in so many way, and finances are no longer a problem.

We finally have an opportunity to have time to ourselves, real quality time, and we're young enough to not only enjoy it, but our relationship will greatly benefit from it!

There are as many sincere and legitimate concerns about this issue and the million and one other contingencies that challenge the heart and thinking of all of us regarding this subject matter every day of our lives. That's exactly why we cannot judge, and why we must pray one for the other!

You've decided, and you've failed. You can't hide it any longer. You blew it; you were so wrong. So many people who would never have thought it, were so surprised and so hurt. Instead of standing in confidence and facing this issue, you stepped back, fear took over, and you blew it. The one thing you never thought you'd ever do is exactly what you did!

This is exactly why we don't judge! With our LORD, there are no *big* sins or *little* sins. There aren't any *white* lies, or just a teeny, tiny falsehood! To God, sin is sin!

Another example, to the casual observer you may appear to be wrestling with nothing, and yet your heart is being pulled and tugged in so many different directions. There are waves of terror mingled with tears and guilt. There's a hopelessness and confusion so strong, so powerful, you feel as if you're being smothered with a pillow that's been placed tightly over your face. When you suddenly fall on your face, crying out to God, "LORD, please help me, I know what's right, but I also know who I am, and You declare in Your Word, You will not put on me more than I can bear, well, I can't bear this!"

What you need to do is to stop what you're doing, stop everything, get quiet, and name your child! I know that sounds bizarre, but who and what you're praying about and crying out to the LORD about, it is your child. Name it! Right now! Immediately your seed of life has distinction! Only don't just give them any name, go to the Word of God, and call your child a name according to His Word. Believe me, it will also be His will!

As long as you continue to refer to the baby as "this pregnancy" or "this baby" or even worse, your child and you will always be at arm's length, and Satan wants to keep you and your thoughts as far from your child as possible. By doing this, there's no attachment, no bonding. You may ask, what if I don't know the gender of my child? As you go before God in prayer, He'll lead you to the proper name for your child. He certainly knows their gender! Don't you trust Him? This entire process is one step at a time! Forgive my play on words, but you must take baby steps!

I've never been more serious about anything. You are literally fighting for the life of your child, and right now, the biggest threat to her or his safety is you! So it's you we must first bring around to clear, sound thinking.

I told you to name your child, and when you've done this, from now on, every time you go to God, with questions in your heart, refer to your child by their name and He'll do the same. When others come to you with a Word of knowledge from the LORD, God will also give them the name of your child.

I would like to give one scripture here that might also help to keep you in focus when Satan comes with his lies and deceits. The scripture is found in Genesis 38: 8-10. "And Judah said unto Onan, go in unto thy brother's wife, and marry her, and raise up seed to thy brother. (9) And Onan knew that the seed should not be his; and it came to pass, when he went in unto his brother's wife, that he spilled it on the ground, lest that he should give seed to his brother. (10) And the thing which he did displeased the LORD: wherefore He slew him also."

This was an immoral act, where a man took the control from God, and claimed it for himself. Whenever we take anything from God's control, we're moving in the wrong direction, and only heartache will be the results.

Sometimes we look at our tragedies, inconveniences, and set-backs, as injustices or as punishment for some unknown fault or sin, rather than, especially in this particular case, God taking something that may have been conceived in anger, abuse, or even in sexual sin, and using the opportunity to bring not only life, but joy! Only He knows how many unforeseen miracles this child will bring to mankind.

Every life is a miracle, but what miracle do you have in your care? Is it the cure for cancer? Perhaps another Billy Graham or even another Paul? What Satan thought would destroy you, God is using to bless you!

The Word of God tells us in Romans 8:26-27, "Likewise, the Spirit also helpeth our infirmity; for we know not what we should pray for as we ought; but the Spirit, Himself, maketh intercession for us with groanings which cannot be uttered. (27) And He that searcheth the heart knoweth what is the mind of the Spirit, because He maketh intercession for the saints according to the will of God. (28) And we know that all things work together for good to them that love God, to them who are the called according to His purpose."

Our LORD is our help. He and only He is our assurance! It is our destiny to be like Jesus. God is committed to producing in all of us, the love, the joy, all the patience, the long-suffering, all the goodness, and gentleness of Jesus! He paid for this with His own blood, and as stated earlier, is committed to seeing it through.

When He declares that "All things work together for good to them that love God," do you love Him? Is it your desire to please Him, and to be only in His will? Then trust Him and them that are the called according to His purpose! Is that call only for you, or does this also include your child? How can you possibly know what your child is destined to be? Will the world be blessed with the genius of Amadeus Mozart, whose brilliance and musical genius allowed him to hear any music score, just once and play it, in its entirety, from memory, and in many cases improving upon its interpretation, not to mention writing his own scores in ink, with no mistakes? Or maybe another Dr. Paul Ehrlich, whose scientific genius and tenacity has given us the cure for syphilis. Dr. Ehrlich also discovered a coding process using dye that allowed research scientists and doctors to determine and separate the different bacteria and viruses that cause certain illnesses and disease, such as typhus.

Wouldn't you love to be the mother of a daughter with the heart, generosity, and charity of a Mother Theresa? None of us know what we're blessed with when we're expecting a child; only the LORD knows. The very thought of terminating your pregnancy is a Goliath-type challenge. But Goliath must be slain or you run the risk of becoming a slave and victim to this sin, maybe for the rest of your life. What we must do, especially when Goliath rears his ugly head, is not just kill him: cut off his head!

What Satan doesn't tell any of us when we sin or when we fail to do what we know is the will and purpose of God for our lives, are the consequences we'll have to pay as a result of our disobedience. For example, how many times when traveling down our highways have you notice a billboard showing all the beautiful people holding what seem to be tall glasses of the most refreshing and satisfying drinks in their hands? It looks so perfect, so fitting, and the smiles and laughter seem to jump out at us, sometimes causing us to sigh softly, "Wow, that looks like fun!"

Or maybe you may have traveled a little further down the road and noticed another billboard, this time lots of young couples are pictured, looking dreamily into each other's eyes, with smiles, dimples and beautiful figures, to boot! They look as if they would just die if they were not in the arms of the person holding them…smile! And years ago, you could even see billboards advertising tobacco and cigarettes, using the most rugged and handsome men they could gather up. They looked as if they could pose for any artist that needed an idea of what Adam looked like in the Garden of Eden (smile): just absolutely perfect!

All of this is done to sell a product that doesn't produce the beauty, happiness, and ruggedness portrayed on these billboards. Satan never shows us the drunkard on skid row that has lost his entire family and future because of wine and liquor. You never see the clinics that deal with the pain and withdrawal of these victims to chemicals, or to sexually transmitted and sometimes incurable disease and viruses.

When you see all the beautiful people laughing and dancing as if there were no tomorrow, Satan doesn't show us the results of fornication, i.e., AIDS, venereal diseases, unwanted pregnancies. He doesn't show us the courtrooms filled with marriages that have been destroyed by the ravages of sin! Satan never shows us the dead-end roads that a permissive life style leads to; he only shows the beautiful facade, never the certain results.

Look at the life of King David, and the terrible sin that overwhelmed his life and caused such pain, and heartache, a sin that left him reeling from its effect and sting! Satan prepared a silver platter, a tailor-made temptation just for the king, catering to David's obvious weakness for beautiful women. Satan served up Bathsheba. There are many conflicting opinions about Bathsheba; some authorities refer to her as being as much a victim as her husband, Uriah. Others see her as the plotting seductress. It really doesn't matter; what does matter is that before God, "All have sinned and fallen short."

What also matters, however, is that the act of killing Uriah, Bathsheba's husband, was not a conspiracy. David arranged for the death of her husband, Uriah in battle. This action was even more despicable because Uriah was one of his own companions. David, desiring her for himself, ordered that Bathsheba be brought to him. Reading in 2 Samuel 11:3-4, "And David sent and enquired after the woman. And one said, is not his Bathsheba, the daughter of Eliam, the wife of Uriah the Hittite? (4) And David sent messengers, and took her; and she came in unto him, and he lay with her; for she was purified from her uncleanness: and she returned unto her house."

David had no idea of what this one moment of pleasure would cost him. Yes, he knew it was sin, but after all, he was king, and shouldn't he have whatever he wanted? Satan knew that David was accustomed to indulging his fancies freely in the matter of attractive women, and he was immediately attracted to Bathsheba as she bathed on the rooftop of her home. His obsession with Bathsheba, and the resulting consequences buckled the knees of God's anointed and brought shame and heartache to the kingdom and household of this wonderful man.

The story of David and Bathsheba is a familiar one, and heart wrenching to say the very least. Their act of infidelity and adultery produced the fruit of sorrow, despair, remorse and murder! Some may say, "What about Bathsheba? Wasn't she also guilty? Well, according to the laws of this era, Bathsheba could not have resisted had she even desired to do so, for a woman in these ancient times was completely subject to a king's will. If he desired her, he could have her; it was as simple as that. Consequently, her part in the story is neither praiseworthy or blameworthy. Remember when Sarah, some centuries before, because of her beauty had been taken into the harem of two kings, Abimelech and Pharaoh? Remember how Abraham feared for his life because of her beauty? Well, this is the same thing, only David knew better.

David was destroyed when faced with the reality of what he'd done! It was almost more than he could bear, not just because of the selfish cruelty that caused the act, but the pain the emptiness and separation he obviously felt from his God was almost more than he could bear.

David's great penitential Psalm was written after his adultery with Bathsheba. The 51st Chapter of Psalms is probably the most beautifully written script for repentance I've ever read! David is horrified at the thought of losing fellowship with his God! Nothing about his life mattered anymore; he was in the pit of despair! Satan thought, "Surely he won't recover from this." And that's what he's always hoping, surely they won't recover from this!

David did what we all have to do, *get over it!* We need to, "… confess our sin, acknowledge that He is faithful and just to forgive our sins, and to cleanse us from all unrighteousness." (1 John 1:9) It hurts, but we can't stop there!

I've used the sin of David not simply because it so graphically paints the horrors of self-indulgence, but also the gravity of his sin should encourage us all that God is more than faithful, not only to deliver us from all sin, but to restore and restore absolutely! See how beautifully God blessed David with Solomon, whose wisdom and personal wealth has never been equaled? Yes, to take a life, at any stage of that life, is a terrible act, indeed, but it's not the act alone that destroys us; it's our ability to recover from the blow, the quake of such a sin to our relationship with Christ that matters most.

David had to be confident in the assurance and the love and mercy he knew was God's alone. There is no pit of sorrow so deep that the blood of Jesus and His love and mercy towards us is not deeper still!

Let's take another look at David that will show us how much he loved and trusted his God to always act in love and mercy towards his children.

Remember in 2 Samuel, 24th chapter, when David fought and was facing multiple battles and decided to take a census? Joab, his right-hand man in battle, asks David, why do this thing, why insult the LORD with counting our men to determine our strength? Only David insisted, and Joab counted the men and gave the total to David, the Bible tells us in 2 Samuel 24:10, "And David's heart smote him after he had numbered the people. And David said unto the LORD, I have sinned greatly in what I have done; and now, I beseech thee, O LORD, take way the iniquity of thy servant; for I have done very foolishly."

David showed how very human he was, that after so many battles, he wondered, like we all might, did he have enough men to be successful? Well, David's success was not in the might and number of men, but in the might of his God!

The word came to David the next morning by the prophet Gad, David's seer, saying at verse 12, "Go and say unto David, thus saith the LORD, I offer thee three things; choose thee one of them, that I may do it unto thee." The choices were: Seven years of famine upon the people, his armies running from their enemies for three months, or would David prefer that God visit the people with three days of pestilence?

David knew the heart of his God. He remembered how the LORD was merciful with Adam and Eve, with Noah and the flood. God had withheld judgment from the earth in the midst of its moral darkness. David also knew of Abraham's interceding on behalf of Sodom and Gomorrah, and his nephew Lot. David knew of the boundless mercy of God, and decided accordingly.

David says it all in verse 14 of 2 Samuel, the 24th chapter. "And David said unto Gad, I am in deep distress; let us fall, now into the hand of the LORD; for his mercies are great. And let me not fall into the hand of man." Praise the LORD; David knew that no matter what sin of disobedience he'd committed, that the mercies of our LORD endure forever!

There is no pain or sin that you can inflict upon yourself or upon His will that will separate you from His love and willingness to not only forgive but to restore! Not even the tricks, the wiles and schemes of Satan, can separate us from the love of God! We are secured in Christ and in the finished and perfect work of the cross of Calvary!

Paul reminds us in Romans 8:35-39, "What shall separate us from the love of Christ? Shall tribulation, or distress, or persecution, or famine, or nakedness, or peril or sword? (36) As it is written, for thy sake we are killed all the day long; we are accounted as sheep for the slaughter. (37) Nay, in all these things we are more than conquerors through Him that loved us. (38) For I am persuaded that neither death, nor life, nor angels, nor principalities, nor powers, nor things present, nor things to come, (39) nor height, nor depth, nor any other creation, shall be able to separate us from the love of God, which is in Christ Jesus our LORD."

Nothing can separate us from His mercy, His love, His grace, His willingness to not only forgive but to also do the impossible…forget!

Through Christ Jesus, we can conquer and become victorious over every snare, every pitfall, every stronghold Satan may attempt to imprison us with! What matters to the LORD is not the act, as much as our actions afterwards.

Repentance for abortion is no less worthy of the blood of Jesus than the sins of adultery, fornication, lying, manipulation, jealousy, gossiping, not forgiving, and the list goes on! If God doesn't weigh our sin in scales and balances, don't allow Satan or anyone else to take you there!

I cannot imagine the pain and emptiness caused by this sin, but I know that our LORD wants you to get over it! He cannot heal what is not opened to Him, nor can He take from us what is not given to Him. Satan wants to keep us hurting and weeping over our sin, our past, our pain for as long as he can. By doing this we are only half, or even less than half as effective as God wants us to be. This is what I believe is as painful to the LORD as David taking his census to determine if whether or not he had enough men to fight his battles. This was an insult to God, so He smacked him for it! (Smile)

We can know that our LORD is merciful, full of grace, that He's faithful to cleanse us from all unrighteousness. We can know that His love for us has no measure, that His thoughts towards us are more than the sand of the seas. We can even understand that what He wants from us and for us is our very best, and that He is able to do exceeding abundantly above all we can ask or think! Only knowing all of this is not enough; we must also act accordingly, and do so with confidence.

The thing that makes abortion such a tremendous deed to recover from is that it's committed against the body and the spirit and the soul of two lives! And it's hidden from everyone except you and God! There's no place to go for help, encouragement, or even comfort, because Satan doesn't allow for us to do that; he tries to strip us of any support system, and he does this by saying, "No one will ever know," and, as usual, he lied. Or he might says that today's political environment is just too much for you to deal with so just keep it to yourself.

It's like having a bomb go off inside you, and proclaiming there is no damage. That's crazy; you're blown up inside, you're bleeding and hurting in ways you never even imagined! The fact that a tree is chopped down in the forest and no one is there to hear it when it falls, doesn't lessen the fact that it created a loud, thunderous, and even destructive result when it fell. This tree killed whatever happened to be in its path when it fell. Satan wants to do the same to you; he wants to destroy you and everything that God has planned for your path of life.

But the decision to fight your way back to the peace and joy, and even powerful ministry that is yours for the asking, is all up to you. Don't stand still, and don't stand in the middle of the road! If you allow yourself to stand still and make no move in one direction or the other, you're an easy target. See, Satan as the bowling ball that will simply knock you over into the gutter, or into another lane or just put you out of commission all together! If you stand in the middle of your decision, you can be hit by traffic coming from either direction. Those that don't really care, and those that think they know it all, when they z-o-o-o-m by you, you'll find yourself reeling and spinning from your indecision.

We will never know or understand all that God has in store for us. It's not only difficult to imagine that He can do anything with this mess we've all made of our lives, and yet the miracle is that He not only can do, He also wants to do!

We're told in Jeremiah 29:11, "For I know the thoughts that I think toward you, said the LORD, thoughts of peace, and not of evil, to give you an expected end." He not only has these thoughts towards us for good, but He expects these thoughts to come to pass in us! Whatever it is for you, He sees it, has planned it, thought it, and is only waiting on you to set your will in alignment with His so that He can perform it! Again, you are your only hindrance!

Whenever God begins dealing with us, He begins or starts with the things that are the most difficult. He usually starts with our fear, the fear we have of ever being able to feel the joy and peace we once felt with such frequency! We are like David when he cried out in Psalms 51: 1-3, "Have mercy upon me, O God, according to thy loving-kindness; according unto the multitude of thy tender mercies blot out my transgressions. (2) Wash me thoroughly from mine iniquity, and cleanse me from my sin. (3) For I acknowledge my transgressions, and my sin is ever before me." Isn't that beautiful?

Understand that our LORD will begin by bringing back to you an understanding of *who* He is, and that He is *not* your judge…He is your Savior your advocate, your intercessor your solution. He doesn't have to judge you, just like David; you're doing that well enough on your own! You really don't need His help! That's the reason you have so much pain; your judgment is severe enough for the both of you.

Next He will deal with your human nature, that part of us that is either too unworthy of forgiveness, or more than deserving of whatever befalls us. This is called self pity. Yes, it's there! When the Holy Spirit of the LORD erases and empties you of yourself, He can begin to refill you with His love, and His presence in your life. You see that that void within you caused by your doubt and fears must be filled with something else. The only thing that will fill a void like this is more of Jesus and His love than you can hold.

Believe it or not, it's like being born again, again! That's what has to take place: a spiritual rebirthing!

God's only desire right now is to make you free. Free from the guilt and pain of sin, free from the burden and heartache of sin, free from the condemnation of Satan and possibly others, and free to praise and worship Him exactly the way you've done so often before!

Our LORD wants to destroy the 3-Ps of Satan, his *plans* for your life, his *pain* for your life, and his *price* for the sin you'll never feel equipped to pay. Satan's plans to destroy you and your ministry, to fill you with so much pain that all your joy is gone, and he keeps you constantly trying to pay the cost for something that's already paid for!

God wants to give you His 3-P's; *peace, power and praise*! His *peace,* is described in Philippians 4:5-7. "Let your moderation be known unto all men. The LORD is at hand. (6) Be careful for nothing; but in every thing by prayer and supplication with thanksgiving let your requests be made known unto God. (7) And the peace of God, which passeth all understanding, shall keep your hearts and minds through Christ Jesus." That's the secret of the peace of God. In Philippians 4:8-9, "Finally, brethren, whatsoever things are true, whatsoever things are honest, whatsoever things are just, whatsoever things are lovely, whatsoever things are of good report; if there be any virtue, and if there be any praise, think on these things. (9) Those things, which ye have both learned, and received, and heard, and seen in me, do: and the God of peace shall be with you." Now, that's the presence of God's peace!

My dear friends, you must determine your own thought life. *Do not* allow others do it for you. Keep your mind on those things that bring peace to you and glory to God. Surround yourself with those whose hearts are right before

God, and whose lifestyle and ministry you can most benefit from. Dear one, right now you're a recovering wounded, and you need the spiritual support and encouragement of those who see only the Christ in you, and His perfect will for your life! Allow the LORD to readjust your friends and confidants if necessary; the last thing you want is a Pharisee-type spirit around you.

God wants your life filled with *power*! To accomplish this two things must be present in your life, and the first is the infilling of the Holy Spirit according to Acts 2:4, "And they were all filled with the Holy Ghost, and began to speak with other tongues, as the Spirit gave them utterance." Also, you need to know the power you possess when you will dare to use His name! All things are possible through the name of Jesus! Philippians 2:9-11 says, "Wherefore God also hath highly exalted Him, and given Him a name which is above every name: (10) That at the name of Jesus every knee should bow, of things in heaven, and things in earth, and things under the earth; (11) And that every tongue should confess that Jesus Christ is LORD, to the glory of God the Father."

Hallelujah! All Glory to God! Well, honey, there's your carte blanche! The name of Jesus will destroy every attempt of Satan to revisit you with this sin that is covered in the blood of Jesus! You have a supreme confidence that through His name and through the power of His name, we have access to God. Learn that God's Word can never fail us, so if His Word declares that every knee should bow and every tongue confess that Jesus Christ is LORD, believe it! If His Word declares, according to John 14:13-14, "Whatever ye shall ask in my name, that will I do, that the Father may be glorified in the Son. (14) If ye shall ask anything in my name, I will do it."

God not only answers our prayers, He always does more than that. He always gives "exceedingly abundantly above all that we ask or think" (Ephesians 3:20). Never listen to the plans and schemes of man or Satan. God can work mightily when you persist in believing Him despite the discouragement from anyone else's standpoint.

In the name of Jesus, you are equipped with more power to resist the lies and slanders of Satan and all the demons of hell, and also the so-called saints that may have a word for you from the LORD. If that word doesn't line up with His Word, it's a lie, and I don't care who's speaking it.

His *praise* in your mouth will destroy the voice of Satan and keep His presence close to your heart! Without question, one of the most remarkable and exciting things about songs and sincere praise is given to us in Psalms 18:3. "I will call upon the LORD, who is worthy to be praised; so shall I be saved from mine enemies." Also, Psalms 22:3-4, "But thou art holy, O thou who inhabitest the praises of Israel. (4) Our fathers trusted in thee; they trusted, and thou didst deliver them."

Praise will always bring the presence of God. Although God is everywhere present, there is a distinct manifestation of His rule which enters the environment of praise. When at times you'll feel alone, deserted, or even depressed, praise God!

Sing a new song unto the LORD; that's what I said; compose a song of testimony and praise to God for His goodness in your life, for His delivering and strengthening power, for the way He did battle for you against the attacks and discouragements of Satan and gave to you the victory!

God does not merely visit us when we praise Him, but He abides with us, and His presence will live and inhabit your life! Let this truth create faith and trust and lead to your complete healing and deliverance from satanic harassments, torment, or bondage.

We're told in Psalms 50:23, "Whoso offereth praise glorifieth me; and to him that ordereth his conversation aright will I show the salvation of God." Don't you just love David, and the way he loves and worships his God? It's simple; when you offer praises unto God, the attention and focus is on Him, and off of you! When we praise God, we also glorify Him, and our praise becomes the vehicle for God to come to us and to minister to us and through us!

Another beautiful psalm of praise, and one of my favorites, is psalm 63: 1-5. " O God, thou art my God, early will I seek thee; my soul thirsteth for thee, my flesh longeth for thee in a dry and thirsty land, where no water is, (2) To see thy power and thy glory, as I have seen thee in the sanctuary. (3) Because thy loving-kindness is better than life, my lips shall praise thee. (4) Thus will I bless thee while I live, I will lift up my hands in thy name. (5) My soul shall be satisfied as with marrow and fatness, and my mouth shall praise thee with joyful lips." Don't you just wish that you'd written that? (Smile...me too!)

Never forget that perfected praise will also produce strength! It is powerful! You know how is feels when we enter a service of true praise and worship, our worship begins to grow intensely, as we magnify our LORD, and shackles and chains fall off, people are delivered, and lives are touched and healed, all in the atmosphere of perfect praise!

There is only one price you must sometimes pay for your praise. Praise often requires that we kill our pride, fear or laziness, anything that threatens to diminish or interfere with our worship of our LORD. The foundation of all praise, is remembering the cost that Jesus paid, that we might have perfect access to the throne of God, with every petition being given to Him, and left in His presence, and to never be picked up again!

Friends, forget yesterday. No matter what happened, and no matter what you did, when it's confessed, all is forgiven because of Christ. "Rejoice in the LORD always; and again I say Rejoice!" (Philippians 4:4) It's over; it's covered, and it's forgotten! God bless you!

Chapter XI

Father…Knows Best

Honestly, I really can't imagine a more difficult and yet honorable position for mankind, than that of father. God reveals Himself through the love, protection and provision of our earthly fathers. This office of ministry has no equal, and the upside potential for growth and development is limited only by a father's willingness to surrender his own agenda, for that of the LORD's.

Fathers who allow themselves to be open vessels for the directions and instruction of our LORD will find both the inspiration and the power to be everything for their families, for the very attributes of God's character will flow into their lives, fill their lives, and be the umbrella of covering over their lives, that is so necessary today.

The roles of father and mother are not self-chosen, nor are they assigned by the culture in which one lives. They are established and ordained by God as a means of manifesting the life of Christ on this earth, through His children, through the body of Christ, through the Christian family.

For the father to be in direct alignment to our LORD, he must also be in total submission to the same. Exactly as the wife, or mother, must be in submission to her husband, and the father of her children, so it is with the father: his head of authority is Jesus Christ, and as with any corporate organizational chart, all power and all other authority trickles down from there.

This explains my opening statement with regard to this position of great honor and responsibility! To have to answer directly to God the Father for all the matters that affect and concern your family, your children, is for me, a frightening prospect, not because of any dread or terror I have of our LORD. On the contrary, it's because of His love and trust towards us that He would entrust the welfare of His body to man. That's exactly what He did with Jesus.

He said to His only Son, everything is in your hands now, Son; the future of all mankind rests upon you!

To every father that lives today, will live tomorrow, or ever shall be, if you're a child of God, the welfare of the body of Christ, your particular vineyard, rests on you! The church is as effective and as prosperous as every family represented by it, and at the head of every family is the father.

Let's take a look at the first father, the father of all mankind, Adam, the first human son of God, God's masterpiece and the crowning work of His creation. Every man should be interested in the history of the first man who breathed, man's great ancestor, the head of the human family, the very first man to walk on this earth!

Can you imagine the world that Adam found himself in, or a part of, a world filled with all the beauty and wonder that only God could have created, a world where there was no sin, no sorrow, no sickness or disease of any kind, and fathers, guess what...no taxes! (Smile)

The word of God doesn't tell us how long Adam and Eve's paradise lasted, this state of blissful blessedness and innocence, for it was cruelly interrupted by the whispers and seduction of the tempter, Satan. I'm not sure, but I think we all know the rest of the story! (Smile)

Anyway, our first father Adam lost his first and only job. He was fired from his position as CEO for the Garden of Eden and was forced to take an entry-level position as laborer, tilling the now-cursed and stubborn soil of the earth to put food on the table.

God made the earth for man, to shelter, protect, feed, and totally provide for his comfort and amusement. Now this same earth turned its back and refused to yield of itself without the sweat, tears, and back-breaking sacrifice of man. How the roles of authority changed! First the earth was made for man, and now man was made for the earth. Without the earth and its willingness to yield, man would die, and his family with him.

The sight of all this must have torn the heart of God. Like all good fathers He wanted the best for His children and did everything within His power to provide the very best for them. But like all good children (smile), we rebelled! Our heavenly Father told us to not touch the stove because it was hot, He turned His back, and we touched the stove! We were not only burned, but everything in the house, in this beautiful Garden called Eden, everything went up in smoke!

As it is with most children, when caught with their pants down, (I couldn't resist saying that...smile) we began to point the finger at everybody else. In other words, nobody really knew what happened; the forbidden fruit just fell into their mouths when they weren't looking, and they were forced to swallow it to avoid choking, or something to that effect! (Smile) It doesn't matter because the lie didn't work, and we were sent to our room without supper!

So Adam was not just the first man, he was the first everything, i.e., the first man evicted, the first man to find himself unemployed, homeless, dressed in hand-me-downs (clothing that was provided by someone else), and last but not at all least, heavily in debt, with no means or ability to pay the debt owed!

Whew! our first father had no way of knowing the bind and the pain he was causing his children. If he'd known the repercussions of his disobedience, I earnestly believe Adam would have assumed his role as covering and interceded on Eve's behalf before God rather than partaking and becoming a part of the sin with her. The commandment was given to him as the head over his wife, and just as the Second Adam, Jesus Christ, stood in the gap for us and took upon Himself the penalty of our sin, I fully believe that Adam could have done the same, perhaps lessening the effects of their disobedience. Of course this we won't know until we see him in glory.

A father should never leave his family unprotected, uncovered, and open to the attack of the enemy. This is exactly what Adam did with Eve, and then with his sons, Cain and Abel. Why was Cain able to slay his brother Abel? Where was the teaching, training, and love that God had so obviously shown to him? Adam and Eve still had the hook-up with God; they were not abandoned. Their fellowship with God was perhaps more distant than up close and personal, but God was still there for them. Why didn't Adam notice in Cain the character trait of envy and evil? As their father, he should have seen it, and sought God about it.

What Adam shows us is not only our need to seek God for everything about our lives, but also our need for His complete covering and provision. We have not the knowledge, or understanding, to effectively raise and train a child without our LORD, it just can't be done. Children, even when they are the only two children on the earth, are totally different from one another, and sometimes those differences are not seen with the naked eye, only the discerning eye of the Holy Spirit.

Adam had only Cain and Able, and he failed because he obviously neglected to go to the only possible source available to him, the only possible source available to us all, God the Father!

Dads, when it comes to your children and Satan, you're in a no-holds-barred wrestling match! Satan won't care what he uses to draw your children from you, and neither should you care what it takes for you to keep them protected and secured in your love, and in Christ! Never neglect to use the power and authority you have in our LORD, to not only stop but also to prevent any attack of Satan against your home, against your children! Know this, he'll always hit below the belt, so you must go for the throat! Go for the jugular!

I think Adam thought that his only problems would be finding food for everybody to eat, and this seems to be the supreme concern even today: putting food on the table. Only, just as it was with Adam, it can't be your only concern; if you're to be the provider God needs you to be for your children, you must consider the office of fatherhood as a multi-faceted, task-oriented position, smile!

Providing requires forethought. You must determine exactly what needs to be done by you for your children every day. You seek the LORD early, and constantly on their behalf, never leaving one corner of your home uncovered and vulnerable to the attack of Satan.

When your wife discovers that you have a child coming, all the prayer, financial provision, and the proper shelter should be in place. Ask God, from the beginning of day one, for His divine will and guidance regarding your child. Lay your hands upon your child and upon your wife daily, asking for God's favor and blessings of health and protection upon them. You stand spiritual guard over them, according to the Word of God, using God's Word to speak into their life those things that you desire of God for them, and that God may desire of you on their behalf.

Be alert, and be not deceived by the many ways the enemy may attempt to steal the joy and blessings God has for you and your family. Your responsibility as a father is deeper than deep, and wider than wide, and you have nothing to meet its challenge but the Holy Spirit as your guide and tutor. I know this sounds so simple, and maybe to some, even elementary, but whenever we are presumptuous in regards to anything God has given us to do, we've already made the first step towards failure.

As a father you not only need forethought, you'll also need foresight! Again, not just looking ahead, but seeing ahead! Our heavenly Father refers to Himself as a high tower which enables Him to see afar off concerning His children. It's a matter of positioning, a matter of visual perception! The Word of God tells us in Psalm 18:2, "The LORD is my rock, and my fortress, and my deliver; my God, my strength, in whom I will trust; my buckler, and the horn of my salvation and my *high tower*." Psalm 61:3 says, "For thou hast been a shelter for me, and a strong *tower* from the enemy." Also Psalm 144:2 says, "My goodness, and my fortress; my high tower and my deliver; my shield, and He in whom I trust; who subdueth my people under me."

So if the ability to see ahead is this important, whose vision and positioning do you want when it comes to your children, yours or the LORD's? What would you rather have working for you, hindsight, foresight, instinct, or insight? You can always depend on God's sight! The LORD must always go out before you, and your family; His eyes are the only eyes that will never fail. With God as your high tower Satan cannot surprise you or your family. Trust in what HE sees, when it comes to your children, not…in what you think!

The only wall that separates all of us from the will of God…is built on our own *pride*! Pride kills. It destroys everything in its path. Pride is a pharisaical sin, characterized by a superior attitude. Pride always tells you, "I can do it, I don't need any help!" Pride says, "No thanks, I'm just fine!" Pride says to a broken leg, "Be still; you're not in pain!" Pride never needs help and is always more than capable of doing it alone! Well, as a father you're not able to do it alone, and God knows it. To be the best father you can be, you must be willing to plan ahead, prepare ahead, see ahead, and trust "The Head."

Sometimes fathers really can't help themselves, and will show favoritism when it comes to their children. This tendency is probably more common in fathers than mothers, so it's something that as a father, you must really guard against. One son may be more athletic than the other, or you treat your daughter like the son you've always wanted. There may be various reasons why distinctions may be made between your children, but no reason is good enough, and you can cause untold emotional and spiritual injury to your child by doing so.

To avoid having to deal with the fallout from this type of problem, don't allow Satan to keep your thoughts on the gifts or talents of just one of your children; you must become concerned and equally motivated to bring out the best in all of them, or you just might end up losing someone as a result.

There is probably no better illustration of this than the one found in Genesis 37:3-4."Now Israel loved Joseph more than all his children, because he was the son of his old age: and he made him a coat of many colors. (4) And when his brethren saw that their father loved him more than all his brethren, they hated him, and could not speak peaceably unto him."

It's obvious that Jacob couldn't hide his feelings from the family, and that more than likely he'd been told about the situation from his sons, because they were all grown men. However, when Jacob gave Joseph the garment or coat of many colors, his partiality towards Joseph was then really shouted from the rooftop, for all the world to hear: "He's number one; he's number one!"

It was one thing for Jacob to show his obvious partiality towards Joseph every day, his other sons could always rationalize that maybe it was just their imagination; after all, their father was such a holy man of God, also a part of such a wonderful covenant, they had to be mistaken. However, when Jacob gave Joseph the coat of many colors, he was not only telling his sons, "Joseph is my favorite," but the entire world at that time would have known it; this brought such a severe hatred between all of them that they wanted to kill their brother Joseph!

Jacob was out of order in more ways than one. First, he placed the youngest above the eldest. In ancient Israel the real and personal property of a father normally was divided among his sons. A larger portion usually went to the eldest son, who would assume the care and responsibility of the mother and unmarried sisters, as head of the family.

Secondly, the birthright of the firstborn son could only be denied because of a serious offense against the father, which of course, initially, wasn't true. Lastly, to the children of Israel, the term *inheritance* had both a strong spiritual and national associations extending far beyond the family estate. The land of Canaan was regarded as an inheritance from the LORD because of God's covenant with Abraham and his descendants. I'm certain Jacob's sons saw not only their pride being dumped on, but their portions being drastically reduced!

Our heavenly Father has made no distinctions between His children, and as our perfect example, we must do likewise. We're told in Acts 10:34-35, "Then Peter opened his mouth, and said, of a truth I perceive that God is no respecter of persons: (35) But in every nation he that feareth Him, and worketh righteousness, is accepted with Him." Likewise the biblical concept of a spiritual inheritance for believers is primarily of Jewish origin.

Because we are joint heirs with Christ, our inheritance was immediate upon receiving Him as our LORD and Savior. Our spiritual inheritance is equal among us. It doesn't matter if we were saved fifty years ago, or the next minute from now. It doesn't even matter if we are two years old, or one hundred and two, our portions are equal. What is that portion? It's found in

1 Corinthians 2:9. "But as it is written, eye hath not seen, nor ear heard, neither have entered into the heart of man, the things which God hath prepared for them that love Him."

Also, in John 14:1-3, "Let not your heart be troubled: ye believe in God, believe also in me, (2) In my Father's house are many mansions: if it were not so, I would have told you. I go to prepare a place for you. (3) And if I go and prepare a place for you, I will come again, and receive you unto myself; that where I am, there ye may be also."

We are more than provided for and can be confident that in Him there is no respecter of persons. Having favorites of any type will cause pain and grief, and can create anger and bitterness, and this we definitely don't want in our homes and families. It's a weapon in the hand of Satan that's just too powerful; don't give it to him, and never allow this ugly thing to be used to destroy your children.

A father must also be willing to accept the weaknesses of his children as well as their strengths. Remember, God's love for us is not based on our perfections. Romans 5: 8 says, "But God commendeth His love toward us, in that, while we were yet sinners, Christ died for us." God's love for us is based only on Himself, it has nothing to do with us, or our ability to be worthy of such love. God's love is always sufficient, and it stands alone. It doesn't need our support, only our willingness to partake of this great love that's ours for the taking!

That's your responsibility as a father, that the love you have for your children must never be based upon their performance as your child, only on the fact that you're their father. Nothing else matters.

In Luke, the 15th chapter, we have several examples where the love God has for His children is depicted. The first being that of the lost sheep, where the shepherd leaves the ninety and nine to restore the one sheep that left the flock. Then we have parable of the lost coin that was found through great effort. Lastly, the parable of the lost son, most commonly referred to as the story of the Prodigal Son.

The father's love for his youngest son is tested and stretched seemingly beyond measure and yet, there seems to be more than enough to meet his son's need for forgiveness and patience. We are left with no doubt about the love of the father for his son—really for both his sons. But we also see in this story the unforgiving attitude of the older brother, who was obviously under the impression that his father's love could be earned!

The young son is given the freedom he demands by his father, but the choices he makes lead to personal disaster as he spends and spends, living as if there was no tomorrow. When all his earthly fortune is wasted, he's forced to live beneath the privilege of his birth, rather than as the heir and son of a wealthy man. Finally this son comes to his senses. He returns to his father ready to confess his sin and hoping to be accepted as a servant.

The true beauty of this story is the portion that we read at verse 20 of Luke the 15th chapter, "And he arose, and came to his father. But when he was yet a great way off, his father saw him, and had compassion, and ran, and fell on his neck and kissed him."

First of all, the father had to have been waiting and watching for his younger son for months. I can imagine him telling the servants, "Please keep an eye out for my son; I expect his return any day now." Can't you see him pacing back and forth on the road, straining to see a far off, thinking that every figure coming his direction was his son, that it would finally be his son! Yet another day would pass, and still no word or sight of him, but he kept on watching, praying, and believing that any day now, he'll come!

Can't you see and feel the love and compassion this father has for his son? The Word of God tells us, "But when he was yet a great way off...!" This father probably saw him coming a mile up the road, and started running towards him! His love didn't allow for the dignity of waiting until a servant brought him before him, nor the dignity he obviously dropped when he lifted his robes to his knees so that he could run as fast as possible without his clothing impeding his progress. In fact, if a servant was out there, this father, most likely passed him in a cloud of dust! (Smile) Isn't it just wonderful? Such love, such priceless love!

Just like the Prodigal Son, we also rejected God, our heavenly Father. We've wandered in far countries, spent the good gifts He has given us in selfish and often sinful pursuits. When we finally do come running back home, the Father comes to greet us. Stilling our confession, He assures us of His changeless love. And He prepares abundant life for us: the fatted calf of restoration!

That's a father's love for his children. The question is not *if* they'll mess up...it's *when* they mess up! It's not *if* they'll disappoint you...it's *when* they disappoint you! It's not even *will it be painful*? It's *how long will the pain last?* (Smile)

Dad, you just be there to pick up the pieces. Allow the love of Christ, the love and compassion He's extended to you again and again and again, to shine through to your child. There's something so special about the love and compassion a father shows towards his children. We sort of expect a mother to love us, dote on us, and, well, spoil us; but a father is the stern figurehead of authority; he's there to pay the bills, pat you on the shoulder, and make good the old familiar threat of, "Wait until your father gets home, young man!" (Smile)

Don't take the attitude of the oldest son, who represents the pharisee, standing by, waiting and expecting the worse. The oldest son's attitude of stubborn, open hostility and resentment was sad. He was angry and criticized his father, and in his anger the older son refused the love and compassion the father offered him, even though the father entreated him to attend the feast.

Allow your heart to be full of compassion, not hardened and resentful because of all you expected from your child. The cost and sorrow it may have caused the family, especially the mother, try to let it go; it's so superficial. Trust your spirit; believe me, when our children fail, when they disappoint us, they've already beaten themselves with many stripes; they really don't need any more, at least not right away. If something needs to be said to them our LORD will tell you how and when it should be done. For now just enjoy their return; give a party of celebration!

It's so exciting when we've experienced a father's sincere love, when we're accepted just as we are, free from the pressure of trying to be anything more than we're capable of ever being. All that we are, or all that we'll ever be depends on our heavenly Father. Try not to be too anxious over the future of your children; God has them, and He will finish the work and the faith He has established for them. Your only task is to be there for them, with them, and behind them, pushing a little when necessary. (Smile)

Whose character do you want to manifest as a father? Our heavenly Father's, whose love overcomes and makes the dead to live again, who brings hope out of hopelessness, and joy out of our sadness, who takes the dryness and emptiness of failure, and causes our lives to bloom and flourish with the hope of a brand new tomorrow. Or the character of a father whose demeanor reflects the I-could-care-less attitude about everything?

Of course not; you want to exemplify Christ in all that you do, so you must find out all about Him; you must really get to know who He is. The more you know about Him, the more like Him you'll become; after all, like father, like son; right? Right!

Sometimes you may not have younger children. Your children are all grown, out of the house (thank you LORD), and they are raising your grandchildren! Well, Pops, you're still needed! You can't sit down yet! (Smile)

You've actually graduated in responsibility, because now, you're not just a father, you're a mentor! The office of counselor, teacher, and spiritual advisor, actually it's still much like a father, only I want to deal with another dimension of a father.

Let's reflect a little about Paul and his spiritual son, Timothy! Paul loved Timothy, many years his junior. Paul's instruction to Timothy was always encouraging him to be everything he could be for the gospel, constantly reminding him of his Godly and spiritual heritage. 1 Timothy 1:5-6 says, "When I call to remembrance the unfeigned faith that is in thee, which dwelt first in thy grandmother Lois, and thy mother Eunice; and I am persuaded that in thee also. (6) Wherefore I put thee in remembrance that thou stir up the gift of God, which is in thee by the putting on of my hands."

Paul was comforting Timothy and encouraging him, because of the severe challenges he was facing. Timothy was much more than one of Paul's converts; he was the true reflection of spiritual commitment and ministry that we want for all our children. Strength and faith like his cannot be accomplished without tenacity, spiritual integrity, and a superior example to follow.

Our children will have many challenges to face, exactly like Timothy. Opinions and theories, about their salvation that will be extremely difficult at times. They'll need to know they can depend upon you not just to be their spiritual example: you must also be their living example. Timothy could trust the instruction and example of Paul without reservation.

A father needs to be able to reassure his children that what they have in Christ is real. It's great hearing it from the pastor every Sunday, or from the elders as they pray, or from the deacons as they peer over their glasses at them whenever they're out of order. (Smile) But it's never as good, or as effective as it is coming from you as their father.

Times are not only changing, they're changing over night! Our children start every day with a new challenge from the enemy, and different feelings of concern within themselves. It's never easy to know what's right for them at any given time; you can only do exactly what you're asking of them; take one day at a time. As you assure them of your love, and the love that our LORD has for them, it will help them to show more of God's light and His inspiration and influence in their lives, to their peers. It will also encourage them to stand, and when they've done all they can, they must still stand.

It's such a blessing when our children are cradled in the things of God, when from their father's knee, so to speak, the Word of God is read to them and explained to them every day of their lives! Their love for God's Word will only come as they are taught to depend upon it for everything they need in life. The Bible cannot just be a book of stories, even true stories. It must be meat unto them, that will help them to grow and spread their ministry among their friends with a confidence and clarity that only the Holy Spirit can give. They are never, never, too young to hunger after the Word of God!

Paul knew the gifts of his spiritual son; he knew of his call to evangelism. That's why he was always Paul's companion when Paul was in town. Timothy worked right along with Paul in the ministry, and served in ministry faithfully. Never send someone else to do your job! Keep your children involved and in sight as much as possible when you're serving and worshiping the LORD.

Many churches today have what they call youth pastors, and children's church, and other ministries in the local body. Be certain to follow up with what they are learning, and also communicate with their teachers at church whenever possible. Don't depend on them to always care about what happens to your child. They won't, and they don't; your children are your responsibility and your eternal investment. You stay on track with your monies and other investments. Why would you do less when it comes to your children? Hold them spiritually close. When our LORD needs something to take place in their lives, He should not have to go through several people to get a spiritual update on your child. He ought to be able to pull you aside, and find out everything He needs to know about them.

Sometimes fathers rely on the mother, or grandmother, or other family member to take their children to church, or rely on other youth ministries. It should be you! There will be times when work or some other responsibility will prevent this, so any other time you can be there, be there!

You've heard the old saying, "What goes around comes around!" Well, let it be the Word of God, living in you and growing within your children. Our LORD tells us in John 15:1-2, "I am the true vine, and my Father is the husbandman. (2) Every branch in me that beareth not fruit He taketh away: and every branch that beareth fruit, He purgeth it, that it may bring forth more fruit." In other words, the apple doesn't fall too far from the tree! The closer you get to the LORD, and the happier you are in Him, the more like Him you'll look. Also, the closer your children get to you, the more they enjoy being in your presence, you will see the mirror image of your life in your child! It's so beautiful, so perfect, so like God!

You're the first pastoral counselor your child will have in his life. Take the office seriously, enjoying the opportunity to mentor your children, in God's Word and for His glory, you'll feel so blessed when you see the fruits of your labor.

From his youth to the time Timothy was martyred, he lived, preached, and taught the gospel of Christ. He was indispensable to Paul, and an asset to the church. Timothy loved his mentor, and it was his mentor that taught him all he knew, not only about the gospel, also about himself, his life, and how to stand in the midst of severe testing and trials. He learned well, and the body of Christ is all the better because he lived.

All of our lives have purpose, and it's up to us as parents, especially you fathers, to live a life in front of your children that will glorify Christ. When Paul reminded Timothy of the call on his life that came from the laying on of hands it changed Timothy's life!

Fathers, bless your children by the laying on of your hands. Moses was told by the LORD in Numbers 6:22-27, "And the LORD spoke unto Moses, saying, (23) Speak unto Aaron and unto his sons, saying, in this way ye shall bless the children of Israel, saying unto them, (24) The LORD bless thee, and keep thee; (25) the LORD make his face shine upon thee, and be gracious unto thee; (26) the LORD lift up his countenance upon thee, and give thee peace. (27) And they shall put my name upon the children of Israel; and I will bless them."

This is such a powerful thing, the LORD wanting so much to bless His children, that He instructs them word for word on how to be blessed by Him! This blessing, I speak over my children every night of their lives, whether they are home or not, I kneel at the foot of their beds, and proclaim God's blessings upon them, and I don't have little ones. My children are grown; my daughter is even married, yet I turn in the direction of her home and kneel before my God, and bless her according to this scripture, and it works; they've always been blessed, kept, and covered by the LORD! Thank you, dear Father!

Understand, from God's point of view, He is the blesser, the one who gives the capacity for living a full, rich life. The Aaronic Benediction epitomizes God's promise of blessing to His people, to His children. We are also His children, and whatever He promised to do for Israel is available to us if in faith we reach out and claim it.

If you want the best for your children, then you must get the best from the best! Our LORD is waiting for you to claim the blessings He has in store for all of us!

Every child wants and needs the favor of his father. Whether it's his earthly father or their heavenly Father, you want your life blessed, only you can't come to God for blessings unless you understand that He really wants to bless you! God wants to bless His people, only we often don't feel worthy of asking, or we simply think that if we have shelter, clothing, and are not hungry, then it's greedy to ask for more.

The abundant life Jesus died for is so much more than food, shelter, or raiment. It's not just health and happiness either. The more we can handle of God's goodness, the more He desires to pour out upon us, especially if we can handle it! He wants to pour into your children authority, spiritual anointing, power, discernment, and all the fruits of the spirit, and when this is accomplished, He'll bless them with the desires of their hearts.

You can teach them to pray for themselves, and to bless themselves also. In 1 Chronicles 4: 9-10, "And Jabez was more honorable than his brethren; and his mother called his name Jabez, saying because I bore him with sorrow. (10) And Jabez called on the God of Israel, saying, Oh, that thou wouldest bless me indeed, and enlarge my border, and that thine hand might be with me, and that thou wouldest keep me from evil, that it may not grieve me! And God granted him that which he requested."

The name Jabez meant *pain*, and he didn't want pain following him the rest of his life; he wanted God's best, God's blessings, and he got them.

Jabez wanted the LORD to not just bless him, but to bless him indeed! He wanted more territory for himself, and for the LORD! He wanted the hand of God on his life, every day of his life, so that Satan wouldn't, and evil couldn't rule in his life to dishonor him or his God! And God gave him exactly what he asked for!

Fathers, teach your children to want and expect the very best from God! If they see in you a willingness to settle for less, or that you have little or no desire to grow in Christ and in ministry, they will also think the same way. Show them that in Christ, there's always more, and that more of Him is what you want, and they will desire the same!

See God as Moses saw God, "The LORD, the LORD God, merciful and gracious, longsuffering, and abounding in goodness and truth." (Exodus 34:6) Your children will see God through the eyes of your faith until it becomes their faith!

Fathers, it's your responsibility to nurture your children in a way that brings respect rather than provocation, as recorded in Ephesians 6:4, "And ye fathers, provoke not your children to wrath: but bring them up in the nurture and admonition of the LORD."

Satan is actively struggling against the body of Christ, and the families of God: the Christian home. All his energies today seem to be in dismantling the entire family structure! What the Word of God is telling fathers in the above scripture is warning fathers to not so provoke your children, driving them away from the LORD, the home, and all the principles you're striving to instill in them, thereby putting into the hands of Satan your own children, to become the weapon he uses to destroy your home!

The enemy will cripple your home with confusion, heartache and rebellion, so much so that dissension in your family is inevitable, only he won't stop there; he'll stop at nothing until he has totally corrupted and demoralized your entire family, shattering all the hopes, plans and prayers you've invested in their lives.

When we're instructed in Ephesians 6:11, "Put on the whole armor of God, that ye may be able to stand against the wiles of the devil," Paul is reflecting on the armor used by the Roman soldiers of his day, but if we take that armor apart, viewing it with the perspective that would better represent home and family, your divine resources are made even clearer for you.

The *belt of truth*: put off falsehood. Speak truthfully and honestly to your children. Your openness and honestly will gird your relationship together, where misunderstandings and hidden motives will only divide.

The *breastplate of righteousness*: there cannot be even a hint of immorality, or any other kind of impurity, or greed of selfishness, seen in you. It makes you a hypocrite before your children and your entire family. Righteous living is essential, guarding the very heart and core of your family.

Feet fitted with the gospel of peace: if the gospel is effective in your life, and is represented in everything you do, there will be a spirit of peace, that rests in your home, peace that binds and holds you together, in a way that will not only amaze you but will also amaze Satan. When your home is full of peace, unity is maintained by the Holy Spirit, and every opportunity for confusion is destroyed before it can even get started!

The *shield of faith*: always maintain a confident hope before your children, not in yourself but in the reality and power of God. Their trust in this confidence will extinguish all doubt. Teach your children that we are inadequate within ourselves but that we serve a God, who is able to do immeasurably more than all we can ask or think!

The *helmet of salvation*: because of our salvation in Christ, we have a new life and a new identity. Don't allow your children to take for granted the cost and the privilege of their salvation. Satan cannot steal or distort what's bound tightly within their hearts; he simply cannot take what they're not willing to give up! If their hearts and minds have grasped fully the meaning of the salvation we enjoy in Christ, the enemy will never be able to steal their hearts away!

The *sword of the spirit*: teach your children how to fight! The sword of the spirit is the Word of God. They cannot do battle in the spiritual realm with a carnal weapon; you and I both know this. Make very certain that they know it, too! All of their battles will take place on their knees, and according to the living Word of God, you be a strong example in this warfare. God's Word is a vital tool, and one they should be very comfortable in using, one they should get to know as early as possible by learning as many scripture from memory as possible.

They won't always be able to just pick up their sword, but if it's hidden in their hearts, their mouths will speak readily and without hesitation.

Fathers, your own conduct is the most effective sermon you will ever preach. Live a life that will give consistent and undeniable evidence of the truth of the gospel within you. Model your life after Christ's life, imitating Him, rather than others. Christ is your most perfect example of the love of God in your life. Your children will never be confused on how they should conduct their lives, because what they see in you is validated in the Word of God.

Be quick to praise and give glory to God for His manifold blessings to your family. Allow the Holy Spirit to overflow in your heart with worship and thanksgiving that all will see and take comfort in.

Give yourself to constant and faithful prayer. Let the LORD change your prayer life to *a life of prayer!*

With these attributes and others that the Holy Spirit will be faithful to develop in your life, you will be more than just a father, more than just their provider; you'll be like Christ! What better gift of life can you bestow upon your children? Exactly! Nothing! (Smile)

Chapter XII

WANTED…Everything!

How do we as Christian parents teach our children the integrity of moderation in a world that constantly clamors for excess! Endeavoring to teach them the values our LORD has made known to us such as, modesty, temperance, contentment, etc., is something all good parents tend to be a little frustrated about these days.

Children are enticed to excess by every commercial, by celebrities, movies, entertainers today, not to mention the impact that our media plays in luring our children to look, think, and act beyond their years and their means…correction…our means!

The world screams out to them every day of their lives, *more* is better, and sparkle and shine is best, and of course if the name isn't a brand name, then for certain, it's worthless! After all, it's the name that makes the garment, the shoe, or whatever else they want you to buy.

How many of you remember when you were younger, that if you inherited the family car to drive as our own, you were thrilled? Today when you see young people driving beautiful expensive cars that we've worked so hard to own, or have waited a lifetime to acquire, you wonder, who are their parents? Cars driven by young people today are often considered luxury cars, detailed elaborately with expensive wheels, rims, paint jobs, and other personalized features, not to mention the costly sound systems that would be a healthy down payment on a brand-new car. It's out of control!

There is clothing with designer labels most of us parents cannot read or pronounce, and shoes that range from one hundred fifty dollars, to over two hundred and more. Young girls are getting their hair and nails professionally done as early as twelve or thirteen years of age, and are dressed in sophisticated, adult-type clothing that would make almost anyone blush.

Proms once held in the decorated school gym are now held in exclusive hotels. The family car has been replaced by rented luxury cars and limousines. The lovely but modest party dress and white dinner jacket have been shoved to the background for expensively made dresses and suits, dinner jackets, top hats, canes, and just whatever else the glamorous couple can think to wear. It's just insane!

Our children are frantically pursued by every advertisement and celebrity, every athlete, vocal group, rap star and media gimmick known to man, woman, or child today! Their names and their visual images of success are painted across the marques, screens, and hearts of many children around the world. They force our children to run faster, jump higher, to grow bigger, faster, stronger, by any means necessary, as they stretch and reach for the golden ring of success.

How do we keep our children and their feet firmly planted on earth, when their hearts and thoughts are constantly reaching, if not to be a star, to look like one? Everything they see tells them that to be seen you must be *seen*! And being seen today is an extremely expensive venture.

I know you're as concerned about these issues as I am. We all understand that as Christian parents we have a tremendous responsibility to focus and center our children on the things of Christ, and by doing so, causing them to be centered within His will and purpose for their lives.

The legacy we give our children has as much to do with today as it does with tomorrow. If they are to handle tomorrow's economy, they must learn to do so today. In an atmosphere of greed and excess, our task is a great one, but fear not. Make this the confession of your faith, "I can do all things through Christ, who strengtheneth me." (Philippians 4:13) Also, in James 1:5, "If any of you lack wisdom let him ask of God, who giveth to all men liberally, and upbraideth not, and it shall be given him.")

The prospect of handling all these issues can be at times overwhelming. I know, and I'm also dealing with some of these same issues. Today the word *mother* is more than just a household name, (smile); it's more like job description, a job where the necessary skills may range from the most elementary, entry-level-type task, to the high-level, corporate decision making, that in any other arena would bring about great wealth! (Smile) Only, our decision making doesn't take place in the huge, beautifully furnished conference rooms of these corporate offices; it takes place around our kitchen tables or in the family room of our homes, perhaps even in the car as we take our children to and from school or other activities. They take place on our knees as we seek God for His wisdom and direction, surroundings that are not power fronts but powerful, especially if God is at the helm.

If we didn't have to contend with so many outside influences, life would be so much easier, wouldn't it? But we do; we have to compete with the parents of their peers, with the opinions of even their older brothers or sisters, not to mention the pressures of being drummed out of the "Ultimate Mom and Dad Corps," finding yourselves stripped of every medal and Badge of Courage you fought so desperately to gain! (Smile), not forgetting the possibility of losing those precious stripes that tell of your many years of faithful service above and beyond the call of duty. Smile! Well, easy come…easy go! (Smile)

This is one corps we entered into knowing it wasn't a popularity contest, so whenever you are blessed with a quiet and serene atmosphere, savor the moment. It's usually the quiet before the storm; smile! They're coming with their itemized list of "Just gotta have its," or the invariable question, "Hey, Mom, Dad, guess what Jimmy's parents just bought him?" And, oh yes, don't forget the old, "I'll just die if I can't have so-and-so" routine!

Well, parents, don't forget our mission, training up a child! Every child should know that there's nothing wrong with having nice things, we all appreciate nice things. There's nothing wrong with looking nice, but there is an extreme difference between having nice things, and looking nice, than having to have designer labels on anything they wear from their clothing, shoes, back packs, sun glasses, purses, etc. to everything else they may want to wear; not everything has to have a designer label attached.

There's also quite a difference between impressing others with what you wear, and dressing to impress. There's a difference between wanting to look nice, and trying to look rich! Why is there a need to look like someone of privilege, rather than simply being themselves, and not allowing others to dictate who and what they are, by determining how they should dress or package themselves for someone else's approval?

Parents, no one knows better than we do the cost physically, emotionally, and spiritually on our self-esteem when we want the acceptance of others, at any price when we're willing to sacrifice everything we have to attain it, at the high price of our own self worth and integrity. The pain and sorrow it causes will exact a toll on their hearts that more often than not will be just too costly for them to pay. It can and will affect everything from their schoolwork, health, and peace of mind, not to mention their over-all value system for life.

As Christians we mustn't allow our children to rely on anything but their LORD, for help, strength, favor, grace and the respect of their peers. We find in Mark 10:23-25, "And Jesus looked round about, and saith unto his disciples, with what difficulty shall they that have riches enter into the kingdom of God! (24) And the disciples were astonished at His words. But Jesus answereth again, and saith unto them, children, how hard is it for them that trust in riches to enter into the Kingdom of God. (25) It is easier for a camel to go through the eye of a needle, than for a rich man to enter into the kingdom of God."

It's not the wealth that leads to sin, it's the trusting in it, the dependence upon it, the comfort we allow it to bring to our hearts and lives. The desire for great gains, especially gains not greatly achieved, i.e., by work ethics, goal setting, difficult academic achievement, etc., may be causing a snare or pitfall for them that in later years might be extremely corrupting.

In the above scripture Jesus is pointing out the difficulty of the rich who, in abandoning trust in God, trust in their wealth. If we don't teach our children that wealth is painfully deceitful, we give them the kind of confidence that is utterly false. It makes people feel as if they're in control or that whatever needs to be done, can and will be done…by us. Wealth gives the illusion that all is well, by telling us, and others that all we need is the almighty dollar, that we don't need the Almighty God to deliver, provide, and keep us by His power!

Whatever has the greatest value in their lives, they will rely on and come to depend on. If they've learned from an early age to listen to your wisdom and direction as it is based upon the Word of God, they will continue to depend upon it. If they've been allowed to make their own choices and decisions on a regular basis, with little or no adult input, then they will depend upon that. If you have allowed their peers to shape and mold their thinking and choices in life, and you've done little to change this process, they will also depend upon their peers. On the other hand, if all of these factors are a source of input for them, they will learn to seek advice from many sources, weigh the value of each, and make their own choices based on sound judgment and advice, according to the Word of God. This last scenario is a good one when they reach the age of choice and independent thought, but they should never forget, there can be no wise decisions made by them, or by us for that matter, that aren't based upon God's Word.

We must never allow the choices and decisions we make for our children to dip below God's ideal. Many parents wonder where the harm is in allowing our children to be indulged in their every whim. It looks so cute to see a tiny infant in Nikes or little Mike Jordan tee shirts and Lakers Basketball outfits.

Some little babies are dedicated in white Christian Dior from the tops of their little heads to the soles of their feet. They're pushed around in Peg-Perego Strollers costing an unbelievable three hundred dollars or more! My thought about this one is "Walk, my child, walk!" (Smile) It's cute and funny when they're tiny, but as they get older, and the more fabric and leather is required to make each garment, the dollar bills mount up, and then it's not so cute anymore. Only, by then we've created a monster, a monster who demands to be fed! Just think; it all started with us as their parents.

Why were we dressing them this way and buying these expensive pieces of furniture and necessities? Was it necessary to purchase items based on what it looked like, and how many neat features it had, rather than for the safety and comfort that's so easy to pay for? When you're purchasing items for your children that will be used by many and maybe even passed on to others, this is a good thing, you'll want something that will last. However, if you have only one child, and are not planning others, why spend needlessly?

Friends, what we're really talking about here for ourselves and our children, is stewardship. That's the bottom line. Stewardship is the subject matter of this chapter and it's a crucial dynamic to the Christian lifestyle. It can never be cultivated too early in their lives; in fact, the sooner they master this quality, the better: the richer and fuller their lives for Christ will be.

What is a steward? By definition it means simply a person who manages another's property, finances, or other affairs. Now we'll look even closer at this definition and how it reflects on us as parents. According to the Word of God in 1 Corinthians 4:1-2, "Let a man so account of us, as of the ministers of Christ, and stewards of the mysteries of God. (2) Moreover, it is required in stewards, that a man be found faithful." Also, it says in 1 Peter 4:10, "As every man hath received the gift, even so minister the same one to another, as good stewards, of the manifold grace of God."

We know that our children are gifts from God. We know also they are loaned to us by God for a season. Our responsibility is to be good stewards over God's property and His investment with us, and that the management of His children covers everything from their spiritual needs to their physical, emotional, and educational needs. We are to mold and shape their moral and ethical character as well as teach them how to not only survive in today's society, but to become productive contributors to it, and to do so without compromising their Christian values. This is indeed no easy task. But you're a parent; you must be a master of juggling by now! (Smile)

The believer's stewardship incorporates accountability for the way in which we manage all of life's affairs, as given to us in Matthew 25:14-30, the parable of the talents. Our LORD gives the parable about the master leaving, making his servants responsible for his possessions. While he is away, the servants are to use the gifts and talents they have been given for benefit of their master. One day the master will return, and then there will be an accounting.

God expects us to nurture our children in such a way that they will not only benefit Him, but will benefit the gospel of Christ and the body of Christ. Within each child whom God blesses us to raise for His purpose, will be strengths that should be increased, and weaknesses that should be controlled, if not completely corrected.

As I've stated earlier, when God comes for our children, or when they reach the age of accountability and ministry, He's expecting an increase on His investment. He does not want to find exactly what He left us with. And, who would? Why would anyone want a fifteen- or sixteen-year-old toddler? What could be more bizarre that seeing a twenty-year-old, or even thirty-year-old, sucking her thumb while sitting in a playpen! Sounds crazy? Well, when we neglect to train and nurture our children spiritually, and allow them to remain infantile in their spiritual behavior while they mature and develop as an adult in every other aspect of their lives, we're asking God to use something that must really look more like a freak to Him, than anything else!

Take a look at Matthew 25: 26-27. "His lord answered and said unto him, thou wicked and slothful servant, thou knewest that I reap where I sowed not, and gather where I have not spread? (27) thou oughtest, therefore, to have put my money to the exchangers, and then at my coming, I should have received mine own with interest."

Our LORD is expecting much more than what He gave us; after all, why shouldn't He? He's given us a seed. That seed became life, and that life must become all that it can be for the cause of Christ!

This will never happen if we don't have a clear perspective on what God expects from us in every detail of our care for our children. We cannot think that anything that involves them will take place in their lives automatically simply because they belong to Him! Romans 10:14 says, "How, then, shall they call on Him of whom they have not believed? And how shall they believe in Him of whom they have not heard? And how shall they hear without a preacher?" The preacher in this instance is you! They cannot understand and know the will of God for their lives, nor the purpose that God has for their lives without your instruction. Teaching them the principles of stewardship is as important as your understanding the weight and value of your stewardship in regards to them. Does that make sense? I hope so, (smile).

Nothing is more valuable than achievement through hard work, goal setting, and proper respect of these ethics. With that in mind, imagine your child at age seven or eight years old. You and your husband have decided to start teaching him the value of life, and of responsibility. You do some background on family pets and have decided upon a puppy for the family. Everyone is excited and thrilled at the new family member. You sit your child down and begin to tell him as much as you can, and as much as he can adsorb about their new friend.

After you've given him some detail about the type of puppy he is, you allow your child to name him. He thinks for a bit, and after some deep thought decides to name his puppy, "Puppy!" Well, you and your wife sort of look at each other, smile a little, and proceed to tell him how important a name should be. You tell him that a name tells everybody what you want everyone to know about your pet every time they see him, that he'll not always be little, that someday he'll be big and strong and able to protect and take care of him. He'll play all day with him and see to it that no one will do him harm, and that he'll keep him safe. Then you ask him again, do you still want to call him "Puppy?" After a little more thought, he decides to name his new pet, "Friend." Well, with that in mind, and all that you understand the word to mean, you smile and tell your child what a great name that is!

What you've accomplished here is so crucial; you've given your child some background on the pet you've chosen and told him as much as he is capable of understanding; you've even explained the importance of a proper name for anything. You don't just name something because of what it may look like, or because it sounds good, or because it's your grandmother's name; the name should have meaning and purpose to you and everyone around you. A name will always mold and shape the personality, character, ,and even the destiny of your child, so it's great to start with the first thing that they will have to assume care and responsibility for.

After your child has named his new "friend," you tell him of the chores he will assume in his care, to make certain that his friend will grow up healthy and strong. You tell him of the importance of feeding him every day, and giving him fresh water, that his friend will need someone to play with him to help keep him well and strong, and that as he becomes older and bigger, Friend will require more food, water and exercise. You tell him that he must be certain that he is clean, and that he doesn't ever go for a walk without his leash, and that he doesn't jump and play rough with others.

Much of what you're explaining will be done initially by you, but allow your child to take part in what's being done for Friend whenever possible, and never do anything for Friend without his at least watching you do it. This will teach him early how much work and care goes into taking care of someone you love, that it's not always easy, and that you don't always feel like it, and that even at times, Friend may make you tired or even unhappy, but to never forget, he will always be his Friend.

Naturally, the older your child becomes, and the more efficient he becomes with his chores, your part in the pet's care must and will lessen. When your child gets to the place where he's also a lot older, release all responsibility and care of Friend to him, and you'll only be there for health or care issues he cannot attend to alone.

As your child gets older, lawn cutting, paper routes, and baby sitting can and should be implemented to increase their understanding and knowledge about responsibility, and how important it is to share in the maintenance and care of the things they want and enjoy.

One of the very first things they should do whenever they begin to earn money towards their own hobbies, fun, and extras, is to help them open their own savings account. It makes them feel so grown up to have a money account of their own, and to watch it grow and multiply before their very eyes. As they begin to earn their own extra money, please be sure to explain to them the gift and value of tithing.

Tithing is a discipline that many Christian adults still have trouble with, and find it almost or at least for some, an insult to have their pastor or minister tell them again and again the importance of such a holy ordinance. They want to control what they earn and how they'll use it, and don't want the help of any other man dictating to them what they are responsible to do. I'm also certain that our LORD doesn't want anything from them that they are not willing to surrender to Him.

The Bible gives us clear guidelines for the wise and careful use of the many gifts God has bestowed upon us. Tithing, giving ten percent of our income, is the physical manifestation of Christian stewardship. Tithing is important because it is the recognition of God as the sole possessor of heaven and earth. Tell your children that according to the Word of God found in Deuteronomy 8:18-19, "But thou shalt remember the LORD thy God; for it is He who giveth thee power to get wealth, that He may establish His covenant which He swore unto thy fathers, as it is this day. (19) And it shall be, if thou do at all forget the LORD thy God, and walk after other gods, and serve them, and worship them, I testify against you this day that ye shall surely perish."

Explain to them that the health they possess, only God can give. That the favor to get the job was also given by Him. That the ability they have to work, to remember the task of their job, and to even get better and faster and more efficient, comes from God! Tell them that our LORD asks only one dime from every dollar they may earn, that our LORD will take that one dime and place it in a heavenly bank account where the interest and investment rates are greater than any bank or investment company on this earth, that our LORD will take the ninety cents that is left, and bless it so much that it, too, will grow and grow, and stretch to buy more than they thought possible, through sales, discounts, special bargains, and that God will allow for people to give to them things they never thought possible! He will cause people to bless them, even when they're not praying for or expecting a blessing!

Encourage them to trust their God to always do and know what's best for them. If they don't trust Him, then they are trusting in their own ability to accomplish what they want, and that they are not big enough or smart enough, to know what's best. They cannot see far enough, or even make enough, to take care of themselves without God's help and His blessings upon them.

Help them to understand that reaching for things is like worshiping and serving other gods, and that this not only displeases God, it causes Him great pain and sorrow. He wants to be the most important thing in their lives, because they're the most. 1 John 1:9 says, "If we confess our sins, He is faithful and just to forgive us our sins, and to cleanse us from all unrighteousness. (10) If we say that we have not sinned, we make Him a liar, and His Word is not in us.") important thing in His life!

The older your children get, the more responsibility they can handle, the more responsibility they should handle. Here is where they begin to start paying for those things they think they need so badly! Once they start really looking at the value of their dollar and understand how difficult it is to earn it, and as they watch their savings account either grow or diminish due to reckless spending, when they understand the importance of giving to God and allowing Him to take what's left of their finances and multiply them so that they can be blessed, they will sit and think a long, long, long time before they get foolish about their money. Your money is one thing, but theirs, well that's something else all together! (Smile)

You'll find them waiting and watching for sales and values just as you do.

They'll plan for larger, more expensive items, just as you do. Their friends will have to wait, or plan events around pay periods, just as you do. Lastly, they will see more, do more, and enjoy more, just as you do!

Our attitudes for service and being a servant to one another, are also a very important part in the lesson of stewardship. Our children must realize that whatever God has placed in our hands, belongs first to Him, without exception. From the crown of our head to the soles of our feet, we belong to Him. What He blesses us with, and gives us the ability to earn, belongs to Him. But it's these gifts, talents, blessings, and goods He will also take, use, and multiply for our good and His glory.

Acts 4:32-35 says, "And the multitude of those that believed were of one heart and of one soul; neither said any of them that any of the things which he possessed was his own; but they had all things common. (33) And with great power gave the apostles witness of the resurrection of the LORD Jesus; and great grace was upon them all. (34) Neither was there any among them that lacked; for as many as were possessors of lands or houses sold them, and brought the prices of the things that were sold. (35) And laid them down at the apostles' feet; and distribution was made unto every man according as he had need."

I love two lines in this scripture, "they had all things common," and "neither said any of them, that any of the things, which he possessed, was his own"! If we could help our children to grasp these two very simple principles, that we should have nothing that we're not willing to share, because nothing really belongs to us, what a blessing to us and the body of Christ they would be, and what glory God would gain from their lives!

Here we don't see only the principle of tithing, but a people and church willing to give a hundred percent of their lifetime accumulation of wealth, while too many today hesitate even to give ten percent of their weekly income.

One other thing we must teach our children as early as possible is that even their bodies and the health they possess, belong to God. They must be good stewards over their bodies, and not allow friends, peers, or society's *dos* and *don'ts* to force them into living in a way that does not please God. They are not to indulge their bodies in sin, sinful acts or deeds. They must not pour into their bodies foul and unclean substances that will impede their physical health and strength. They must take excellent care of their bodies while they are young, so that when they are older their bodies will take care of them!

Paul told young Timothy in 2 Timothy 2:22, "Flee also youthful lusts, but follow righteousness, faith, love, peace, with them that call on the LORD out of a pure heart." Also in 1 Timothy 4: 12 says, "Let no man despise thy youth, but be thou an example of the believers, in word, in conduct, in love, in spirit, in faith, in purity." Paul was instructing his spiritual son that as a young man, he should live the life of a Christian in such an exemplary manner that he did not bring reproach upon the church. Earlier in the above scripture, Paul admonished Timothy to live his life in such a way as not to be despised as a Christian youth, but rather be an example of purity.

As others, young and old alike, watch the life of your children, they will not only marvel at the hand of God that rests upon their lives because of your obedience, continuing in His will for their lives, but they too will benefit from what they see, and will seek to do and to instruct their children likewise.

As Christians, your sons or daughters must be made to understand that his or her body belongs to God, and therefore, he or she has no right to do anything with it that is not approved by God.

Paul tells Timothy to flee; run away from fornication, to run from youthful lusts, for the body is not for sexual immorality, but for the LORD, and the LORD for the body. This is a commandment of God as we're told in Deuteronomy 6: 4-5, "Hear, O Israel: The LORD our God is one LORD; (5) and thou shalt love the LORD thy God with all thine heart, and with all thy soul, and with all they might."

Going a little further down in this same chapter, Deuteronomy 6:13-14 says, "Thou shalt fear the LORD thy God, and serve Him, and shalt swear by His name. (14) Ye shall not go after other gods, of the gods of the people who are round about you."

The world has established a kingdom of gods, deities, thrones and idols that Satan would demand that our children bow down to and worship every day of their lives. The gods of this world are athletes and celebrities, their kingdoms are stadiums, and the theaters, and the sound studios. The world's idols are cars, clothes, jewelry. Celebraties, labels, all the flash and show. The currency is not only the dollar bill, but the bodies and health of our children, and because the years fly by so quickly they end up spending into their future health and strength!

Satan is bidding high for our children, and we must therefore stand guard over their lives as good stewards, teaching and training them in the things of God at every possible opportunity. The lives of our children are not ours to give or loan to anyone but God. And when we fail to do all that we can do to train them up in the way they should go, we are allowing Satan to come in and steal from God what we were charged to keep in our care and instruction.

Lastly, Paul admonishes the church in 1 Corinthians 6:19-20, "What? Know ye now that your body is the temple of the Holy Spirit who is in you, who ye have of God, and ye are not…your own! (20) For ye are bought with a price; therefore, glorify God in your body and in your spirit, which are God's."

Our God purchased the believer's body and spirit with the precious shed blood of Jesus Christ. There can be no substitute or greater value of riches, than the life of Christ, and His witness in the life of your child.

Be the good steward God would have you be, and give great increase to the property and life He has loaned to you. As you invest your life and wisdom in the life of your child, he will not only have the benefit of the things our LORD has taught you, but he will have the benefit of your experience that will keep him from making the mistakes that were made by you, allowing for them to grow at a more rapid rate of interest than you did. (Smile) This will give our LORD tremendous benefit also, because the sooner their lives are matured in Him, the sooner the body of Christ will be blessed by their gifts.

Don't allow your child to be trapped in the trappings of this world! 1 John 1:14 says, "I have written unto you, fathers, because ye have known Him that is from the beginning. I have written unto you, young men, because ye are strong, and the Word of God abideth in you, and ye have overcome the wicked one."

Remember, the fads of this world will fade, and the customs of the times as seen and passed on via mass communication will also fade and change with the demands of Satan's whims. But the believer's mind is renewed by adherence to God's Word that changes not!

There's a scripture in Jeremiah 9:23-24, that says it all perfectly, "Thus saith the LORD, let not the wise man glory in his wisdom, neither let the mighty man glory in his might, let not the rich man glory in his riches, (24) but let him that glory, glory in this, that he understandeth and knoweth me, that I am the LORD who exerciseth loving-kindness, in the earth; for in these things I delight, saith the LORD."

Teach your child that the lifestyle of a Christian is holy, not worldly, that it must be God conscious and God centered; nothing else is acceptable to God. Stewardship is doing *all* we know to do with what He has given us. Only this will delight the heart of God!

Chapter XIII

Different Strokes...Different Folks!

I'm certain most of us have heard the old adage, "Good help is hard to find." Well, when it comes to our children this is more than just an old adage...it's the truth.

There are so many reasons parents may have to entrust their children to the care and knowledge of someone else, i.e., both parents may work out of the home, the parents may decide to take a much-needed holiday away from the children, illness may prevent your being able to care for your children for a short period of time, and sometimes a family member or neighbor may just decide to give you a little break and offer to help with the kids for a while.

It really doesn't matter what the reason, what matters is who you allow to care for your children, and how long they may be in that person's care. There is no getting around it, extended family, loved ones and friends will invariably make a contribution to the care and even raising of your children. Only there are two things you must understand right now, and that is; 1) age doesn't mean wisdom, and (2) their having multiple children of their own doesn't mean experience.

Being able to have someone share in the care and watching of your child is a marvelous concept in itself, but it must also be done with great thought and guarded trust. Naturally, as with all issues there are the inevitable pros and cons...the yeas and nays, and dos and don'ts!

Everybody needs help. We need the advice, counsel, and wisdom of those whose opinions and judgment we not only trust but have come to rely upon when things get just too crazy.

Age does not factor into this equation at all. One can neither be too young to offer help or advice, nor too old to need it. What we're looking for here is not just wisdom and knowledge about your child, but what they may need. What is essential however, is that you not allow anyone, and I do mean anyone, who does not have a heart for children, to touch the heart of your child! Honestly, people who are not saved should not keep or care for your children. I know this sounds a little severe, but the Word of God tells us in 2 Corinthians 6:14, "Be ye not unequally yoked together with unbelievers; for what fellowship hath righteousness with unrighteousness? And what communion hath light with darkness." What closer yoke is there for your family, than with the one who cares for your children?

Dear friends, when we allow anyone to care for our children, and they're not saved, it creates an environment of discord and confusion for our children, and inevitably, the entire family. Why would you entrust your children to someone who has told you by the life they live, or the confession of their mouths, they haven't trusted your heavenly Father with their lives!

Friends, trust begets trust! The simplest meaning of the word beget is to cause to exist. And we as Christians know that without God there is no life, physical or spiritual! Why delegate the responsibility of caring for your child to someone who either doesn't care, or who hasn't realized the critical and precarious state of their own eternal welfare? It's not only scary, but it could also be dangerous. Anything they could offer your child would be based on their carnal understanding of the circumstances, rather than spiritual wisdom or insight. We really don't even want to go there! (Smile)

Help and advice for your children can come, and will come from a plethora of sources. Some will be constructive and a blessing, others, you'll have to toss out. And still others you may have to sincerely pray about and think about before implementing. Be very cautious and not quick to jump to conclusions when it comes to your children. Always wait on the leading and instruction of our LORD.

We have many examples of help and guidance given to God's people from many sources and for many reasons, sometimes help and advice we've even asked for. (Smile). When we look at Moses and the help and guidance he received from his father-in-law Jethro, as described in Exodus the 18th Chapter, we can clearly see the hand of God protecting and preserving the health and welfare of His servant. Moses' wife and sons, and his father-in-law joined with him as Israel camped near Mt. Sinai. Jethro noticed the heavy burden of responsibility that Moses was under. Moses was judge in settling all their disputes, their teacher in that he imparted to them God's Laws and Commandments. And he was also their intercessor before God. Moses was overwhelmed!

Reading at verse 19 of this chapter, "Hearken now unto my voice; I will give thee counsel, and God shall be with thee: be thou for the people to

Godward, that thou mayest bring the causes unto God." Moving down to verse 21-22, "Moreover thou shalt provide out of all the people able men, such as fear God, men of truth, hating covetousness; and place such over them, to be rulers of thousands, and rulers of hundreds, rulers of fifties and rulers of tens. (22) And let them judge the people at all seasons; and it shall be, that every great matter they shall bring unto thee, but every small matter they shall judge; so shall it be easier for thyself, and they shall bear the burden with thee."

Moses was working very hard, doing everything that God had ordained for him to do, but by attempting to do it all alone, two things were evident; 1) he was killing himself, and 2) by not allowing the people to share in their progress and their success, they had no spiritual investment nor incentive in their outcome.

God never wants, nor needs to drain us of our strength, and will always provide His own solution to the circumstances, just as He did for Moses through Jethro. God doesn't believe in burnout, and if we allow Him, He will prevent it by sending a Jethro to your aide. God used Jethro to preserve His servant Moses. There may be times when the LORD will tell you to rest my son, or rest my daughter, and send someone to be of great help and rest to you in that season.

Whenever we are too tired to think we are too tired! We also become a huge target for the enemy, because everything about us has been weakened and left vulnerable because of our weariness. Needless mistakes and poor judgment will be the result. So when help is offered, and it will be, be certain to check God's Word regarding certain traits that should factor into your decision.

However, your instructions may not come from Exodus; they may come from Proverbs 6: 16-19, "These six things doth the LORD hate; yea, seven are an abomination unto Him: (17) A proud look, a lying tongue, and hands that shed innocent blood, (18) An heart that deviseth wicked imaginations, feet that are swift in running to mischief, (19) A false witness that speaketh lies, and he that soweth discord among brethren." Quite a list, isn't it? Well, if our LORD doesn't want His children among these types of people, who are actually representing the body of Christ, how much more will He resent the unsaved, watching and caring for His little ones?

The book of Proverbs is a collection of all the thoughts on wisdom and knowledge we need to have successful lives, and to live that life within the prudence of God's will and purpose for His Children. Only, wisdom is not shown exclusively in Proverbs, you find her and her effect on the lives of God's people through out the Word of God.

If we are to please the heart of God, we must earnestly desire to do everything within our power to guard against any influence that is not of Him, thereby guarding against anything that would confuse, distract, or even bring pain or harm to His children.

Everything that surrounds our children can influence our children. Another aspect we must learn to concern ourselves with are the words spoken, or the images given by those who may share in the care of our children. Words spoken by us, or words spoken by others can either build their esteem, or destroy and pull up every good seed that the Holy Spirit has deposited within their hearts. Let's look at Proverbs again. At the 16th chapter, verses 23-24, "The heart of the wise teacheth his mouth, and addeth learning to his lips. (24) Pleasant words are like an honeycomb, sweet to the soul, and health to the bones."

If the heart of a person is not in alignment with temperance and compassion, based on the Word of God, that person can rip the will the very soul of your child. Nothing hurts us as much as a cruel word spoken with little or no thought or concern for the feelings of the person on the receiving end of its sharpness! Recovering painful words is like attempting to stuff a goose down pillow in a windstorm…it can't be done! Your child is not only left with the sting of the words spoken, but the atmosphere, violence, or abuse they were spoken in.

And as verse 24 tells us, pleasant words heal not only the soul, but also the body. Pleasant words are life giving, not life destroying. Pleasant words build up and encourage. Pleasant words give hope and light in the midst of pain and confusion. Pleasant words will soothe and calm your children when fear has gripped their hearts.

The last thing you want or need to subject your child to are the ugly words that come from an ugly, out of control situation. People don't intend to be "loud and wrong" it just seems to happen. However, the possibilities of this happening seems to lessen when self control and wisdom is applied in the heart of a Christian.

Wisdom is found within the Word of God, and His Word will teach our hearts those truths and promises that will influence our speech and conduct. His Word, properly used, will help us to transmit this same wisdom and knowledge to our children, thereby influencing their hearts in such a way as to govern their speech and their conduct. The sweetness and health of such speech, as we read earlier in Proverbs, promotes healthy relationships among their friends and with their God. It will lead them in an overcoming, victorious life, through a consistent acknowledgment of the power and might of God to work within their lives and the lives of their peers.

You may say, "Well, of course...I know that, but I'd never leave my child or children to the care of anyone whose conversation would not be godly. Well, maybe not, but what about the teenager that babysits for you, who spends endless hours on the telephone talking with their friends about anything from A-Z, and everything in between? Your child is listening. Whenever the phone rings, they're listening. How many times do you have to tell them, excuse me, I'm talking now. Well, at that very moment, what was your sitter saying? Better yet, what has your anger caused you to say to the party on the other end of the phone, when you were not aware of their presence?

Here's a simple situation. Your very best friend, who may not be saved, has offered to watch your children for the weekend. When you return, you hear a word from your child that was never heard by them in your home. The word may not have been profane, just ugly. How do you un-ring a bell? What they've heard, no matter how innocent or sincere your efforts were to protect them, and to trust your friend, that friend was not saved, and whatever your child heard is now settled in their spirit, and will come out at such a time you think not!

Maybe while staying with your friend, someone comes in who is bi-lingual, only the second language is profanity! In fact, they're so fluent they not only speak it, they also read and write it, with little or no effort at all! Now you really have a mess! (Smile) Perhaps their television habits are not like those in your home, and they spend hours watching family-centered sitcoms. Yeah, right!

There are so many so-called family-centered sitcoms, where the children are allowed to talk back to their parents, call their siblings ugly names, destroy each other things, plot against them, causing them pain and embarrassment, and we're being encouraged to laugh it all off! They show one child who is constantly being ignored by one parent, and smothered by the other.

One family sitcom has its characters and scenery surrounded in a cartoon-type format. The parents are continually at odds with one another. The father portrayed as a bumbling, clumsy incompetent, never getting anything quite right. They have three children, including a loud-mouth son, somewhere between the ages of ten or twelve who is also a brat, a sister who he is constantly bumping heads with, and a baby that's just there, mostly ignored! The poor mother is trying desperately to juggle this crazy, three-ring circus! This is hardly a healthy representation of family and home. And we're told to laugh; it's supposed to be humorous.

Television, sitcoms, cartoons, and even commercials may be delivering messages that are not necessarily profane, but extremely suggestive to children, full of anger, violence and even abuse! Words, words, words…our children are bomb-barded with words and images that can destroy all the hard effort and territory gained by you, can be destroyed in just one over-night sleep over, if we're not careful and vigilant when it comes to what they are exposed to.

On the market today there is a video game that coaches our children on how to commit crimes of auto theft, drive-by shooting, even how to use cars as weapons of murder in the killing of law enforcement officers, pets, or pedestrians. It's vicious, and yet you'll find it in the homes of young people every day. The voice on this video gives explicit instruction to our children on what to do and when to do it and how to do it. Parents are purchasing these types of video games, and our children are being influenced by them directly or indirectly, at club meetings, camp outs, or as stated earlier, at the homes of those they may visit or stay with overnight.

There is no reason for us to panic, but we should be concerned. When dealing with Satan the element of surprise is a formidable weapon in combat, and we are in combat! He's always surprised when we do our homework, when we don't assume that this is just another outing or just another party or something we don't really have to be too concerned about, because Judy is my best friend! The enemy is depending on us, or shall I say counting on us, to be more concerned about hurting someone's feelings than doing what we know our LORD is asking us to do.

Surprise him! You must determine in your heart to not be ordinary when it comes to parenting. Our God is extraordinary in everything that He does, and in everything He expects us to do, in fact. He's counting on us! Do not take lightly your responsibility when it comes to the care of your children. We either believe God's plan for our children, or we don't. His Word declares in Proverbs 4:20-22, "My son, attend to my words; incline thine ear unto my sayings. (21) Let them [God's Words] not depart from thine eyes; keep them [God's Words] in the midst of thine heart. (22) For they are life unto those that find them, and health to all their flesh."

We mustn't allow just anyone to have the ear of our children. For anyone other than another child of God, it's like giving to Satan a member of their body that has too much influence on the rest of the body. Look at Romans 6:13. "Neither yield ye your members as instruments of unrighteousness unto sin, but yield yourselves unto God, as those that are alive from the dead, and your members as instruments of righteous unto God."

What they hear, if it's garbage, lies, profanity, condemnations, bitterness, jealousy, corrupt conversation of any kind, it settles within their hearts and spirits. This causes disinformation and entices them to stumble over things, or to be frightened by things that our LORD never intended.

I never allowed my children to watch monster movies or extremely violent movies when they were growing up. This was our family policy, and we never veered from it. The word I used to teach them this concept was *garbage*. Anything ugly, violent, or extreme in nature we called garbage. One day my youngest was looking at the television, and out of nowhere came this ridiculous commercial selling Michael Jackson's new video at the time called ,"Thriller!" Well, Ethan jumped up, as if shot from a cannon, yelled, "*Garbage!*" and started running blindly down the hall. We quickly turned the channel, calmed him down, and tried to explain that it was only a commercial, but we were sorry he was assaulted with it. Today my family laughs about it, but it works, and even now the tolerance level of my adult children when it comes to movies and T.V. is still highly selective, and involves little or no garbage-level content. (Smile)

It was also a family policy to not allow our children to sleep over, or spend the night with people we didn't know, or with people whose home environments were different from ours. Christians, or non-Christian friends and relatives alike, were critically examined by my husband and me. Our children, like most children, routinely made friends at school and would want to stay overnight. If we didn't know them, know the spiritual and moral convictions of their parents, our children could not stay over. It was just that simple, it was not discussed. It was final.

Sometimes parents are wondering where nightmares are coming from that disturb the rest of their children. Think back; who did they spend time with recently? Most often it's something that they've seen or heard. Children, contrary to popular opinion, don't frighten easily; they have to be frightened by something. Young people, and even some adults, think it's funny to see a child scream out in fear, or jump suddenly from a loud noise, or to be frightened by a mask or make-up, or frizzy hair! You may not be aware of any incident that involved these factors, but what you get are the residual effects…their nightmares!

Satan has a way of making us feel that things are innocent and harmless, that we're being too strict, too protecting, too unyielding. Well, my feelings are that all things, especially for a child of God…are spiritual. Nothing happens in days and times like these that are a coincidence. Nothing just happens; it's either God's blessing us by His divine intervention and mercies, or Satan's attempts to kill, rob, and destroy!

No, I don't see demons behind every bush, neither do I run at every sound, but I also know Satan. And it's God's Word that commands us, according to Matthew 10:16, "Behold, I send you forth as sheep in the midst of wolves; be ye therefore wise as serpents, and harmless as doves." We must be wise when it comes to our children; never give the enemy a leg up! In other words, don't give him any help; he certainly doesn't need it, especially from us! (Smile)

A season may come in the life of your children when God is saying they need to be under the care and guidance of someone special, someone that can sharpen the gift or gifts He has placed within them. That someone may not be a Christian, but if God has said for you to do so, in instances like this, fear not. He's already gone before you, preparing the way for you and your child. Trust Him! Remember, "The steps of a good man are ordered by the LORD, and he delighteth in His way." (Psalms 37:23) Also in Psalms 16:11, "Thou wilt show me the path of life. In thy presence is fullness of joy; at thy right hand there are pleasures for evermore!" Trust Him! God will never compromise the safety and spiritual well being of His children! There are many wonderful, morally sound, and conscientious people that God may use just for a season, to benefit your child. Just because a person is saved, doesn't make them right for your child or family.

Here we can recall the story of Esther. She was orphaned and raised by her adoptive father, Mordecai, after the death of her parents. There was a time when God ordained that she be placed in the hands of those who held her and her people captive at the time, in a gentile nation.

What joy must have filled the heart of this foster-father of Esther, when he saw her elevated to the position of queen, and himself exalted to the high office in the court of the king! Exile and poverty were now past.

Was this what Mordecai foresaw? Was it even in his plans for Esther? I think not. We are seldom aware of the far-reaching plans of our LORD, and I'm actually happy about that; sometimes the plans and dreams that God has for His children can be frightening! (Smile)

But we see Esther crowned the most beautiful virgin in all of Persia, and the queen of King Ahasuerus. Esther was divinely placed by God to protect and intercede on behalf of her people at a time with their lives and safety as a nation were threatened. A time when only the influence of "someone in high places,"could save them from certain destruction.

There is no limit to God's providential care of His children. Nothing takes Him by surprise. Therefore, He may make demands on you and on your family that may not be commonplace in the homes or lives of His other children. You can rest assured, when and if He does, it's for a good reason, and only for a season. God is strategic in His care and plans for us, and He makes no mistakes; we have only but to hear and obey.

I know a young man who is brilliant and gifted, and his desire has always been to serve his country in the military. Sean completed his secondary education, graduated with high honors, and is reaching for his dreams of becoming an astronaut! The only route his life could take was military schools and academies; this required his being separated from the parents and family he dearly loves. When he graduated and was ready for his first rung of the ladder to his dreams, recommendations came from senators and other high-ranking politicians that he might be able to attend the very elite USAF Academy, in Colorado. O-o-o-o-h…how the hand of God moves on behalf of Sean!

His dreams are bright and sure, and yet there is also the sadness of separation necessary to fulfill these dreams. The doors that opened for Sean have been absolutely miraculous; no one could ever doubt the hand and purpose of God on this young man, a young man who is growing and developing in such a magnificent way. There is no question; it's the will of God for his life.

What does God have in store for Sean? Whatever he does, and wherever he goes, it was ordained from birth!

Hannah prayed and believed God for the son she so willingly released into the care and hands of God. Imagine, after having waited for years to hold your own child in your arms, nursing them for a short season, and then because of a beautiful covenant you made with your LORD, you release that son into God's care and into the hands of Eli, the temple priest.

Who is like Samuel, a Nazarite whose vow with God demanded total abstinence from intoxicating drinks; self-denial, and separation from sensual indulgence; he was never to cut his hair, indicating his complete dedication to the power of God as the head, above all things. A Nazarite was also commanded to never touch any dead thing, which signified his purity in life.

Samuel was a prophet, intercessor, priest, and judge over the people of Israel. Samuel was loved and revered by all Israel, as we're shown in 1 Samuel 25: 1, "And Samuel died. And all the Israelites were gathered together, and lamented him, and buried him in his house at Ramah. And David arose, and went down to the wilderness of Paran."

The LORD may establish your children. Sometimes this is difficult for parents to readily accept. They may feel left out when their child depends on the help and guidance of someone, other than the parent. If God has ordained this for one of your children please don't deny them the spiritual growth and influence they may gain from the life of one chosen by God, especially for them.

One of our greatest examples of this is Paul and Timothy. We also have Elijah and Elisha, and I even consider the relationship of Naomi and Ruth in this same light.

A mentor simply passes on to others what God has given to them. Every child of God should have experienced the blessing and influence of a mentor, someone whose love and knowledge of the LORD is so special and so profound, that it sometimes changes the direction and will of a child, to the purpose of God for her life.

God wants mentoring parents also, parents who create in their children a standard of life that is productive, holy, and an example to others of the life of Christ. Parents are to be living examples of what is right and wrong, so that their children will have an excellent sensitivity gauge. They will notice the little red light, or the sound of the buzzer, or the raised temperature monitor in his or her conscience when it comes on, and turn away from what they planned on doing.

The journey of life is not a simple one, and as parents we certainly don't have all the answers. God has placed thoughts, knowledge, and wisdom in the hearts of all his children, but there are some who have mastered the art of wisdom; they have sat at her feet for hours upon hours, and have soaked up like a sponge every ounce of her strength. It's people like these that we pray for, to affect the lives of our children!

Our lives, when it comes to our children, should open with expectation, and close with profit, gain, and growth for them. Children will learn and gain from everything that has touched and influenced our lives. My mother was a good cook who enjoyed good food, and she used to tell me that life was a feast, that I must eat the meat and throw away the bone. I would like to take this a step further: some thoughts and knowledge we impart to our children they will taste of, some they will even chew on, but the very best we have to give them must be digested by them, or they will not grow according to God's plans and purpose for their lives.

Nothing will speak to the heart of your child like the life you live before them. Parents must be on the same page when it comes to their instruction. Your children will feel secure and blessed when you exercise your authority, but they may become fearful if they don't have restrictions or boundaries. Never allow your love for your child to blur the purpose of your role as their parent.

Another perfect example of mentoring is our LORD, with His disciples who established the early church. What they needed to learn from Him had to be learned quickly, and when Christ left them, the Holy Spirit picked up where He left off!

Our LORD told us, "I am the way and the truth and the life. No one comes to the Father except through me." (John 14:6) There was never a mission as important as the mission of our LORD Jesus Christ. Isn't is amazing that He had at His disposal the power and weight of all heaven, including the access of every angel in heaven, yet He chose twelve humble men, and through these men, worked out His ministry, and the miracle of the good news, the gospel.

Have you ever wonder how our LORD determined who He would use, whom He would entrust with the establishing of His church?

These twelve men, of rather simple lives, had teachable spirits. These were honest men willing to confess their need and dependence upon Him, so much so that Luke 11:1 reports, "And it came to pass that, as He was praying in a certain place, when He ceased, one of His disciples said unto Him, LORD...teach us to pray, as John also taught his disciples." With the exception of Judas, their hearts were big; they had a hunger and thirst for righteousness, and they were filled!

Isn't that beautiful? That's all God is asking of us. He wants us to train our children so that they have a teachable spirit, that they are dependent upon His love, His mercy, His provision, and His help...His everything, that they would have generous hearts towards the gospel and others, and a hunger and thirst for the things of God!

All of this cannot be accomplished by you as their parents, but with the help of those whose hearts and compassion are directly in alignment with the will of God for our children...all things are possible, and shall be accomplished. I love 1 Corinthians 1:27-28, "But God hath chosen the foolish things of the world to confound the wise; and God hath chosen the weak things of the world to confound the things which are mighty; (28) And base things of the world, and things which are despised, hath God chosen, yea, and things which are not, to bring to nothing things that are, (29) that no flesh should glory in His presence."

Doesn't this sound exactly like our LORD's disciples? The majority of them were simple, unlearned, and ignorant, by the world's standards, making mistakes in judgment, slow to understand spiritual concepts, their manners awkward, and their abilities limited, but they were perfect for the cause of Christ, and for the cause of the gospel.

We've talked about not allowing just anyone to attend to our children, and to guard against ungodly conversation and images, about the importance of placing our children in the care and guidance of those God may ordain for their lives for a season, about mentoring from others, and the importance of parents who are also willing not just to parent, but to mentor their children. We've looked at our LORD and the tremendous investments He's made to the church through His disciples; now let's talk just a little bit about how to handle and deal with the educational system that seems to be pro everybody but the Christian! (Smile)

There are many things about today's educational system that are sorely lacking. Because a good education can be and most often is the foundation of every successful person, it is crucial that every effort be made by us to satisfy this need for our children.

The world with all its complexities should never place our children in the shadow of anyone or anything else. If this is allowed to happen, their future will always be determined, limited, or restricted by the thoughts, guidelines, and opinions of others. God cannot show you who your children are without your having a clear understanding of the importance God places on knowledge, on understanding, wisdom, and the preparation for their advancement in this world's system.

We're admonished in 2 Timothy 2:15, "Study to show thyself approved unto God, a workman that needeth not be ashamed, rightly dividing the Word of Truth." If this is the standard that God has placed on us, to accomplish the things of God, His work ethic will not change when it comes to the things of this world. "The fear of the LORD is the beginning of knowledge, but fools despise wisdom and instruction." (Proverbs 1:7)

There are many methods of instruction available to us today when it comes to educating our children, i.e., the public schools, private schools, home teaching, tutorial study and preparation, and so on. It doesn't matter too much what option you will choose; we know that all wisdom comes from God, and that it's He that will give the increase on every seed of knowledge planted. But education must not be taken lightly.

The public schools system affords the convenience and structure many of us are more comfortable with, but we have to also contend with any and all legal aspects that will inevitably interfere, more or less, with the teaching and training your child is given at home. The separation-of-church-and-state guidelines are sometimes extremely frustrating to deal with, especially if you've done your job well, and your children are really the salt of the earth among their peers!

My children have had confrontations with their teachers throughout their education whenever they were asked opinions on subject matters that flew in the face of their fundamentalist background...smile. They were always able, however, to handle every crisis with the conviction and respect God empowered them to have at the time. But...with public schools there may be conflicts you'll have to deal with.

If finances allow, private Christian School are a plus, but there are times our privates school become dumping grounds for those students who are expelled from other systems, and the only option available to those parents is the private school. When this occurs, our children must sometimes deal with an element that may be difficult for them, especially when they are older and real pressures to be accepted with their peers become an issue.

The scenario mentioned above is usually the most severe problem you may have to handle, but by all means, parents, handle it! If you're investing in the education of your children at such financial cost, cursing, fighting, vulgar or profane behavior should not, and must not be tolerated, no matter how badly the school may need the finances. If you're paying for a Christ-centered atmosphere and academic program for your children, then you must settle for no less, period!

The thoughts and ideas of others are a crucial factor in the educational process of your children. Some parents I know place their confidence more in the elements of high academics, i.e., reading, writing and arithmetic, never considering the person whose time with their child may range from four to five hours, if they're very young and in a pre-school or kindergarten as much as six or eight hours a day, especially if they study after school, or have outside activities. Now that's a lot of time for your child to be out of your influence and care. Are you aware of what they're getting, and how effectively this time is being spent?

If we carefully look at the things mentioned in this chapter, you can clearly see that your child may be under the influence of more people than you may have previously thought about. Their lives are being touched, inspired, and affected in so many different ways. The only certain thing is that you need the LORD and His guidance to determine what is good and productive, and what is worthless and unfruitful.

Down through the centuries, children have learned through careful observation from those more experienced. Apprentices have learned from craftsmen who took them by the hand. Amateurs emulated professionals. Disciples studied masters. But there is no authority, no wisdom known to man, that can surpass the infinite wisdom and knowledge of our LORD and our Savior, Jesus Christ! It is He you must rely and depend upon, to mold your child and their character into the powerful tool of wisdom and authority they are meant to be.

The most influential person in their lives must be their LORD! For when all else fails them, they will run to His arms for strength and comfort. As they sit at His feet, He will pour into their lives every thought He has for them. According to Jeremiah 29:11-12, "I know the thoughts that I think toward you, saith the LORD, thoughts of peace, and not of evil, to give you…an expected end. (12) Then shall ye call upon me, and ye shall go and pray unto me, and I will hearken unto you." "Neither is there any creature that is not manifest in His sight, but all things are naked and opened unto the eyes of Him with whom we have to do." (Hebrews 4:13) Amen…Amen!

Most people have no argument about being accountable to God. He is our Father. He is perfect; He has every right to check upon His children to see if we are still on course. We have no doubt that God is not only able to help in the training of our children, but He also has a vested interest in the success of that training. Therefore, why would you hesitate to seek Him concerning those who may touch and influence their lives, their education, or the social, moral patterns of their lifestyle?

We all have different attitudes and concerns when it comes to our lives and the way we raise and train our children, but the one common factor for you as their parent is whether or not your child is yoked up with an unbeliever! "Be ye not unequally yoked together with unbelievers; for what fellowship hath righteousness with unrighteousness? And what communion hath light with darkness? (2 Corinthians 6:14)

Now, this verse of scripture alludes to Deuteronomy 22:10 regarding the yoking together of an ox and a donkey for the purpose of plowing a field. In Deuteronomy the LORD also refers to the mixing of seed in the vineyard and the mixing of fabric in a garment. The idea here is quite clear: God's people,

His children, are to be pure and holy. They must invest their lives in relationships that bring glory to God and offer the potential of furthering His kingdom.

There can be no conflict when it comes to the training of your children, not between you and your husband, nor anyone else for that matter, but the two of you must be on the same page! Outsiders don't even begin to factor in to the control and training of your children if they are not saved, not living for the LORD, and do not have a heart and compassion for all children. Not just yours, but a tender heart for all children.

There are many saints who believe that "God is sovereign," and that because of this, they don't have too much to say about how things are done. I've watched parents just sit back and wait for God to change their children, allowing their children to be broken by Satan, and discouraged by the same, thinking that when God is ready to move, He'll move, and that until then they have no power or authority to change the situation. Meanwhile the entire family is held hostage by the enemy and the untamed will of their children, waiting, waiting on God to do something! And like everything else that pertains to our lives, we have a will that our LORD won't touch, and it's the will of our children that must be trained to depend upon Him!

It's true that our biblical teaching declares the sovereignty of God over all things in our life, but sovereignty so balanced; so sensitive that the free wills of our lives are not compromised. This can only be accomplished by God. Understanding that God is sovereign and has the final word in everything that pertains to us, gives us such liberty and freedom that the world cannot begin to understand! It's like faith; faith is not blind; faith does not deny the reality of difficulty; faith declares the power of God in the face of difficulty!

It's the sovereignty of God, balanced with our faith in Him, that gives us the authority not only to determine the course our lives will take, but to stand in the gap for our children until they have the spiritual strength and fortitude to do the same. We must tap into this source available to us without reservation. Pursue with confidence His Word, that cannot lie nor produce a lie or unfruitfulness, and thus proclaim that we are victorious! Philippians 1:6 says, "Being confident of this very thing, that He who hath begun a good work in you will perform it until the day of Jesus Christ."

We can't begin to understand the challenges and pressures our children will and do face, but we are accountable for their lives and for giving them the sound biblical training necessary for them to make the right decisions. Keeping this thought in mind, guard jealously those you permit to deposit words, knowledge, thoughts, concepts, prejudices, etc. into their lives.

If we can remember that the entire new church, this brand-new baby ministry started with a group of frightened men in a second-floor room borrowed for the night to share the Last Supper! Though trained and taught, they didn't know what to say. They'd marched with Jesus for three years, they now sat, afraid. They were timid soldiers, reluctant warriors, speechless messengers, and such were some of ye…smile! I think the Apostle Paul said it first, and in a very different reference, but it still works; smile.

If twelve willing disciples could not only determine within themselves to reach the known and unknown world at that time, if they could muster up enough courage to come together in one accord waiting for the promised Comforter, if Peter could lay aside the past of his own denial of Christ and be used of God in such a powerful way that three thousand people were saved and baptized after Pentecost, surely we can guard the investment God has entrusted to us and multiply the gifts, talents and knowledge He's placed within them.

Despite our prayers and hours of counseling and instruction, we will make mistakes in judgment, methods of discipline, and maybe mistakes by not allowing the direction of the LORD to guide us when His will is not our own. In times like these, repent and move on.

Nothing drags more stubbornly than a sack of failures. Could you do it over again, you'd do it differently. You'd make a better, more thought-out decision. You'd follow through on the convictions of your heart and not allow yourself to be intimidated by the pressure of your youngsters or their peers. But, sometimes you can't, and what's done is done. And in the exact way our children need our love when they've messed up, we want and need the love of God to comfort our hearts when we've messed up, a Father whose love towards us will cover a multitude of faults, not by diminishing His own high standards, but by covering our lower standards with His blood.

Friends, we have a Father whose love will always bridge the gap between success and failure, a Father who is at His best when we are at our worst, a Father whose grace is strongest when our devotion is weakest, and a Father who's awake twenty-four/ seven, three hundred sixty five days out of a year, when we can't even seem to function without at least six hours of sleep! If your mistakes seem to be overwhelming, then you're in for some exciting news: your mistakes…are not fatal! Mistakes in judgment and convictions will come. Never allow that thought or fear to keep you from moving forward in your desire to do God's will. Our LORD has you and your child in His care at all times. No mistake is fatal! He's got your back! Praise Him!

Chapter XIV

Our Children Are...the Latter Rain!

Praise God! We have such a blessed assurance, one that should comfort the hearts of every man woman or child, that proclaims Jesus Christ as their LORD and Savior! There is no need for dismay or frustrated bewilderment every time you wonder if what you're doing, or what you're saying to your children is reaching its target. Well, without a doubt it is! And more than that, you can take comfort in the knowledge that your children will not always appear to be *lost in space*! (Smile)

This promise is so profound, so magnificent that it was mentioned in the Old Testament in Joel 2:28-29, "And it shall come to pass afterward, that I will pour out of my Spirit upon all flesh; and your sons and your daughters shall prophesy, your old men shall dream dreams, and your young men shall see visions; (29) And, also, upon the servants and upon the handmaids in those days will I pour out my Spirit."

Paul gives reference to this same scripture in Acts 2:16. The astonishing fact about this passage of scripture is that the prophet Joel sees a time in the future when the Spirit of God will be poured out on all flesh. Young and old alike, both women and men will experience this outpouring. For prophets and priest to experience the presence of the Spirit in their lives was not a phenomenon, but never had there been such a general outpouring of the Spirit of God. Then, on the Day of Pentecost, the Spirit came with such power and force that it captured the attention and the hearts of the masses gathered in Jerusalem for the festival.

It's this power, this presence of the Holy Spirit, that I'm certain we're looking at among our young people today. It's so refreshing, so like a shower of spring rain among us! They're excited, they're rejoicing and witnessing among all those who will listen with such fervor. It's washing away the dust and cobwebs from the ministries and lives of many saints lost in the traditional, pharisaical-type theology. The Holy Spirit is attempting to strip all tradition away from us, with a last ditch effort so that this new wine, found in the new wine skins of our youth, will cause us all to become intoxicated under His presence and power!

The activity of God's Spirit that regenerates sinful man also regenerated His people with a fresh latter rain of Himself. This latter rain is bringing about such a bountiful harvest of hope and faith, a sheer zeal among our young people. It makes you weep when you witness it in its fullness.

Our churches and congregations have been thirsty for such a long time for this refreshing, and what we need to do is simply prepare ourselves for the arrival of change, the arrival of a new type of boldness that will shock some, confuse others, and even frighten those who are not prepared for this sudden storm.

My only suggestion for all of us is forget the umbrellas, and all other rain gear; rejoice, splash your feet in the puddles, hold your heads back, and let the rains fill you with a new hope, a new power, and a new authority that you thought lost and gone!

The dictionary gives the definition of a *storm* as an atmospheric disturbance manifested in strong winds accompanied by rain, snow, or other precipitation and often accompanied with thunder and lightening. Every congregation, or at least every healthy congregation, will have a strong, effective, children or youth ministry outreach. They offer music, plays, outside ministries, and group outings, inter-church youth activities and games, just about everything that will give its main focus to reaching our young people for Christ.

Whenever these initial atmospheric disturbances begin, some people will resist to the point of changing their memberships. Others may stay for a season, but their grumpy faces and attitudes can hinder or stifle the free moving of the Holy Spirit in the services. Still others will complain aloud, and make no bones about their total displeasure with these goings on. However, whenever the pastor will stand firm and allow the Holy Spirit the liberty He needs to do a new and fresh work among the young and the seasoned alike, the rewards are without measure, and the benefits boundless!

If any child of God is paying the slightest bit of attention to our young people today, you will notice the enemy's attempt to destroy and to discredit them through sin and shame, attempting to disenfranchise our young people of their hope and promise of a new and better way through Christ Jesus. You'll also notice the power, purpose and presence of the Holy Spirit, wooing and drawing His young ones to Himself, with even greater strength and determination. For He is greater according to His own Words: "Moreover, the law entered, that the offense might abound, but where sin abounded, grace did much more abound." (Romans 5:20) Also in 1 John 4:4, "Ye are of God, little children, and have overcome them, because greater is He that is in you, than he that is in the world." Praise the LORD!

The law was a tradition that could not be kept. It weakened the hope and promise of a new and better way! When Jesus, the world's first real revolutionary came on the scene, He was also mocked, threatened, ridiculed, slandered, challenged, and finally crucified to shut Him up. But, all Satan succeeded in doing was breaking up this spiritual molecule into more pieces than he could contain; thus a new church was built on the foundation of the rock…Christ Jesus!

The first mention of this new church came in Matthew, the 16th chapter, when Jesus was asking His disciples "Who do men say that I, the Son of man, am?" and Peter spoke out in verse 16, "And Simon Peter answered and said, Thou art the Christ, the Son of living God." At verse 18, "And I say also unto thee, that thou art Peter and upon this rock, I will build my church, and the gates of hell shall not prevail against it."

Our LORD was declaring to the entire world, that upon this declaration *that I am* (remember Exodus 3:14, And God said unto Moses, *I AM THAT I AM*: and He said thus shalt thou say unto the children of Israel, I AM hath sent me unto you.") Friends, this is that same "I AM" speaking. Hallelujah! Jesus is declaring that as the "Christ, the Son of the Living God," He was establishing a new order of things, and new church, and new way of worshiping and serving Him, a new and better way, built upon better promises, and a new and better relationship between God and man made possible by the precious blood of Jesus!

This is what our young people are declaring, just like the woman at the well: *Come see a man that changed my life, lifted me from drugs, drink, hopelessness, sorrow, suicide, gangs, prison…etc*. They are shouting it from the rooftops, and this wonderful message it's raining down in our congregations and schools and homes, and we must rejoice! Friends, it's raining, and it's raining on us. Don't run for cover; stay out under this shower and get wet. You just might catch something! (Smile) Only it won't make you sick; it just might make you whole again.

Our responsibility as parents is to so educate our children that they will not fear, but will run into the presence of God. To do this, they must know who God is. Reading again in Exodus 3:13-14, "And Moses said unto God, behold, when I come unto the children of Israel, and shall say unto them, the God of your fathers hath sent me unto you; and they shall say to me, what is His name? What shall I say unto them? (14) And God said unto Moses, I AM THAT I AM: and He said, thus shalt thou say unto the children of Israel, I AM hath sent me unto you."

This fundamental declaration by God is the hope and promise of the Church. Whatever we need, desire, or struggle with, I AM, the almighty God, has the power to provide, supply and deliver. By the confession of our faith in Him, according to the Word of God, all things are possible. Our children must be rooted and established in this fact and in this assurance. As they surrender their lives to Him, their victory, miracle, and protection against the flesh and the spiritual attack of the enemy is assured.

There are four basic keys to understanding God, and number one is: Teach them to pursue after Christ who is Holy, and that His life in us makes holiness possible. God calls us to be holy, set apart for Him and His purposes, thereby causing us to be distinguishable in our nature and character from the world, different in the way we think, act, and live. This difference will be visible to others and bring glory to God.

Secondly, help them to understand that Godly living is essential, not impossible. With God working and living in their lives, He is the one that will guide and direct them, and help to establish and build their lives upon His precepts according to His word. Godliness cannot be accomplished without faith and trust in Him; our acts and efforts become vain and religious, encouraging religious tradition, and not relationship.

Thirdly, God calls His people to live according to wisdom. Wisdom is simply knowing and applying the truth. We're told throughout the Word of God, and particularly in Proverbs, how to live wisely and please God. Proverbs teaches us everything from what we learn, and from whom we learn, to how to stay away from the wrong people who bring with them trouble and heartache. Proverbs tells us how to manage, earn, and increase our economic wealth, how to set goals and follow them to success by allowing the Holy Spirit to establish us in the practice of this wisdom that will lead to fullness of life.

Lastly, they must understand and acknowledge the authority of God in their life, and the lives of all His children. All authority is from God, as explained in Romans 13:1, "Let every soul be subject unto the higher powers. For there is no power but of God; the powers that be are ordained of God." To distrust those, i.e., parents, teachers, public officials, and others, is to distrust

Him. God calls His people to a submissive attitude towards His leaders. He cautions us to be careful how we speak about them, to give honor and respect to whom honor is due. If we disregard Godly leaders, and refuse to yield ourselves in prayer to pray for those who are not Godly leaders, it dishonors Him.

Remember when I made early reference to Moses, God established with His children a tabernacle. Moses was to collect an offering from the children of Israel for the construction of this sanctuary, so that God "may dwell among them." God established Aaron and his sons as His priests that would perform the duties of the priesthood, including the leading of the people in worship. There were detailed instructions given for the assembling of both the tabernacle and the priestly garments, and Moses was charged to make everything according to the strict guidelines of God's command.

The writer of Hebrews tells us that this tabernacle was a "copy and shadow of the heavenly things" which would ultimately be fulfilled in Jesus Christ. In Hebrews 8:5, " Who serve unto the example and shadow of heavenly things, as Moses was admonished of God when he was about to make the tabernacle; for see, saith He that thou make all things according to the pattern shown to thee in the mount."

What our LORD has accomplished by His blood is a relationship that could never have been established by any other means. His very presence can abide within us. Nothing made by the hands of man, as in the tabernacle of the Old Testament, but a holy and pure relationship, a one-on-one...relationship, because of Calvary. In 2 Corinthians 4:7, "But we have this treasure in earthen vessels, that the excellency of the power may be of God, and not of us."

When our children understand, not only the importance of their salvation, but what the Old Testament saints had to endure and struggle with, how hopeless and futile their human efforts were towards holiness, that because of Christ we are blessed with not only a relationship, but also a new and better covenant of promises, bought and paid for by the establisher of the covenant, their desire to serve, worship and praise our LORD, will not only be second nature to them, but breath to them!

God wrote His covenant, performed the fulfilling of His covenant, and paid for the covenant with His own blood! Our only task is to reach out and receive this completed, magnificent work. Amen...Amen.

Your children must also learn the importance of Praise and Worship, and being comfortable in the presence of our LORD. We were created by God to live and breathe in the presence or atmosphere of praise-filled worship. The void that so many, saved and unsaved alike, try to fill with so many different things, i.e., academic achievement for the adoration of man, athletic achievement, material trappings, and clutter, even our families, will never fill the void or that place in our lives, that God has reserved for Himself alone! Never!

To not give honor and praise to our LORD is to reject one of the most powerful weapons of warfare we have in our spiritual arsenal! I believe that David was a man after God's own heart for two reasons. First, David knew how to repent with a broken and contrite heart. In Psalms 51:1-3, "Have mercy upon me, O God, according to thy loving-kindness; according unto the multitude of thy tender mercies blot out my transgressions. (2) Wash me thoroughly from mine iniquity, and cleanse me from my sin. (3) For I acknowledge my transgressions, and my sin is ever before me." Secondly, David knew the secret of being a grateful child of God, and to whom all the glory belonged. As we see in Psalms 100: 3-5, "Know ye that the LORD, He is God; it is He who hath made us, and not we ourselves; we are His people, and the sheep of His pasture. (4) Enter into His gates with thanksgiving and into His courts with praise; be thankful unto Him, and bless His name. (5) For the LORD is good, His mercy is everlasting, and His truth endureth to all generations." Praise God!

Tell your children we cannot enter into true praise and worship without a heart that is willing to repent before God, giving Him, and only Him all the glory for everything and anything they are privileged to hold, for a season because of His love, mercy and grace towards all of us. Nothing will last forever, the mountain top or the valley, but it is through Him and by His grace that we are kept through either.

We are to praise God both for *who* He is and for *what* He does. When we praise God for who He is, it's called adoration. Praising Him for what He's done is called thanksgiving. Praise to God may be done through a song or in prayer, or it may be done individually or collectively. Praise might be spontaneous because of an emotional experience or victory, or even prearranged during a group meeting or service called for by the pastor or other congregational leader.

All of our children have a gift for boasting and becoming enthused about a sports team or individual. They'll wear the colors of their school or favorite team. They run from campus to campus, chanting and singing the names and accolades of their team and its members, especially before a big game.

Banners will fly, flags will furl, bands and trumpets blast, drums roll with a thunderous sound that would burst the normal (smile) ear drums!

Sometimes their excitement is so feverish it robs them of sleep, sustenance, and sanity! The phone will ring off the hook as the game draws nearer and nearer to the time and date they have anxiously prepared for. Well, this is praise! And worship; smile!

Or what about that adorable hunk that sits next to them in science or math class, whose muscles go out to here, and whose shoulders reach from there...to there, whose eyes are so-o-o-o dreamy, and who happens to be "All the world" in this, that, or the other! "Oh, and have you seen his car?" (Smile). "Isn't it The Bomb?" "Girl! He's *fine!*" (Smile) This, too, is Praise and Worship!

I could go on and on but suffice to say, I think we all get the message. Our children do know how to praise and worship; our task is to give them a more fruitful option for all this ability.

There was a severance to the bond of blessing through fellowship, worship, and obedience that *sin* brought to mankind in the Garden of Eden. It silenced man's praise filled fellowship with God and reduced us to the self centered, self-pitying, and self-indulging mass of humanity we see in so many of us today. But because of Christ, and upon receiving Jesus Christ as our Savior, our daily communion and approach to God is paved through the pathway of praise and worship.

Although praise and worship are separate disciplines, they are spiritually linked together in such a way that one cannot be truly accomplished without the other. Our God is clever like that. (Smile)

Worship is a reverent devotion and allegiance to someone or something, a ritual or ceremony by which this reverence is expressed. The word *worship* comes from the old English word *worth-ship*, a word that denotes the worthiness of the one receiving the special honor or devotion.

We read earlier in Psalms 100:3-5, that the glory and praise for all mankind belongs to God, because of His mercy towards us. Well, this is truth! The marvelous thing about worship is that as we begin to think about how very good God is, when we begin to thank him for saving our children and for healing our lives and bodies, for delivering us from the pits and valley of sin, we begin to also praise Him!

Our children face situations and challenges that we can't possibly begin to comprehend to the fullest. They must be taught that God, and only God can do for them what they cannot do for themselves! That strength to endure, and the power to deliver comes directly from Him to them! Teach them that when all else fails, and when everyone else fails them, God will never fail them!

Tell them, that when they bow their knee or their will to anything but God, it's worship! Whether it's a friend, family, or Satan, it's worship. No one or anything should ever take that place on the throne of their hearts but God. When we bow or bend our knee, it's an act of submission and reverence. When we fall down and pay homage to God, we are making ourselves low before Him. It's adoration in the highest form of worship. Just as the word "Hallelujah" is the highest praise, to kneel or lay with faces down before our LORD is the highest form of adoration and surrender. Any children that learn to do this with their whole hearts, will be a child after God's own heart. They will, without a doubt capture the heart of our LORD!

Allow me to mention, or take a tiny side-bar right here. *Worry* will destroy and dry up our praise and worship. *Worry* distracts and divides our attention and loyalties (between God, this flesh and Satan). *Worry* causes us to be preoccupied with things, other than the things of God. If we're not thinking on the things of God, how can we praise or worship Him? Our LORD speaks against *worry* and anxiety because of the watchful care of a heavenly Father who is ever mindful of our daily needs.

Where *worry* is, faith is not! And where faith is not, God is not! And where God is not, praise and worship is not! And where praise and worship is not, *fear is!* And where fear is, liberty is not!

This is a spiritually, and maybe even physically deadly continuum, and a snare we must never allow our children to be trapped in. The suicide rate among our young people is at epidemic proportions. Everything mentioned above gives a hopelessness to their lives that is utterly stifling, and must be torn down or cast down when perceived by us immediately.

Praise will cure the dry times in their lives. Look at Numbers 21:16-17, "And from there they went to Beer: that is the well whereof the LORD spoke to Moses, gather the people together, and I will give them water. (17) Then Israel sang this song: Spring up, O well; sing ye unto it." NOTE these four truths: 1) God's instruction: "Gather the people together." There is unity and power in corporate gathering in praise. 2) God's promise: "I will give them water" (life). There can be no life without water: food, yes, water, no! 3) The people's responsibility…they sang, "Spring up, O well!" All of you sing to it. There had to be a *will* to praise God! And, 4) the lesson,: in times of pressure, anxiety or depression, do not stay alone. Gather with God's people, especially a praising people.

We're told in Hebrews 10:25, "Not forsaking the assembling of ourselves together, as the manner of some is, but exhorting one another, and so much the more, as ye see the day approaching." In these last days, the need for fellowship, corporate praise and worship. The exhorting and encouraging one another is at its zenith. We cannot fail to teach our young people, that exactly in the same manner they cheer and yell at pep rallies and football games, and other such events, they must learn to do in services. Exactly the way their enthusiasm and school spirit is heightened when everybody is yelling and screaming for the same event and same goal or purpose, and that is victory, our services and worship for our LORD should be just that intense, if not more!

Regardless of their personal feelings, they must learn to join in the worship and praise along with the saints. As they lift they hands and their hearts towards God, His very presence will over flow their hearts in such a way, they will not be able to contain it! Tears may flow, that songs may rise from their hearts, that they may bow their heads and bend their knees in His presence, that even laughter may come from the sheer joy of His touch. All of this and even more is not only desirable, but normal!

It's times like these, whether at home or at church, or even in their cars, that in the dry places of their hearts are made fruitful gardens of praise and victory. Praise and thanksgiving for God's past blessings, and songs of hope and praise for His future promises in their lives, will blossom into a hope and an authority that will rip off the gates off hell! Where you want them to be parents, in the presence of God, is also where you want them to feel most comfortable! Amen...Amen.

Victory in every area of their lives will be born out of their worship and praise for our LORD. In 2 Chronicles 20:15-22, we have a powerful lesson whenever unity becomes a part of our praise, when everybody is on the same page, so to speak. Judah was facing their mortal enemies, Moab and Ammon. The people sought God in prayer, then the word of the LORD came through the prophet: "Do not be afraid...for the battle is not yours, but God's." (Verse 15)

Imagine this: you're facing your most dreaded nightmare! They not only outnumber you, but your fear or dread seems to have paralyzed you for a moment until you begin to pray. The Word of the LORD tells you to, "Listen up everybody that lives in Jerusalem, and you, too, King Jehoshaphat. I've got something to say. Don't be "scurred" (smile) and don't be shook up, just because you're about to be trampled and sciffilated! This one is on me! (Very loosely translated!) What would you do? I don't think you'd dare to call the praise team and the choir together and tell them, "Hey, you guys, I think you should go out in front of all of us!" I don't think so-o-o-! (Smile)

Well, that's exactly what they did. Verse 19 says, "And the Levites, of the children of the Kohathites, and of the children of the Korahites, stood up to praise the LORD God of Israel with a loud voice on high." They actually appointed some to sing to the LORD and praise Him in the beauty of holiness."And when he had consulted with the people, he appointed singers unto the LORD, who should praise the beauty of holiness, as they went out before the army, and to say, Praise the LORD; for His mercy endureth forever." The result of this powerful praise and complete surrender to the will of God was total VICTORY!

Be honest with your children and tell them that more often than not their need for praise and worship will come at a time when they least feel like it. Sometimes it comes when everything is just great, but it's also true that praise and worship is necessary, in fact crucial when we least feel like talking, let alone praising and worshiping the LORD. This is honest, and it allows them to develop the discipline of the press into the Holy of Holies, that awesome place of God's Holy Presence!

In the tabernacle proper the, holy of holies, the cherubim on both the veil and the curtains were symbolic guardians of the sanctuary. The positioning of the veil made the holy of holies out of reach for anyone but the high priest. When our LORD died on Calvary, the veil of the tabernacle that separated the people from entrance into the presence of God except through the High Priest, this veil (that because of our sin represented the boundary line that could be crossed only at risk of death, even for the Priest, if sin was found in him), was split from top to bottom! The veil not only represented separation because of sin, but was also a constant reminder that sin had produced a chasm that yawned between God and man, that only God, Himself could destroy, He did, Hallelujah! He did!

Praise Him! Look at Matthew 27:50-51, "Jesus, when He had cried again with a loud voice, yielded up the spirit. (51) And, behold, the veil of the temple was torn in two from the top to the bottom; and the earth did quake, and the rocks were split."

The huge chasm that existed between God and mankind, represented by the veil in the tabernacle, was literally snapped shut! That's why the earthquake. It would take an earthquake to close up the Grand Canyon in the natural world. Well, the rumbling that the world felt and heard on the day our

LORD died in our place was only a ripple compared to the shaking, quaking and rumbling that took place in the spirit realm! Hallelujah! Glory be to God! Hallelujah! Thank you, Jesus! Thank you, LORD! Worthy is the lamb!

The price paid by Christ, so that we would no longer suffer the separation and indignity of sin, was tremendous, but to Him...it was more than worth it. To once again have the fellowship and communion of His most cherished work of creation, mankind.

Children and young people face different challenges than most adults, but everything is relative; consequently, it's as painful and testing to them as our challenges are to us. The younger they understand that praise and worship stops the advancement of the enemy, the less painful and severe his attacks will be against them, and definitely the length of their challenges will be shortened.

Praise is always an act of the will. In Psalms 7:17, "I will praise the LORD according to His righteousness, and will sing praise to the name of the LORD most High." Also in Psalms 34:1, "I will bless the LORD at all times; His praise shall continually be in my mouth."

Praise is not merely an exuberance overflowing with words, but a self-induced declaration of thanksgiving, a sacrifice of the will. The praiser chooses to praise.

As our children get older, they seem to always want their space, always need the opportunity to prove they are no longer a child, or "I can do it myself!" Well, this is a great opportunity to explain to them what doing something yourself can mean to Christ! His desire is for all of His children, young and old alike, to come to Him out of their *will*, not always their need.

You can always use yourself as the example. Explaining how it would hurt you if the only time they ever said thank you or that I love you or maybe even that they appreciated your help with something, was when it was brought to their attention by someone else, or because they wanted or needed something. No one ever likes to feel taken for granted, not even a parent. They might have a friend that never comes over to play or enjoys their company, except to borrow something from them or pry something out of them (smile). Or perhaps they never return the items used or borrowed until they are asked for.

All of these illustrations will help to clarify how important our *will* is when serving our LORD, whether in prayer, worship, or praise. It has to be, because we love Him and desire to please Him, and that we want to be in His presence at all times.

I've referred to many scriptures found in the Psalms, because David was a psalmist. His life, even as a boy, was wrapped up in the praise and adoration of his LORD and his God. From a small boy he was a skillful player on the harp, and because of this he often found himself in the presence of the wretched king, Saul, who could only be soothed by David's music. David's poetic genius made him the sweet psalmist of Israel, and no poet has been so constantly used and quoted through the ages. His Psalms are the masterpiece of spiritual literature.

When you look closely at the life of David, you'll find a young man destined for greatness. In his youth, David was trained to tend his father's sheep. He was the youngest of the family, and as it is with many of our young people, especially today, unnoticed and not brought into public view. Yet it pleased God to raise him from a low estate and set him upon the throne of Israel.

Why? His first battle, and open testimony, was to before the armies of Israel and King Saul. He declared before all those men, including his king, that God was his deliverer! David stood before the giant Goliath, and his armies, who represented Satan and all the armies of hell, and again declared that his God was a deliverer and the Almighty God!

Reading in 1 Samuel 17:34-36, "And David said unto Saul, thy servant kept his father's sheep, and there came a lion, and a bear, and took a lamb out of the flock; (35) And I went out after him, and smote him, and delivered it out of his mouth. And when he arose against me, I caught him by his beard, and smote him, and slew him. (36) Thy servant slew both the lion and the bear; and this uncircumcised Philistine shall be as one of them, seeing he hath defied the armies of the living God!"

David was a young man, a teenager, and thought it not strange at all to openly praise the LORD for his goodness and for his faithfulness to him, when there was no one else around that could have protected or delivered him. He thought nothing about standing before the king, that God had allowed to reign over His people Israel, a king who was obviously in the state of fear from the armies of Goliath. David never failed to praise, worship, and adore his God, whether in private on the hill slopes with the sheep or in the presence of a king, or even in the presence of Satan himself! So the question should not be, "Why?" but, "Why not?"

When we look at David, everything necessary to make you proud (as a parent) is there. He's brave, respectful, talented and gifted; a saint of God has the heart and character to repent, was a prophet, over came insurmountable odds, and always looked to the stars. David always looked up to God, never to any man. His trust was in the LORD.

There's a children's hymn that urges us to be "a star in someone's sky." I'm certain that David has lighted many a spiritual traveler on the way to heaven. Has encouraged many a heart when facing one battle after another. David has taught all of us to always remember to whom the glory belongs, and that as man, why does God even bother? When we read Psalms 8:4-6, "What is man, that thou art mindful of him? And the son of man, that thou visitest him? (5) For thou hast made him a little lower than the angels, and hast crowned him with glory and honor. (6)Thou madest him to have dominion over the works of thy hands; Thou has put all things under his feet."

Only in Glory will it be revealed to all of us what David's Psalms meant to Christ and to His followers of all ages. Yet he is *nothing* compared to the Son of Righteousness, Himself. None can compare to the LORD Jesus Christ, who died and rose again to become our Savior, friend, and king.

Teach your children that to know Him is to love Him! And that like David, the younger they really determine to live for Christ, the blessings and high places that God has for them will be realized. I've said it before, but I'll say it again, "God will never bless His children with a life or a lifestyle that makes Him unnecessary!" The sooner they rush to Him, praise Him, and worship Him, the longer they will enjoy and dwell in His presence, and reap accordingly.

I mentioned earlier that at times it might be difficult or seem impossible to praise our LORD because of the pain or the challenges we sometimes face. Help them to understand that praise often requires personal sacrifice. According to Hebrews 13:15, "By Him, therefore, let us offer the sacrifice of praise to God continually; that is the fruit of our lips giving thanks to His name."

The word *sacrifice* means to offer up, but first, something must die. Praise often requires that we kill our pride, fear, or laziness, anything that threatens to destroy or distract from the worship and praise of our LORD. But, as mentioned in the verse above, this can only be accomplished through *Him*! Imagine that! He desires our praise so deeply that He's willing to come into our hearts in such a way that He can empower or enable us to worship and praise Him! He's amazing, He's just so-o-o- deep!

The basis of all our praise: the sacrifice we offer up to our LORD, as a sweet-smelling perfume, is by Him, in Him, with Him, to Him, and for Him. Praise can never be hindered by Satan if we keep our focus on the LORD, the author and finisher of our most holy faith.

Here we go with David again (I simply love David) as he tells us to teach our children to praise and worship the LORD. Psalms 145:4, "One generation shall praise thy works to another, and shall declare thy might acts."

That's what it's all about, parents. As our children see and hear, as they watch and listen to your open love and adoration of our LORD, as they begin to ask the whys and they will always ask why, it opens up an opportunity for you to testify about the goodness of the LORD to you and throughout your life.

This scripture emphasizes the importance of passing on the praise of God from one generation to another. Praise is to be taught to our children. The Bible enjoins us to raise up a generation of praisers. We cannot merely suppose or presume that our children will grow up and desire God.

We cannot hinder the latter rain that's starting to fall upon our children. Whatever we posses of God's blessing and revelation can be lost in one generation. We must consistently teach them to praise Him, and do so by example. The rain will only fall, or continue to fall upon us, as we remain in His presence, and teach our children to do the same. We're told in Psalms 22:3, "But thou art holy, O thou who inhabitest the praises of Israel."

As they learn to press into God's presence, temptation to sin and the desire to live wickedly will soon disappear in the face of sincere, powerful and audible praise. This will bring the glorious presence of Jesus Christ, wherever they are, and His presence will drive out the desire to identify with anything other than Christ.

They must understand, to be in God's presence is not waiting for favorable conditions, during a storm or rainfall. It may not be fair weather but, when a storm strikes, good sailors will know how to anchor deep.

Tell them and love them into understanding that their lives and their efforts are not futile, their failures are not fatal, and their losses are not final! If they will dare to stand in the presence and the outpouring of His Holy Spirit, their lives will never be the same, and neither will yours! (Smile)

Chapter XV

Sanctified…Unto God!

There is no greater honor nor fact more sobering and staggering, than the knowledge that you are so special, so privileged that you were chosen from a tremendous number of people, set apart, as it were, for something or for a purpose not given to anyone else!

From Genesis to Revelation we are witnesses to this awesome truth beginning with the father of all mankind: Adam! Adam was not only chosen, he was God's masterpiece and the crowing work of His creation.

Adam was the first man to ever breathed, man's ancestor, the head of the human family, the first being whoever trod the earth. God created this beautiful paradise for him, with all the comfort and pleasure possible in this garden called Eden, this world without sin and without sorrow, completely furnished with everything needed to make life content! There was not a single need God had not satisfied, except the only thing Adam's offspring seems to remember is the fall of mankind, as if anyone else would have done differently.

Why man? The poets and writers of the ages have written volumes on the theories of God being lonely. God's need for fellowship and communion, also those that are of the opinion that He created man because He could, not for any other reason. I don't know when I look at the awesome beauty and wonder we experience every day of our lives; maybe all of these scenarios are true. Personally, I believe that God wanted to bring just a little bit of heaven down. Satan's crash landing must have created an ugly mess, and God never leaves anything without His touch of mercy, grace, and healing!

Listen to the Word of God in Genesis 1:1, "And the earth was without form, and void, and darkness was upon the face of the deep. And the Spirit of God moved upon the face of the waters." God looked at the dark, hopelessness, of something He could change with just a spoken word, and maybe He wasn't quite finished with Satan yet. God created a brand new paradise, and put His own man right in the middle of it, to tend it, have dominion over it. (Satan hated that dominion part; after all, wasn't that what got him kicked out of Heaven?) In Isaiah we find the Word telling us in the 14th chapter at verses 12-15, "How art thou fallen from heaven, O Lucifer, son of the morning! How art thou cut down to the ground, who didst weaken the nations! (13) For thou hast said in thine heart, I will ascend into heaven, I will exalt my throne above the stars of God; I will sit also upon the mount of the congregation, in the sides of the north, (14) I will ascend above the heights of the clouds, I will be like the Most High. (15) Yet thou shalt be brought down to Sheol, to the sides of the pit."

So our LORD created a beautiful place for His creation to live and dwell in. He placed within his hands the power to reign over and above this creation, right smack dab in the face of Satan. So, Satan thought, "I'll get my kingdom after all; I'll take it from man!" And, for a split second he did, but God…there's always a "But God!"…had a better plan, a second Adam, praise God, and this one was set apart for a new season that only God had determined.

Set apart or *sanctified*! The dictionary defines the word *sanctify* as the quality of, or condition of being considered sacred; inviolability.

At the beginning of this chapter I stated that we find those very special people set apart for God's purposes from Genesis to Revelation, to fulfill the plans of God, for the season and purposes known only by Him. We have Noah, set apart or sanctified for the saving of the people from God's Judgment on the earth. There's Abraham, set apart to establish His people, Israel. We have Joseph, set apart for the saving and building up of that people, Israel. We can't forget Moses, who was set apart for the hand of God to deliver His people from bondage.

The beautiful masterpiece of salvation and redemption goes on and on, with the one common thread of His Grace towards mankind, His Love that will not let us die without hope, nor live without purpose!

For all of God's children, every gift of birth, there is a purpose and a call of destiny for their lives. The lives of our children are sacred, sanctified, set apart for the purpose and will of God, only we must find out what the purpose of God is for their lives.

It's the custom of most Christian parents to dedicate their children soon after their birth. In some churches it's a big ceremony; in others it's a simple ceremony that takes place during the main service where the congregation witnesses and enjoys the occasion along with the family; still others may meet with the pastor in his office before or after service with only the immediate family as witnesses. It doesn't matter what they choose, their desire is to offer their child up to God for His protection and His will in their lives.

Only, how many of us have a tendency to forget what it is we've actually done, that before God and man, we've stated that His will for our child comes first? Instead, we leave services thinking of the family and friends that are coming to share a specially prepared meal to further reverence the occasion. We forget how holy and sacred the act of dedicating our child to God really is. According to the church, to sanctify something or someone is to hallow, set apart, consecrate, separate, and to make holy.

We are saying to the LORD that no matter what my trust is in *you* for my child, that it's your will that reigns supreme in our lives for them. As I stand before my family and my friends, I'm saying, that until salvation becomes a part of their knowledge and understanding, I, as their parent, will stand in the gap for them in prayer, fasting, intercession, spiritual warfare, consecration and devotion to your will and purpose for their lives. You're telling God, "I will establish a wall of prayer and anointing for them that the 'gates of hell shall not destroy,' by the Spirit of the Living God!" You're telling God that you relinquish your will for His, and that you are willing to seek His face concerning the direction their lives should take.

Often as parents, we seem to focus on what career and college or athletic future we want our children to take. We haven't sought God about anything! The entire subject of this book is devoted to helping us understand the importance of training up a child in the way that he or she should go. To accomplish this we must fully understand and accept the responsibility that when children are dedicated, they are a holy thing, a consecrated life, something set apart, for the will, call, and purpose of God for their lives.

Sanctification is completed by the work of God's grace in the lives of all believers, especially our children. Upon salvation we are separated from sin and from the world. Our problem comes when we don't accept the fact that "we're in the world but not of it!" Sanctification is instantaneous before God through Christ. In 1 Corinthians 1:2-3, "Unto the church of God which is at Corinth, to them that are sanctified in Christ Jesus, called to be saints, with all that in every place call upon the name of Jesus Christ, our LORD, both theirs and ours: (3) Grace be unto you, and peace, from God, our Father, and from the LORD Jesus Christ."

When our children are dedicated to the LORD, they are covered with a spiritual seal, a mark that only the eye of God can see. How often have you heard the tremendous testimonies of young people who told of all the things that came across their lives to steal their lives or cause them death or harm. The many temptations they may have even tasted, the pressures of peers that surrounded them, and yet, through it all, they could go so far and no further. Escaping death many times over, or maybe in times when they were in prison they seem to walk about insulated, and unmarred, from the horrendous world that engulfs our penal system? They belong to God, separated for His purpose, and dedicated to His glory; even when they strayed, His hand was upon them!

When your child is dedicated to God, it's not just another custom of the church. You are reaching up and taking the hand of God, and literally placing it upon the life of your child! You're saying, "I can't, LORD; please take care of my child, for your glory!" You're telling Him that it's your desire to separate them for whatever purpose He may have for their lives.

Two mothers who gave up the right to raise their children were Hannah, the mother of Samuel, and Jochebed, the mother of Moses. What more perfect examples can we have than these two unselfish visionaries, who chose the will and way of God for the lives of their children above their own?

Hannah was the prayerful mother, who consecrated her son, before he was even born, who lovingly tended to his needs in his formative years, and prepared him for temple service. Hannah waited and longed for the comfort and warmth of her own child. She sought God with her whole heart, and then let the most precious gift she had go into the hands and care of her LORD. Hannah personified the ideal in motherhood. It brought such heartache to the women of biblical times to be barren, just as today, only these women wanted to have the son or the daughter that would change things for their people. That would bring the messiah, the deliverer, the next king, the next Solomon or David, maybe another Elijah or Elisha!

In her consecration as a mother, Hannah might have even inspired Mary, mother of Jesus, who lived almost twelve centuries later. Everything was recorded in the Chronicles and in the Old Testament. Think about Hannah's Song of Triumph found in 1 Samuel 2:2-10, "There is none holy like the LORD; for there is none beside thee, neither is there any rock like our God. (3) Talk no more so exceeding proudly, let not arrogance come out of your mouth; for the LORD is a God of knowledge, and by Him actions are weighed." It goes on through to verse ten. Then we have Mary, who speaks her own beautifully inspired praise and adoration to the LORD in Luke 1:46-

55. "And Mary said, my soul doth magnify the LORD, (47) And my spirit hath rejoiced in God my Savior. (48) For He hath regarded the low estate of His handmaiden; for behold, from henceforth all the generations shall call me blessed." And it goes on. The similarities between these two songs of exultation are not coincidence; I believe this young teenager was inspired and mentored by her predecessor.

Mary knew that her son was to be the Son of God, and that God's son was separated and consecrated, and destined for the will of God and purpose of God, and for mankind. Just as Samuel was to restore the dignity and prestige to the temple of God and the people of God, they both knew and understood the price and sacrifice of sanctified children, children set apart to be used of God and by God.

Then, there is the rarely spoken of, and even little-known Jochebed, who was the mother of Moses, Miriam, and Aaron, who realized that Moses was a baby whose destiny and purpose had been ordained and mapped out by God! She released her son into the hands and care of God. She made an ark and hid him; during his formative years she nursed him in the court of Pharaoh. Moses was adopted by Pharaoh's daughter; how many mothers could release the care of their child, including the influence and input into their lives, to another woman? You're so right, not many. (Smile). But Jochebed did, for the love of her son, and the love of her God, even the love of her people; no sacrifice was too great.

Her faith in things unseen gained her strength and force. A mother who learned to trust her God and not to doubt, she seemed to be tied to the promises of God, absorbed by them and exhilarated by them. She was no ordinary mother. Jochebed was no stranger to holiness, the kind that strengthens faith. She was the daughter of Levi, in Numbers 26:59, "And the name of Amram's wife was Jochebed, the daughter of Levi, whom her mother bore to Levi in Egypt; and she bore unto Amram, Aaron and Moses, and Miriam, their sister."

The Levites were charged with the care of the sanctuary. These were her descendants. She handed down the priestly tradition of her family to her children. Her son Aaron was set apart to be a priest and become the center and founder of the Hebrew priesthood, in which he served for almost forty years. Her daughter Miriam led the Israelites in a moment when their faith came alive as they crossed the Sea of Reeds, or the Red Sea, the more commonly known name to many of us.

These examples and others will show us that though our children are dedicated, set apart for the purpose of God, it's the lives of the parents that must be consecrated and dedicated also to the will of God before those children are able to assume that responsibility for themselves. You cannot possibly understand and know the will of God for your children without a commitment to prayer, worship, and the consecration that comes from self-denial.

It's our heads that God must first deal with! In the womb, your child must be prayed over, must hear you read the Word of God, and must hear the sounds of worship and praise through you. The spirit man does hear and understand everything; he's familiar and accustomed to hearing and doing in the heavenly realm. The soul of man in not something that is merely snatched out of nowhere! Before our souls became a part of us, they were a part of the heavenly realm. So that seed within us is growing day by day, but the soul has always been eternal! It's not getting any older; it's accustomed to everything eternal, the Word of God, the songs of God, the praise and worship of God, the faith and proclamation of God, etc. We're not waiting on that child to understand; when the child is born, she is ready to understand from her birth the things of God, because of the very breath of God that breathed life into us from the Garden. The only hindrance to the program of God is the parents.

When researching the qualities of these extraordinary mothers, or parents, the common denominator seems to be a willingness to be used by God in an extraordinary way, to accomplish extraordinary feats for His glory and His honor and for the cause of the gospel. They seem to have a contagious and inspiring faith, with hearts and minds so focused on the will of God that nothing else seemed to matter.

Nothing is impossible for God to accomplish in the lives and through the lives of those who are ready and willing to so commit themselves to Christ is such a way that even their children are not withheld from Him.

God cannot fulfill the promises and covenants He may make with us if we're not willing to lay aside all doubts and trust completely in Him, and His love for us. Just think about Abraham, how long he and Sarah waited for the promised heir, and when the promise finally came to them, he was asked of God to offer that promised child up to Him as a willing sacrifice!

The faith and trust that Abraham possessed didn't come through the quiet, blissful times of comfort and plenty; it came from the struggles of a gentile, who became the first Hebrew, who would tear himself away from everything he knew and understood in the way of family, friends, and religion, to follow a voice that called him by name. Genesis 12:1-2 says, "Now the LORD had said unto Abram, (2) get thee out of the country, and from thy kindred, and from thy father's house, unto a land that I will show thee." God, was separating Abram from his familiar influence. How often does family influence us over God?

Friends, that's all! Imagine, a voice you've never heard before, calls you from a people and family you've always known, and commands that you go to a place He will not disclose, to become a part of something you never asked for! Sounds like God; Amen!

Abraham was called the "Father of Faith," because of the trials and testing that made him so. Being a Christian does not mean that trial is impossible or unnecessary. The greater the faith, the greater the trial; faith shines through the clouds of trials and challenges, and faith will always, always glorify God!

From the beginning of time Abram was chosen by God to become Abraham, the "father of a multitude," Abraham, a man of faith, with the flaws to match! He was as subject to his failures as we are. His character, like the sun, had its spots. Abraham's conduct to Hagar on two occasions in sending her away is painful to remember. Then his departure from Canaan into Egypt, when the famine was in full swing, was definitely not the act of faith. And, let's not forget the lies he told on more than one occasion with regard to Sarah his wife, to protect himself from what he thought would happen if it were told to the kings she was his wife. We can see the natural character of a somewhat cowardly, deceitful, and distrustful man. Such as is *common* to man! Amen? Amen.

God is not seeking for perfection in us as parents, with regards to blindly obeying and trusting Him, but what He does need from us is a willingness to trust Him and be willing to stumble into the pathway He has ordained for our children.

Our LORD has a way of linking His children up with those people whose hearts and lives are more mature in the things of God than ours, just for a season. You may not always know what to do, how to pray, or even where to go for the spiritual leadership and guidance you may need. Know this, that as you sincerely seek God in prayer and commitment to His Word, clear direction and insight will come.

The capacity for training your children and knowing God's will for their lives, is not easy, and like anything else, success will come with trial and error, but it's the heart towards doing God's will that will cover your error and cause all things to work together for the good of your child and for the purpose of God.

God's only consistent requirement from us is that we love Him with everything we have, and that we steadfastly commit to Him and to His Word, to not rest until we see for ourselves the hand of God moving in and through the lives of our children. Remember, God never needs perfection, only our *will*.

In the same way you would not allow your child to just go anywhere, with anyone, at any time, seek God for the *what, when, how* and *why*, of their lives. The what to do; the when to do it; the how it should be done, and the never-to-be-forgotten why it shouldn't be done.

As we look at the life of Solomon, we're given the perfect and best example of how to be successful in any task placed in our hands to fulfill. May God help us to understand more as we use this simple prayer of Solomon to guide and pattern our lives. "In Gibeon the LORD appeared to Solomon in a dream by night; and God said, Ask what I shall give thee. (6) And Solomon said, Thou has showed unto thy servant David, my father great mercy, according as he walked before thee in truth, and in righteousness, and in uprightness of heart with thee; and thou hast kept for him this great kindness, that thou hast given him a son to sit on his throne, as it is this day. (7) And now, O LORD my God, thou hast made thy servant king instead of David, my father; and I am but a little child: I know not how to go out or come in. (8) And thy servant is in the midst of thy people whom thou hast chosen, a great people, who cannot be numbered or counted for multitude. (9) Give therefore, thy servant an understanding heart to judge thy people that I may discern between good and bad. For who is able to judge this thy great people?" (1 Kings 3: 5-9)

The Word of God tells us in verse ten, "that the speech please the LORD, that Solomon had asked this thing."

When we take apart the prayer and request of Solomon, there are six predominant or paramount elements of focus for us. First we must first acknowledge God's faithfulness to us, to others, even to Himself and His Word. As you look around you at the lives and ministries of other families and their children, understand within your own heart that God is no respecter of persons, and what He's done for others He'll do for you!

When we're able to acknowledge that God has always been faithful to His children, never leaving us, or of forsaking us (Hebrews 13:5), always there to give wisdom when wisdom is asked for (James 1:5), that no task or hurdle is too much for Him to accomplish or help us over (Ephesians 3:20), and that nothing that Satan will attempt to do will ever be successful (1 John 4:4), you'll begin to praise Him within your heart, and with everything that is in you. Your mind will take you back to the places and times He has proven Himself to you again and again. Flashbacks of heartache and sorrow that only He could heal and comfort you in, and the many, many times He created something from nothing will cause you to extol and magnify Him for His goodness, then you will rest and trust, and be quiet from fear, and again see the salvation of the LORD!

The second element is knowing without doubt that God honors the faithfulness of His children. As in the case of Job, when God set apart Job for the challenges and testing of Satan, He was also more than able and ready to honor Job's faithfulness to Him.

Job's name means *hated*, or *one ever returning to God* or *he that weeps*. Job was the man God called blameless and upright, and a man that fears God and shuns evil. In a single day all that Job had was torn from him. Job's oxen and donkeys, were, rustled by Sabeans, and his herders were killed, his sheep were destroyed by fire falling from heaven. His camels were lost to a raiding band of Chaldeans. A tornado struck the house where his 10 children were feasting, and all the young people were killed. The Bible tells us, "Job got up and tore his robe and shaved his head (signs of mourning in the East). Then he fell to the ground in worship. (Job 1:20)

This tremendous battle between God and Satan, with Job as the helpless pawn, was not over; for his own physical suffering and personal battles with family, friends and all the powers that were of that region was just the other side of an already-too-sharp sword thrust out against him. But Job remained faithful! And God honored that faithfulness, as we see in Job, the 42nd chapter. When we approach God with trust in His love and His righteousness, and that His purposes will be just and righteous, we will also trust that what He does in our lives will be for the good of our lives.

Third, God will always remember His Word and covenant with us. Joseph was a man whose dreams and visions came true. At the age of seventeen, Joseph had dreams that indicated he was to have authority over his brothers and his parents.

We all know the story and foolishness of young Joseph, but we must also remember that his visions given to him by God were right, and God honored what He promised to Joseph in his visions.

The lives of our children may take a multitude of detours, and surprises, and even disappointments, but if we can hold fast to the fact that God declares, according to Proverbs 22:6, "Train up a child in the way he should go and, when he is old, he will not depart from it," we will always have good success.

As with Joseph, even though his family failed him, or at least his brothers did, and he was sold into a life and culture and a people that were totally foreign to him, God fulfilled His Word concerning Joseph, remembered him, and saw him, when no other family member could or would, and did exactly what He foretold He would do, through his dreams.

There may come a time when you feel as if you've lost control and sight of what the dreams and visions were that God has given you regarding your child, but never give up on God, He always sees and knows and is ever present, even when you can't be. Our LORD will not fail to establish the thing you're trusting in Him to do for your child or children. And exactly as it was with Joseph, whatever seemed to be lost in the way of time, relationships, or substance, God, and only God, can and will restore!

The fourth element is: you must also acknowledge who God is to you, and that without Him you are nothing! One of the most difficult things for any of us to say, other than, "I'm sorry," is, "I can't." And, one of the first things our LORD needs for us to understand is that "We can't!"

Honestly, when we think about all the failures we've chalked up just for ourselves, and we won't even think about the mess we've made with our children, what makes us think we can get anything right the first time, even with sound advice and instruction?

Let's see. Who's the best example of this truth? Well, what about Abraham and Sarah? They waited on God to fulfill His covenant with them, and waited, and waited, and waited. Finally Sarah thought, "Hey, maybe God meant for us to use our own source of supply and do this thing, and we're to stand back and watch Him bless it?" Wrong! We're always wrong when we don't wait on God. Because of Abraham and Sarah's impatience, we have the Middle East, with all its sorrow, pain, suffering, and tragedy.

Never allow the enemy to cause you to think that this is impossible for even God, that whatever your children need to take place in their lives, cannot be accomplished in this life! Just think, what if Mary hadn't grasped the possibilities of God doing what He declared through the angel Gabrielle He would do? The entire plan of salvation would have been destroyed. Mary was set apart specifically because of who she was and the heritage she bore, and the faith and trust she possessed, even as a young girl!

Mary had to be willing to acknowledge *who* God was, and say what she said in Luke 1:38, "And Mary said, behold the handmaid of the LORD; be it unto me according to thy word. And the angel departed from her." Are you willing to tell the LORD, "Behold the handmaid, the vessel, the mother, the servant of the LORD?" Are you willing, to release your will in exchange for His? Do you really understand *who* He is, not just for you, but also for your child? When you can totally rest in *who* He is to you, you'll say like Gabrielle said, at verse 37, "For with God nothing shall be impossible!"

The fifth element is that you're honored to have been set apart for the task, He has placed in your care, and that you completely understand your inability to successfully complete it, and with that thought in mind you're willing to release every thought, every opinion, every fear, even every capability into God's hands.

Lastly, tell our LORD, that your desire is to do the very best job possible, and that to please and honor Him is your only desire! With a willing heart and out-stretched arms towards Him, you'll find that exactly as He told Solomon after his prayer, you'll more than please God! After all, His only desire is to be God in your life, and in the lives of all His children. Why would He ever fail to develop and nurture this relationship, or do anything that would destroy it?

One more thought on the beauty and splendor of the sanctified life, or the one set apart for the purpose of God, and that is Christ, Himself!

What better example of the sanctified life, and lifestyle do we have? Christ, the *anointed one*, or in the Hebrew *Christos*, translates *Messiah*..The more complete and accurate understanding of His name, Jesus the Messiah, or Jesus the anointed one, emphasizes the fact that the man Jesus was God's anointed one, the promised Messiah. He was not only anointed, but even His word or calling was anointed and set apart from everyone and everything that would every touch or affect our lives.

The Word of God declares in 1 Peter 1:20-21, "Who verily was foreordained before the foundation of the world, but was manifest in these last times for you, (21) Who by Him do believe in God, who raised Him up from the dead and gave Him glory, that your faith and hope might be in God."

That word, *foreordained*, means that God the Father made a sovereign choice in His election and divine decision based on His eternal omniscience, of all possible plans of action. Friends, there was always a Second Adam set apart for the will and purpose of the Almighty, all knowing and ever-present God, and Christ, the Anointed One, was He! Our God knew Adam would fail! Adam didn't know he would fail! Jesus, was set apart to be our *Savior*. We read in Ephesians 1:4, "He hath chosen us in Him before the foundation of the world, that we should be holy and without blame before Him, in love."

As our Savior He is also our deliverer, preserver, benefactor and rescuer! This title certainly describes both God the Father and Jesus the Son. In John 3:16, "For God so loved the world, that He gave His only begotten Son, that whosoever believeth in Him should not perish, but have everlasting life." As our savior we are rescued from danger or eternal destruction. Physical healing and cleansing belong to us, because of Jesus Christ, our savior, we have new life and a new heart towards all things in this life and the life that is to come.

He is also our LORD, meaning *master*. As His children, we must see Him as "*Adonai*" a plural form that is used only in reference to the glorious LORD in all His powers and attributes. The only way to fully confess Him as LORD of your life, is to not accept substitutes! In John 6: 66-69, "From that time many of His disciples went back, and walked no more with Him. (67) Then, said Jesus unto the twelve, will ye also go away? (68) The Simon Peter answered Him, LORD, to whom shall we go? Thou hast the words of eternal life. (69) And we believe and are sure…that thou art that Christ, the Son of the living God."

The world, your flesh, and the enemy of your soul, will pull and attempt to twist you in more directions than you ever thought possible. But will you be determined to say as Peter said, and as the other eleven disciples also declared, "Where can I go LORD, for only you have the words of eternal life?"

Your children will see in you a behavior towards your LORD that is dignified, honorable, decent, August, and worthy of respect. You must set a good example, displaying a deportment that commands respect not only for you, but for your LORD and Savior, Jesus CHRIST, who is our supreme example of the set-apart and sanctified life and lifestyle.

Parents, you must be first sanctified in your thoughts and purposes towards your child and the will of God in their lives. When you dare to see Christ, the Anointed One, as the only power for us to live and shape the lives of our children, you fully understand that as he is our LORD, and we must rest in His sovereign authority when we are willing to release our struggles. We must not attempt to, "Do it our way!," and instead, surrender our will and the lives of our children into the trustworthy and more than capable hands of our God. Then every personal battle will cease.

Remember Ephesians 1:4-5, "According as He hath chosen us in Him before the foundation of the world, that we should be holy and without blame before Him, in love. (5) Having predestinated us unto the adoption of sons by Jesus Christ to Himself, according to the good pleasure of His will, (6) To the praise of the glory of His grace, through which He hath made us accepted in the Beloved;"

Friends, we were set apart from the very foundation of the world for the pleasure and will of God the Father. As we prepare our lives and the lives of our children with this truth in our hearts, also being aware of His second coming, we will live and dwell in the High Places of spiritual maturity, and success by the supernatural power and provision of the Holy Spirit. The human heart and mind are incapable of grasping the dimension of Christ's purpose for His people.

All things have been placed under Christ's feet. Now, it remains for the church to walk in the same authority given to us as Christ's body here on earth, and each of us acknowledge,"I can do all things through Christ, who strengthens me." (Philippians 4:13)

Chapter XVI

And They All Lived…Happily Ever After!

One of the most amazing things, and probably one of the most unfathomable concepts for mankind, is Eternal Life. What more perfect end to any good book, or in this case, the outcome of your child or children's life story, than the fact that they all lived, parents children, grandchildren, etc., happily ever after?

It is an assured fact that if the Word of God is established in the hearts of our children, and if God's laws, or His Word is the spiritual barometer to all things that govern their lives, that if the Bible has supreme place as the only constant rule of thumb to life's decisions, you can rest assured, the eternal outcome of their lives will be that of rest, joy, beauty, health, and happiness. This eternal bliss will be shared and celebrated with all those they have known and loved, including their LORD and Savior, Jesus Christ.

With this thought in mind, allow me to give you two powerful scriptures that must become a part of your thoughts and efforts, when teaching your children to have to proper respect for the Word of God, and His love towards us all.

The first scripture is rather common to our ears, well, at least the first part of the scripture, but we must understand and consider the entire verse and its meaning as it applies to life and success, for not only our children, but for their children, and their children's children, if the Second Coming of our LORD so determines.

In Hosea 4:6, "My people are destroyed for lack of knowledge [this is the familiar portion]: because thou have rejected knowledge, I will also reject thee, that thou shalt be no priest to me; seeing thou hast forgotten the Law of thy God, I will also forget thy children." Whew! I don't know about you, but that scripture is extremely unsettling to me!

Now the atmosphere or the spiritual climate that reigned in Israel at this time, was one of gross sins that warped Israel's relationship with God and called for judgment. No one could complain that God failed to make His ways plain to His people or to His people even today, nor that He is horrified at unrighteousness, which is still a stench in His nostrils.

The prophet Hosea denounces Israel's actions and explains those sins, and brings judgment against Israel, as they stand before God…guilty. He charges that Israel's bold and rebellious deeds range from everything imaginable: cursing, lying, murder, stealing, and adultery, all of these and more have replaced faithfulness and love for God in Israel. Israel has ignored God's law to the point of practicing ritual prostitution at the sites where they committed idolatry! In today's climate of adultery, divorces, fornication, murder, stealing, rape, kidnaping, dishonoring authorities, disrespectful to parents, drunkenness, drugs, and the list goes on and on, we cannot afford to take lightly this scripture we just read in Hosea.

I'm certain many will say, "Well, that was then, this is now." But the list I just gave you is now! Things haven't improved; if anything, they've gotten worse! It compels us to not be ignorant, careless, or unaware of the times that will affect and shape the climate that our children are forced to contend with, especially when we may not be around to guide them in their choices and decisions most of the time.

Just as our LORD is tied to Israel, He is also tied to us, and His commitment to us and to our children has not changed, nor will it ever change, even if for a season, we are unfaithful. At the end of all life, that is life as we know and understand it, God will restore to Himself those who have been found faithful unto death. And there can be no faithfulness without the understanding and knowledge provided for us in His Word.

Encourage your children to read their Bibles on a daily basis. I'm not really a believer in the many translations we have available today, sometimes the translations are so diluted that the complexion of the scripture verse or its meaning can tilt just a little off center, at times. But any translation that will encourage them to read and study their Bible is a good translation, especially if it is read in conjunction with a good King James translation. Without the fiber of the Word coursing through their lives on a daily basis, they cannot be successful in their walk as a Christian. Teach them early to read, as you read to them.

The other scripture I want to give you at this point, has a different tenor to it; it's not one of stern judgment for a lack of obedience to the Word, but one of encouragement when you abide by the principles given, according to God's Word. Isaiah 59: 20-21 says, "And the Redeemer shall come to Zion, and unto those who turn from transgression in Jacob, saith the LORD. (21) As for me, this is my covenant with them, saith the LORD: my Spirit that is upon thee, and my Words which I have put in thy mouth, shall not depart out of thy mouth, nor out of the mouth of thy seed, nor out of the mouth of thy seed's seed, saith the LORD, from henceforth and forever."

Praise the LORD! Hallelujah! Isn't it wonderful to know that if we have repented of our sin and stand before God redeemed, that as the redeemed of the LORD, we will have His Spirit upon us, and that the Word He has established within us and placed in our mouths will not depart from our mouth, nor the mouths of our children, nor our grandchildren! He has declared that our mouths will always be filled with what He declares to be truth! Our mouths, just like His Word, will be filled with words of health, blessings, prosperity, peace, joy, authority, victory, healing, deliverance, courage, and faith, and the good news; so will the mouths of our children and grandchildren! The success of each generation depends upon the generation that preceded them!

If we can keep these two scriptures close to our hearts and the hearts of our children, much of life's battles will be simple, for it is the Word of God that establishes and strengthens our faith, and it is also that Word that restores those places torn or battered by testing and challenges. It's God's Word that changes the tide on all of life's stormy seas, and the Word of God that *cannot* lie!

We're told in Jeremiah 23:29, "Is not my Word like a fire? Saith the LORD; and like a hammer that breaketh the rock in pieces?" His Word also declares in verse 23 of this same chapter, "Am I a God at hand, saith the LORD, and not a God afar off?"

We can take comfort, and rest in the absolute assurance, that God is not only faithful, but He is always at hand, and is never, as the enemy would love for us to feel, out of touch with our pain, heartache, or challenge of the moment. Whatever stumbling block Satan would attempt to block our path, and the paths of our children, God's Word, like a hammer, will break it into a billion pieces. And this same Word will burn like a furnace against every and any stronghold the enemy may attempt to devise against us. Remember the fiery trial that tested the companions of Daniel, how they were protected when the Word of God, Himself, came and stood in the midst of that furnace with them, proving that He was the God that is always at hand, and never afar off, and that the presence of His fire within us is greater than any furnace the enemy may push us into!

In Jeremiah, God was speaking to those prophets who mis-spoke His Word to His people, who used their own words to bring fear and judgment to those around them, and then said to them, "God said this" or "God said thus!" Our God declared His anger against His prophets for doing these things, and for using Him to beat and frighten His people. But the fact still remains, it's God who declares that His Word is powerful, and that He is ever present on our behalf! That's what you can't forget, and what we must always rely and depend upon when endeavoring to teach our children the faithfulness and sovereignty of our wonderful LORD!

As parents we know that life is a journey; to put it a little more biblically we are considered sojourners here on this planet called earth, especially in the condition it is now. We're all aware of what the Bible declares about a new heaven, and new earth, but until the millennium, that period mentioned in connection with the description of Christ's coming to reign with His saints over the earth, don't build your home in this earth too soundly, or at least, don't nail down the foundation. After all, we must be prepared to leave at a split second's notice (smile).

Reflect for a moment on the first few chapters and the introduction of this book, where your child was compared to a priceless book you were given to read, and you were instructed to increase its value to the author many times over. I explained that as you turned the priceless pages again and again to new chapters, it would open a wealth of information and instruction, that would better help you to increase the value and worth of the book placed in your hands. You were told the reading material might differ from the expansive novel-type reading, to maybe the more casual, but highly informative news or digest-type reading material. Whatever the reading material was, the author, our LORD and Savior, Jesus Christ, regarded each book and its pages to be of extreme value, delicate to the touch, and full of possibilities.

The one and only crucial factor about the book you were given, was that eternal life and the welfare of the Gospel of Christ, must never cease to be paramount in all your thoughts, efforts, and commitment to the development, and training process of your child. Every effort and devotion to the pages and chapters of their lives will result in eternal salvation for them, and for their children, and their children's children, and so on! Know that because God was faithful, and we were obedient, we shall live and dwell together in Glory with Christ and our loved ones forever!

But first things first; have we read thoroughly the book, or books, handed to us? Or have we skipped chapters, or a few pages, because things seemed to be going along just fine, and all was quiet on the home front! Then, suddenly you're startled when you're confronted with a sudden detour in their personality or their thought processes, and wonder where all of this came from. One minute your son or daughter was a perfect, sweet, dimpled child, and suddenly, all too suddenly, she became *that* child from the galaxy *far* beyond! Well, it wasn't sudden; you simply skipped those pages that would have clued you in on the up-coming events of your child's life, and you were caught off guard!

The lives of our children can and should be a vivid, inspiring, personal odyssey marked by faith, tears, praise, joy, and sometimes, sheer panic! We're to travel through chapter by chapter, page by page, shedding a little light in the dim or darkened places, and reaffirming truths already permanently established in our hearts by His Word as we look afar off into their futures, times when we've learned to bow humbly before our LORD, and dream aloud for our children.

The life of every child of God, even our children, is an uplifting spiral and spiritual quest to this awesome and longed for place called heaven, or paradise. Our LORD reminds us in John 14:1-6, "Let not your heart be troubled; ye believe in God, believe also in me. (2) In my Father's house are many mansions; if it were not so, I would have told you, I go to prepare a place for you. (3) And if I go and prepare a place for you, I will come again, and receive you unto myself, that where I am, there ye may be also. (4) And where I go ye know, and the way ye know. (5) Thomas saith unto Him, LORD, we know not where thou goest; and how can we know the way? (6) Jesus saith unto him, I am The Way, The Truth, and The Life; no man cometh unto the Father, but by me."

That's it, as my brother Kenneth would say, "simple as that!" The Word of God will keep and establish within them 1) "The Way" of God. David tells us in Psalms 16:11, "Thou wilt show me the path of life. In thy presence is fullness of joy; at thy right hand there are pleasures for evermore." 2) Because it's His Word, that remains the truth; they will find confidence in Revelation 3:7, "And to the angel of the church of Philadelphia,1 Kings 3: 5-9 says, write: These things saith He that is Holy, He that is true, He that hath the key of David, He that openeth and no man shutteth; and He that shutteth, and no man openeth." With these two factors firmly rooted in their hearts, they will receive Jesus as their savior thereby, guaranteeing "the life" as seen in 1 John 5:12. "He that hath the Son hath life; and he that hath not the Son of God hath not life." And this life gives them total and complete access to the Father through Him! Hallelujah!

Our comfort has been, and should always be in the fact that God has sent His Son, before us, and that He and only He is *the way, the truth, and the life,*. and if we are to have eternal life, and prepare our children for the same, it will only be found in Him!

Eternal Life is found *in* Him, *through* Him, and *by* Him! The children of Israel were instructed that, as parents, they were to keep before their children the laws and commandments of God, so that in times of prosperity, they would not forget *who* delivered them, *who* provided for them, *who* healed them, and *who* fought the enemy for them!

I believe with all my heart that as parents we have a spiritual and moral obligation to teach our children to always be grateful, thankful, and humble in the presence of God. In Deuteronomy 6:6-9 says, "And these words, which I command thee this day, shall be in thine heart; (7) And thou shalt teach them diligently unto thy children, and shalt talk of them when thou sittest in thine house, and when thou walkest by the way, and when thou liest down, and when thou risest up. (8) And thou shalt bind them for a sign upon thine hand, and they shall be as frontlest between thine eyes. (9) And thou shalt write them upon the posts of thy house, and thy gates."

God is telling us simply, that from the rising of the sun until the going down of the same, He must be glorified, magnified, and lifted up in our lives, and by doing this we are teaching our children to do exactly the same thing. They will not think it strange when eating out that you bow your head in the presence of God and man, giving thanks to Him for the provision of the meal. Neither will they wonder why, when they ask you a simple question about a decision they need to make in regards to friends, relationship, or even how to dress, when you go to the Word, or quote the Word to them as your answer. And they won't think it strange when they get up each morning, and they have a greasy spot of anointing oil on their forehead...smile. For them, life will just be normal! Isn't that what you want for them, for the things of God to be normal and not *weird*?

Well, it will take everything you just read in Deuteronomy and then some! After all, when you think that your child has arrived at that spiritual plane you have determined for their lives, that's when Satan will have you exactly where he wants you, in the dark! In the dark is where we never want to be when it comes to our children. We must always be in the know so that we can be prepared for whatever needs to be done for them in the way of protection and defense against the enemy.

We must take nothing for granted, not the mercy and faithfulness of our

LORD, and not the quiet self-assured feeling your child may give you. You must remain watchful and ever vigilant in the care and instruction of your children.

There were times as a young girl I'd find my mother sitting quietly with her Bible opened and on her lap, and sometimes with her eyes closed. I'd walk quietly into the room, thinking she was asleep, and she'd open her eyes. They were as sharp and as alert as a cat, and I'd say, "Mom, I thought you were sleeping." Her comment to me would be, "I'm watching, and I'm praying." I'll never forget it. I didn't understand her then, but I certainly do now, because there are times when my children say the same to me, "Mom, I thought you were sleeping." My comment to them is, "I'm watching and I'm praying." The morning my mother went home to be with her LORD, I found her sitting on the edge of her bed, with her Bible and her eyes closed, exactly as I had seen her so often before, only this time I knew that the days of her watching and praying for us in this earth were over. Now was the season where the prayers of the righteous would bring forth much! Mom never took anything for granted!

Trust me, neither God nor man ever wants to be taken for granted. How long would you be silent, if your child never said, "Thank you" or never appeared to be grateful for the sacrifices you made. Perhaps even the times they seemed to think that they deserve, or have earned everything you've given them? It wouldn't take long before the paddle shed would be open and under new management. I don't know about you, but I've experienced the LORD's paddle shed and I don't want that for my children. It's just too painful. Teach them to be grateful to the Father for His Son, grateful to the Son for His sacrifice, and grateful to the Holy Spirit for His keeping and sustaining power.

Help them to keep a clear picture in their hearts and lives of not only *who* God is, but what He can and will do for those who love Him, and for those who look for His appearance. Eternal life is not impossible; it's a fact. What is impossible, however, is our attempting to accomplish victory over sin, *without* Christ!

Never give up on your child, and certainly not the LORD. 1 Corinthians 15: 57-58 says, "But thanks be to God, who giveth us the victory through our LORD Jesus Christ. (58) Therefore, my beloved brethren, be ye steadfast, unmovable, always abounding in the work of the LORD, forasmuch as ye know that your labor is not in vain in the LORD."

The life of a Christian is oftentimes referred to as a race, and it is; it's a race best run one step at a time. We're told in Hebrews 12:1, "Wherefore, seeing we also are compassed about with so great a cloud of witnesses, let us lay aside every weight, and the sin which doth so easily beset us, and let us run with patience, the race set before us."

The Bible tells us that the LORD calls the young, because they are strong. He never said they were patient! That's where we as parents come in; we must teach our children the discipline of patience if they are to be successful in their lives and their quest for eternal life with Christ.

Patience: what a word, what a powerful and crucial asset to the life of every Christian, and when it's present in the life of a child of God, there is no mistaking it. By the same token, if it's missing in their life, the entire world will know it! (Smile) Patience determines our ability to bear up under suffering, and helps us to endure in the face of adversity. Children need to develop patience with themselves, with others, with the issues of life, with just about everything. Patience is a discipline in some, and a gift in others.

The only way patience comes is by sitting at the feet of Jesus. We have a simple, yet beautiful example of two lovely sisters, Martha and Mary, found in Luke 10: 38-42. "Now it came to pass, as they went, that He entered into a certain village; and a certain woman, named Martha, received Him into her house."

Now Martha and Mary were as dissimilar in disposition as Esau and Jacob had been. While Martha was practical and unemotional, Mary on the other hand was impassioned and imaginative. Martha was probably the older, and mothered Mary; and she took the lead as homemaker. Verse 39 says, "She had a sister called Mary, who also sat at Jesus' feet, and heard His word. (40) But Martha was cumbered about much serving, and came to Him, and said, LORD, dost thou not care that my sister hath left me to serve alone? Bid her, therefore, that she help me."

Martha was running all about impatiently doing this and that, probably over-planning her meal instead of doing something simple and pleasant so that all could enjoy the presence of the LORD. Martha strove for perfection around her house, especially when guest the family loved came to visit, but she was just too busy!

Continuing with Verse 41, "And Jesus answered, and said unto her, Martha, Martha, thou art anxious and troubled about many things. (42) But one thing is needful, and Mary hath chosen that good part, which shall not be taken away from her."

People who are impatient are usually running about attempting to do so much more than is necessary at the time. Rather than taking one project, one thing at a time, and doing it well and thoroughly; they attempt to do too much, and end up short-tempered, resentful, and maybe even angry.

Martha loved her LORD so much that she wanted the best *for Him*. Mary loved her LORD so much, that she wanted the best from Him! That's the difference; we must be able to determine what it is that we want from the LORD, and how it can best be accomplished to His glory.

It cannot be accomplished running to and fro, juggling everything and anything with one hand, while with the other attempting to stay afloat when things get too deep!

Mary wasn't selfish by not wanting to do housework when Jesus was in their home teaching. The Bible tells us that, "Mary hath chosen that good part." She had chosen what was best for her at the time, and that was, sitting at the feet of Jesus.

Remember when I made the comparison of Mary and Martha to Esau and Jacob? Mary, like Jacob, knew the value of a birthright. She knew and understood who Jesus was, and like a sponge, she wanted to soak up everything He could offer her that she might become all that she needed to be, and that by doing so, her life would be changed and be all the richer because she sat at His feet. Esau, like Martha, thought it more important to continue on with life as usual, working from sun up to sun down, and at the last minute, with no resources left, asking for help. Like him, we are sometimes willing to pay a price that is much too high, thereby jeopardizing our birthright, or the right that we all have as Christians: the abundant life through Christ Jesus.

If our children understand at an early age to prioritize their day, always beginning with prayer and thanksgiving, and at the close of the day completing whatever tasks and assignments they may have in the home and from school, reading their Bible, having prayer again, and thanking God for everything He's provided for them in their day, they will not just be blessed, but they will be a blessing to others.

If they will sit and learn from whatever mentor God has placed in their lives, be it their parents, a Sunday School teacher, youth pastor in whom sound spiritual wisdom can be found, they will flourish, and become strength to all those that are blessed with their presence.

Patience is a fruit of the Spirit. Galatians 5:22, "But the fruit of the Spirit is love, joy, peace, long-suffering, gentleness, goodness, faith. (23) meekness, self-control; against such there is no law."

When we look at the term *long-suffering* it is firmly based in love, and is a by-product of patience. Look at 1 Corinthians 13:4-8, "Love suffereth long, and is kind; love envieth not; love vaunted not itself, is not puffed up, (5) doth not behave itself unseemly, seeketh not its own, is not easily provoked, thinketh no evil, (6) rejoiceth not in iniquity, but rejoiceth in the truth; (7) beareth all things, believeth all things, hopeth all things, endureth all thing. (8) Love never faileth; but whether there be prophecies, they shall be done away; whether there be tongues, they shall cease; whether there be knowledge, it shall vanish away." Moving down to verse 13, "And now abideth faith, hope, love these three; but the greatest of these is love."

What is the LORD telling us here? Simply that to accomplish anything for Him, our motives must be based in our love for Him, and because we love our neighbors as ourselves, His love abides within us.

We will be *patient with them*, and with ourselves, until we have successfully accomplished the things of Christ, in our lives and for the gospel's sake.

Make certain that your children understand that everything takes time! That love for their LORD and Savior is the only thing that will give them strength and courage to endure to the end.

This generation has often been referred to as a microwave generation. Well, some meals, or foods, are fine for the microwave; others are better when prepared by conventional means. As parents we don't ever want to run the risk of our children being only half prepared for life's issues. We don't want them to look as if they've got it all going on, and on the inside, they are hardened, or frozen, or too raw for anyone to digest!

Take the prime rib, for an example. I prefer to season it really well, sear or roast it at a high temperature for about forty minutes or so, depending on its size. This process seals in its vital rich juices. Then I turn my oven down low and allow it to cook the remainder of the time at a much slower oven until it has been cooked to desired doneness. This gives a beautifully roasted, medium-rare prime rib that I just love! That looks as good as it is.

Now for our children, teach them the fundamentals of this Christian life. Read to them the Bible as quickly as they can effectively absorb it, while they are very young. This will seal in the goodness of our LORD to their hearts, before Satan can come and destroy them with his lies! Then as they grow, teach them more slowly, step by step, precept, upon precept, teaching them and preparing them for our LORD's desired readiness, and they will not only look good enough but be good enough...for Him to use!

Faith is another part of this eternal equation that needs to be developed, and reinforced within the lives of our children. For some, faith seems to be another difficult concept to obtain, but extremely crucial to the walk and life for the child of God. Faith is the divinely implanted principle of inward confidence, assurance, trust, and reliance in God and all that He says, and declares to us, in His Word. More simply put, faith is a belief and confident attitude toward God that involves commitment to His will for one's life.

That's what we want to teach our children. We want them to have a faith in their God, in their LORD and Savior, Jesus Christ that is so rooted in confidence, that His will for their lives, is never a question, never an option to be or do otherwise!

It's faith in God, and in our LORD, that will bring them to Christ. Saving faith involves personally depending on the finished word of Christ's sacrifice on Calvary, also the only basis for forgiveness of sin and entrance into heaven! Faith is the very essence of the believer's life from beginning to end.

The words we speak will determine what our hearts will come to depend upon. For whatever is in your heart, will more than likely, come out of your mouth. This is not a speak-it-and-claim-it kind of concept, it's much deeper than that. Let's look at Luke 6:45, "A good man, out of the good treasure of his heart, bringeth forth that which is good; and an evil man, out of the evil treasure of his heart, bringeth forth that which is evil; for of the abundance of the heart his mouth speaketh."

Our children must understand that it's the Word of God that cannot lie or bring forth evil. It's the Word of God that will accomplish good and not evil in their lives. It's faith in God's Word that will settle itself within their hearts, and that their ears will be reminded of His power, His authority, His sovereignty, His will!

Let's take a quick look at Abraham in Genesis 17:4-5. "As for me, behold, my covenant is with thee, and thou shalt be a father of many nations. (5) Neither shall they name any more be called Abram, but thy name shall be Abraham; for a father of many nations have I made thee."

Now, one of the explicit teachings of the Bible is the importance of the words we speak. In this text God changes Abram's name to Abraham and promises Abraham that he will become the father of many nations. *Abram* means *high father* or *patriarch. Abraham* means *father of a multitude.* So in this very specific instance, God was arranging that every time Abraham heard or spoke his own name, he would be reminded of God's promise.

God might not change the name or names of our children today, but He has given us a name more powerful, and more influential than any other name in

Heaven above, or in the earth beneath us, or even in the sea beneath the earth, and that is the name of *Jesus*! "At the name of Jesus every knee should bow, of things in heaven, and things in earth, and things under the earth, (11) And that every tongue shall confess, that Jesus Christ is LORD, to the Glory of God, the Father" (Philippians 2:10-11)

We're also told this by the prophet, Isaiah, in Isaiah 45:22-23, "Look unto me, and be saved, all the ends of the earth; for I am God, and there is none else. (23) I have sworn by myself, the Word is gone out of my mouth in righteousness, and shall not return, that unto me every knee shall bow, every tongue shall swear."

Jesus used the words of His mouth then and now, to declare who He was, and what we must do to not only honor Him, but become His very own. When He declares in Isaiah, "There is none else," then there is *none else*!

Faith is such a tremendous tool, and an effective weapon that our LORD has provided for us, but if our children do not become expert in its use at a very early age, or at least comfortable in its use, they might find themselves stumbling over and over again, and becoming discouraged and disgruntled, and tempted to give up, and we cannot have them giving up.

Our children must be taught that faith will help them to stand when facing delays. Remember in Numbers 13:30, Caleb saw the same giants and walled cities as the other spies, but the ten spies brought back an evil report of unbelief. Caleb's words declared a conviction, a confession before all Israel. "We are well able to overcome." Caleb knew the land, and it served as reminder that faith is not blind. Faith does not deny the reality of difficulty; it simply declares the power of God in the face of that difficulty.

Caleb stood his ground in faith and still moved in partnership and support of Joshua for forty years. He stood beside many whose own unbelief delayed his own experience of blessing. What patience and faith! His eventual possession of the land tells us that even though delays come, faith's confession will ultimately bring victory to the believer.

Faith is an extremely powerful ally for our children to have in their arsenal, especially when facing the delays that may sometimes come with their confession. They may become discouraged by the unbelief of others, or with the challenges of the enemy. Caleb, along with Joshua, gives strong examples about standing alone before the many. But the young man, Joseph, shows how standing alone against even family, can be more than painful; it may be even life threatening.

The point we must really focus on with Caleb and Joseph is their refusal to speak doubt and fear. The truth was what kept their hearts more inclined to trust in what God could do rather than to what they could not do.

Joseph had all the faith in the world, and knew the vision that God had given him meant that he would someday have favor over his brothers and his parents. He foolishly told his dreams to his brothers, which further exasperated his relationship with them. His dreams came at the young age of seventeen, and his impatience for the fulfillment of these dreams, came right along with this age! (Smile) Remember patience; teach your children, patience! We're told in Proverbs 30:32, "If thou hast done foolishly in lifting up thyself, or if thou hast thought evil, lay thine hand upon thy mouth." Well, for Joseph it was just a little too late for those words of wisdom! (Smile)

Anyway, Joseph possessed the faith and integrity that as a slave, kept him faithful in the hard places. It gave him comfort in the presence of God, and favor with his master. Although he was very handsome, his looks never became a snare to him. Joseph was able to resist temptation and to remain silent when foul accusations were made against him, causing him to be punished for these accusations unjustly, again and again. Still, his faith in his God was never wavering.

Faith is not something that is measured by what can be seen with the natural eyes. Faith can only be weighed and measured by the spiritual slide rule of God's Word! If your children completely understand from the time they are small that faith is not some shiny, bright, glittery magic lamp, but a personal relationship built on trust, love, confidence, and a reverence for the LORD and Savior they have come to know, that cannot be severed, they will not fail.

Although faith may not seem to be tangible in many respects, or as I mention above by the tape-measure of this life's standards, its effectiveness and results are definitely visible and measurable by even the youngest eyes and intellect. So don't be afraid to use whatever gifts God has given you to teach your children all of His principles, even, or especially, faith!

When we think about heaven, that word that expresses several distinct concepts in the Bible, and sometimes causes us to feel a little overwhelmed by the possibility of somewhere other than this place called earth. Our mind's first thoughts are usually of a beautiful place we are striving to reach, that place where we'll live forever with our children, and loved ones, and other saints, where pain and sorrow do not exist, that place where songs, poems, and beautiful words seem to capture the impossible existence of a painless, ageless, fearless, abundant, world.

Then there are those who just imagine the harrows of hell with its eternal pain and torment, enveloped with a darkness so thick and so heavy it cannot only be felt, but only tasted. They imagine a constant visual replay of their life and the hundreds of opportunities they were given to receive Christ, and would not surrender their life. Thirst would be so intense that water was not only a constant thought, but also a constant source of pain, a scorching reality that only increased your agonizing existence. People in hell would be fighting against the mocking, and vicious, brutal, profane taunts of every demon and spirit that hardened your heart against the gentle wooing and tugging of the Holy Spirit. Being able to hear the voices and cursing of those lives you caused to stumble and fall into their own pits of torment, because they listened to you, hearing over and over again every message of salvation, and every altar-call you failed to respond to. The absence of this and so much more would be heaven!

Then simply try to imagine what it would be like to just look into the face of Jesus for as long as you wanted, to really never have to leave the beauty of His face, or the music of His voice, or the gentleness of His touch, to actually hear Him laugh out loud, to really hear Him laugh, to understand the journey of your life, through the lips and heart of one who loves you so-o-o-o much! He gave His life just for you! He would show you the many, many times you felt so alone, thinking that He wasn't even aware of your need, or that He never heard your call, because Satan told you lies!

Jesus would show you how very close He was, or what the outcome would have been had He not snatched you from the claws of Satan, or shown you the plans that Satan had for your life, that salvation completely destroyed, because of the blood of Jesus! This too, would be heaven.

Then imagine the absolute beauty, my LORD, the colors, the sounds, the vastness, the clarity and brilliance, the smells and tastes, the true sound of music and worship everywhere you turned, joy so over whelming, that joy alone would seem to be too much to bear!

Actually imagine seeing God the Father, face to face, and not being destroyed by His presence, watching as He and His Son talked and laughed while looking at the joy and happiness of all those who were redeemed by the blood of the Lamb, and as they looked on the awesome wonder and beauty of their very creation! They would be talking aloud to the saints and patriarchs of old, calling the names of those whose service and sacrifice were a part of our lives and strength, as we read of their tremendous feats and exploits on a daily basis in the Word of God! They would be calling these saints into their presence, and you would be standing right there among the "Who's Who" of heaven! (Smile) This too, would be heaven!

Imagine…just imagine! Heaven can only be described by the Word of God, as penned by the Apostle Paul in 1 Corinthians 2:9, "But as it is written, eye hath not seen, nor ear heard, neither have entered into the heart of man, the things which God hath prepared for them that love Him."

As we look through the Word of God, we discover that the Kingdom of God and the Kingdom of Heaven are often spoken of interchangeably. Matthew 4:17 says, "From that time Jesus began to preach, and to say, Repent; for the Kingdom of Heaven is at hand." This was when the baton, so to speak, was being passed from John the Baptist, to our LORD, Jesus Christ. Also in Mark 1:15, "And saying, the time is fulfilled, and the Kingdom of God is at hand; repent, and believe the gospel."

At the end of time as we know it, a new heaven will be created to surround the new earth. This new heaven will be the place of God's perfect presence. "And I saw a new heaven and a new earth: for the first heaven and the first earth were passed away, and there was no more sea. (2) And, I John, saw the Holy City, New Jerusalem, coming down from God out of heaven, prepared as a bride adorned for her husband. (3) And I heard a great voice out of heaven saying, behold, the tabernacle of God is with men, and He will dwell with them, and they shall be His people, and God Himself, shall be with them, and be their God. (4) And God shall wipe away all tears from their eyes; and there shall be no more death, neither sorrow, nor crying, neither shall there be any more pain; for the former things are passed away!" (Revelation 21:1-4) Now this too, is heaven, as recorded in the Word of God. Heaven dear friends, is a real place, a place prepared for God and His people to live together forever!

This is our goal in life as Christians, not only for ourselves, not only for our loved-ones, but for as many as the Holy Spirit will help us to win for the gospel's sake. This is not a difficult choice for the sane mind to make, but those whose eyes have been blinded and whose hearts have been hardened, will not only find it difficult,, perhaps impossible, especially if they refuse to listen to the voice of the LORD calling to them.

It's not customary for our LORD to give up on anyone, and His desire is that no man would perish. His attitude toward the lost is one of longing and compassion. In Revelation 3:20, "Behold, I stand at the door and knock; if any man hear my voice, and open the door I will come in to him, and will sup with Him, and He with me. (21) To him that overcometh will I grant to sit with me in my throne, even as I also overcame, and am set down with my Father in His throne."

Our children must understand that Christ's blood and cross are our only source of redemption. To gain heaven and avoid hell, will take patience, faith, and endurance with the help of the Holy Spirit.

The young have a tendency to rely on their own capabilities, and this can be a mistake. When you're teaching them about the life of a Christian, the best way to go about being effective is showing them that they are not alone, that others have gone before them, including our LORD, and have been successful. Encourage them that even though your part as their parent may seem to place you apart from them, it does not place you above them in the eyes of our LORD.

"Wherefore, seeing we also are compassed about with so great a cloud of witnesses, let us lay aside every weight, and the sin which doth so easily beset us, and let us run with patience the race set before us." (Hebrews 12:1) Faith, is the key principle to endurance. Faith believes what God says and acts in line with His Word. Acts in line with God's Word! The discipline they must learn is not to permit themselves to be separated from the Word of God! They, like us, cannot enter into the rest of God that gives us the joy necessary to sustain us, by becoming our strength, if we're frantic and anxious about everything all about us.

God's discipline is a family matter. A father, (or mother) only accepts responsibility for the training of legitimate children! Moving down to Hebrews 12:7-8, "If ye endure chastening, God dealeth with you as with sons; for what son is he whom the father chasteneth not? (8) But if ye be without chastisement, of which all are partakers, then are ye bastards, and not sons."

If we want to live with Him in eternity, and share that eternity with our children, they must realize, they cannot do this alone, that it takes time, faith, endurance, and a discipline that at times may bring chastisement, even from God.

I know that in the heart of a child, heaven seems a far-off prospect, and also the hope of the aged or the more mature saint. Well, there was a time when this may have been true, at least in concept, but today news media reports a different matter all together.

When we read the headlines of the newspaper every day, we see a spirit of murder and violence claiming the lives of our youth at school, at home, and at play, a violence that leaves them crippled, bitter, and without hope. Youth as young as age twelve and sometimes even younger are killing, stealing, using drugs, and spending too many years too young in the prison system that only cripples, kills, and destroy their young lives.

Infants are coming into this world with addiction to drugs that will sometimes affect their lives for the rest of their lives. Babies are crying for a drug they never asked for; children are being left behind by fathers they never knew. Mothers are being forced to work ridiculous hours in a society that refuses to acknowledge their needs because, "She brought it on herself!"

Very young men have become fathers, not because it's what they wanted or needed, but because they were never told, or taught about the sin of fornication, that it's not only a sin against their own bodies, but against a God that loves and wants the very best for them.

Still younger teenage mothers are strapped with children making demands on a young life that doesn't even know how to take care of itself. In our society grandmothers are getting younger and younger every year, also the other side of the sword, many older grandparents, maybe two or three generations removed from the children, are attempting to raise children, whose parents are either behind bars, or because of an addiction or some other tragedy, have been removed from the home.

Then there are the places young people go today, places that their parents would never approve of. They face pressures from their peers, many that determine life-and-death issues for them on a daily basis.

Yes, there was a time when only a freak accident or some childhood illness would claim the life of a child, but not so today! Satan has so distorted the values and character of today's society that only the Word of God can put it plainly enough for all to understand, even the young. Proverbs 27:1 warns, "Boast not thyself of tomorrow; for thou knowest not what a day may bring forth."

As our young people stand before us today, two things are certain: 1) Never, since the time of man have they been more needed, more crucial, and more essential to the cause of the gospel, than they are today; and 2) Never have their lives been so threatened or destroyed at a more fragile time in their young lives than today.

There are lives to reach and touch that only our children can reach, because most often, adults are not allowed! (Smile) It's my firm conviction that this present generation of young people, are chosen by God to usher in the second coming of our LORD. These are the last days, spoken of by the prophets and men of old. It's this bright and powerfully anointed generation that the enemy is doing his very best to distract, destroy, and derail, by the flash and show of a materialistic, celebrity-driven, spiritually comatose people who refuse to, "Repent, for the coming of the LORD is at hand!"

As always, our very best example for anything is Christ! So, probably the best comparison I can make right here is when Jesus was about to leave this earth and His beloved disciples. His hand-picked little army was left with the responsibility of His brand new baby: the church! This group consisted of twelve men, who up to this point had nothing more to think about than fishing, tending to their families, or other properties, or collecting money from the poor! These twelve men had sat at His feet for three years, and were still in desperate need of a crash tutorial program, taught by Professor Holy Spirit!

These twelve men before now thought that fishing meant *fish* not *people;* that sacrifice meant an *altar*, not Calvary; that *broken body* and *blood* meant *injury* or *crutches*! And, when Jesus said, "The poor you will have with you always," He meant *uninvited* houseguest! (Smile)

Yet, His confidence in them was firmly placed and established within these twelve men. Jesus had to know that when they were not looking, the spirit man was seeing. When they weren't listening, the spirit man was hearing! When they appeared to be ignorant, the spirit man wasn't stupid, and when they seemed fearful, they were not cowards! Jesus had to rest in the knowledge that even when they'd shown their human flaws and frailties, as did Peter and Thomas, that their love for Him and what He'd taught them would rise above even their greatest fears, for failure was not an option!

When Jesus left this earth, He gave His disciples one important message, found in Matthew 28:18. "And Jesus came and spoke unto them saying, all authority is given unto me in heaven and in earth. (19) Go ye, therefore, and teach all nations, baptizing them in the name of the Father, and of the Son, and of the Holy Spirit. (20) Teaching them to observe all things whatsoever I have commanded you; and lo, I am with you always, even unto end of the age. Amen"

There was nothing left for Jesus to say or to do. He'd given His all for His church, and taught them from Himself; the rest remained for the Holy Spirit to do, and for them to fulfill.

The baton was now passed, and they were left with a task that if we really look at it from a human standpoint, was utterly impossible. But as Gabrielle told Mary in Luke 1:37, "With God nothing shall be impossible."

The Apostle Paul told his spiritual son Timothy, when his youth was an initial fear to him and a stick in the hands of others to discourage and distract him, "When I call to remembrance the unfeigned faith that is in thee, which dwelt first in the grandmother, Lois, and thy mother Eunice; and I am persuaded that is in thee also. (6) Wherefore, I put thee in remembrance that thou stir up the gift of God, which is in thee by the putting on of my hands. (7) For God hath not given us the spirit of fear, but of power, and of love, and of a sound mind." (2 Timothy 1:5-7)

Timothy could either use the gifts of God present in his life, or allow them to remain useless. Spiritual ministry demands the use of spiritual gifts, and Timothy is encouraged to move beyond the realm of convenient, familiar, and earthly boundaries, as he performs his ministry.

Dear friends, this is exactly what you'll have to do with your children, encourage them to 1) stir up the gifts within them; 2) not be afraid because of their youth; and 3) always know that God is ever present to protect, direct, and strengthen them.

Paul tells Timothy in 2 Timothy 4:7-8, "I have fought a good fight, I have finished my course, I have kept the faith; (8) Henceforth there is laid up for me a crown of righteousness, which the LORD, the Righteous Judge, shall give me at that day; and not to me only, but unto all them also that love His appearing.

It's a comfort to know, and it will be to your children, that the rewards for faithfulness and for keeping the confession of our faith are far greater than the task set before us. The righteous have nothing to fear on the day of Christ's return. The reward for our service and faithfulness to our mission in Christ will come from Jesus, our judge. Our salvation is *free*! However, for enduring temptation, there is the crown of life for those who do His will faithfully.

Family and friends, our children are never too young to understand that heaven is a glorious promise, and that someday, all our work and effort will be more than worth the moments of embarrassment we thought we'd never forget. It will be more than worth the rejection from our peers we were certain would cause us a lifetime of grief, and the many times we stumbled so often we thought we'd never recover.

This Christian walk is a marvelous obsession. If we allow the Spirit of God to direct and cover our steps, and if we remain intensely earnest about the things of God, in order that our will, our minds, and our hearts will be centered in God, nothing shall be impossible for us, for our children, and for our ministries.

No person is ever able to talk about victories without battles. All victories are battles that have been won! You will fight, you must fight, for without battles there can be no growth or patience. Without patience there can be no experience, and without experience we will not have the faith it takes to bring hope, healing, restoration, and deliverance to a lost and dying world.

God has placed all of us on this earth for a purpose, and that purpose is the great commission. The "Go Ye" found is Matthew 28:18-20 that we read earlier. We want that crown of life Paul talked to Timothy about. We want it for ourselves, and for our children, for our children's children, and so on, and so on. But we could never want it for ourselves, as much as our heavenly Father wants for us, for after all, He wants to spend eternity with His children, too!